AF230473

Powder River Publishing
www.powderriverpublishing.com

SADDLING UP TO RIDE IN COWBOY COUNTRY

Dave Campbell

Published by:
Powder River Publishing LLC
1014 Black Mountain Road
Thermopolis, Wyoming 82443

Copyright © 2026
ISBN: 978-1-956881-64-6
Printed in the United States of America

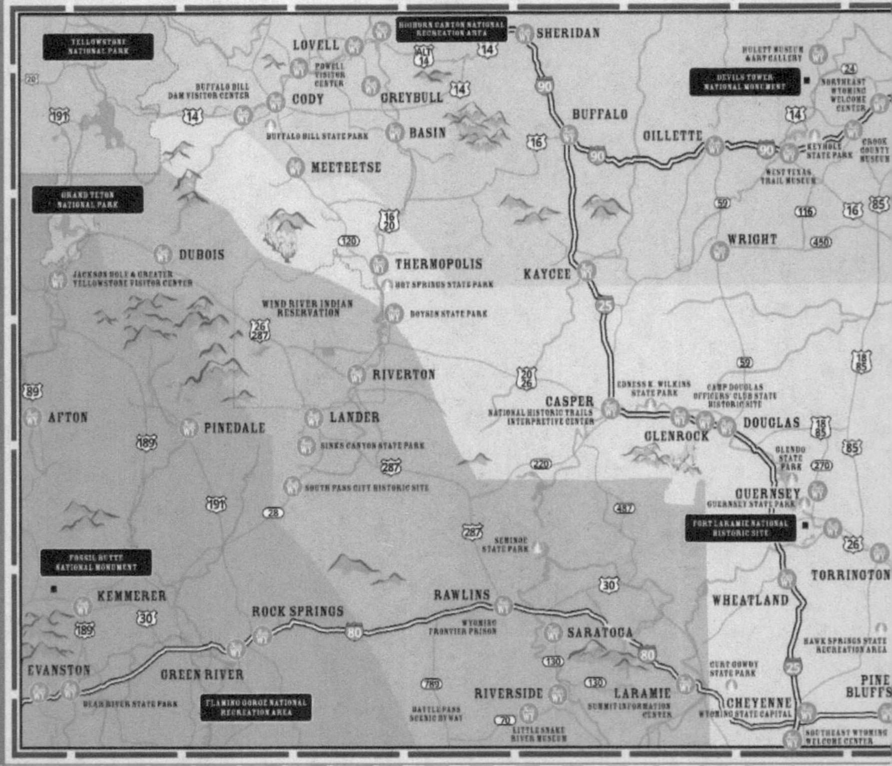

${\cal I}$NTRODUCTION

Like many people in America in the 1980s I fell in love with cycling, an amazing sport that I still enjoy today. A sport that brought me freedom, independence, and adventure while fitting in nicely with my love of outdoor activity. This love was cultivated by growing up in an active family in Lander, Wyoming at the foot of the Wind River Mountains. Cycling gave me an identity and helped me escape from what I saw as the trappings of small-town life. I would come to understand as I grew up, however, the immense support and comradery that both my little community and my sparsely populated state gave me as I struggled to learn the nuances of my new sport and find success.

Cycling seemed to provide challenge and excitement in equal measures and required us to always keep working at it. Cycling in the 1980's had a soundtrack too, that was as alternative to mainstream American music as our sport was to the established youth offerings. Both required diligence and a small close-knit community to gain access to all they had to offer. Growing up in a remote part of the country meant I had to doggedly built a support network and be creative about how to learn about and participate in this exotic new European sport, sometimes even promoting events so that my friends and I had races to compete in.

My generation enjoyed unprecedented support from the US Cycling Federation and the US Olympic Committee, with the opportunity to attend free camps at the Olympic Training Center and learn how to train year-round like elite cyclists. This allowed field sizes and quality of competition at domestic races to explode over a very short period of time. The United States had only one true annual showcase event in Colorado's Coors Classic where our riders could race against the world's best at home and the rest of us could see our heroes perform in person. The Coors was critical to educating the American public and helping our best riders develop. As the 1984 "home" Olympics approached, more of our finest riders were given the chance to compete internationally in the World's most competitive and difficult races with the National Team program. The talented and dedicated athletes that came through these programs initially struggled against the mighty Europeans but ultimately achieved historic successes at the highest levels. And the ascension happened quickly with the first Americans riding the World's two biggest races-the Giro d'Italia and the Tour de France in 1981...and then breaking through to win them both by 1986 and 1988 respectively.

The development of American racing cyclists like me was inspired by both the exploits and accomplishments as well as the trials and tribulations of riders like George Mount, Greg Lemond, Ron Kiefel, Davis Phinney, Andy Hampsten, and the 7-Eleven team. These trailblazers overcame enormous hurdles to compete with the Europeans in a sport we did not grow up with. These rugged individualists defied the odds to learn and achieve in a sport that was strange and confusing to our fellow countrymen. They were riders who all helped each other train, travel, race, improve, and succeed. There was a symbiotic and positive feedback loop of inspiration and information among all American cyclists during this magical time. Everyone in American cycling from the top professionals down to the weekend warriors just wanted to learn and get better and see the sport grow in this country.

Throughout my cycling journey, I met and ultimately competed against most of those pioneers who made history in the world's most famous and storied bike races, when they came back to America to race in a thriving scene that they inspired and helped to create. This proximity and accessibility between the local heroes and the national and international stars make cycling unique. For those of us who love the sport, it makes it absolutely extraordinary. The bond we share is the unfettered passion for cycling: not just racing but riding. No other sport really has this connection like cycling, and it was most profound during American cycling's heyday of the 1980s, a veritable golden age, the spirit of which I have tried to capture here in "Saddling up to ride Cowboy Country".

DEDICATION

This book is dedicated to the beautiful town and amazing people of Lander, Wyoming. But it is especially dedicated to the memory of those cycling friends, teammates, competitors, and supporters from Wyoming aka "Cowboy Country", and later Oregon that we have lost over the years: Clint Ashcraft, Michael Bair, Danny Birkholz, Jim D. Boxell, Aaron Daywitt, Doug Desrochers, Ben and Michele Eder, Carolyn Gilbertson, Bruce Gresly, Terry Hayes, Clay Hendrix, Bill Holcomb, Kevin Hildebrand, Shirley Jones, Danny Knudsen, Tammy Milleson, Lavinia Norris Exton (Vini Scott), Tim Rutledge, and Eirik Schultz. Special thanks to "Coach" Kristy Aalberg for editing, advising, and guiding my writing.

Thank you to my wife Giselle Renee Albertson for her patience, love, and support. I couldn't have done this without you! I will forever be indebted to Alessandro Colnago and his legendary grandfather Ernesto for understanding and embracing my passion for cycling and sharing theirs with great generosity. Special thanks to Topher Downham for recording all those cassettes for me and Marin Asbell and Clay Appleby for providing many of the albums. They fueled a lot of miles of training and travelling to races!

TABLE OF CONTENTS

FOREWARD

We gathered on the team Garmin-Sharp bus for the morning strategy session and our director's words hit me like a truck, "boys, we didn't come here to get second place." I finished second on stage one, second on stage two and our team leader was sitting second in the general classification. We had ridden our hearts out for six days and 700km of racing over the high peaks of Colorado. The 2014 USA Pro Challenge had taken its toll on everyone, and I expected those words to thump the team, but to my surprise, all I saw were smiles. We had one more shot, and my teammates all believed in it.

We saddled up and rolled out into the crowd. Thousands upon thousands of fans sent us off from Boulder, CO. The race was fast paced and aggressive from the start, but our team remained calm and conserved energy. As we approached the main climb of the day, the fellas got to work. Our team amassed at the front and set a furious pace up the climb, ripping the peloton to shreds. The fastest sprinters had been dropped and our crazy plan to pull off a win on the final stage was beginning to look a bit more realistic. From the top of Lookout Mountain to the city streets of Denver, our team used every last ounce of strength to keep the pace high and prevent those sprinters from rejoining. One by one our riders fell off the pace, utterly exhausted in the completion of this task. There were still roughly forty riders left in contention for the win and the final push for victory was a gamble at best. As we came ripping into the final kilometer, my race radio was a flurry of instructions, but all I could hear in my head was, "we didn't come here to get second place." Rounding the final bend, I put my head down and gave it everything. No tactics, no craft, just force, hope, and a very well-timed bike throw to finish it off. We won by six millimeters.

I was in such disbelief that I nearly crashed after the finish line. There were high fives and back slaps all round as I was whisked off to the post race media tent. As I cleaned up for the podium ceremony a close friend of mine came stomping in and exclaimed, "Dude, what a finish! Crazy! Seriously, what are you doing in here? You HAVE to get back out there! This is some Coors Classic sh*t out there right now! Once in a generation energy man! Leave the dirt on your face. GO!" I wasn't allowed to go out just yet, but once the podium ceremony commenced, it was clear as day how right he was...over ten thousand people were cheering out in the parking lot! The noise was deafening, and the energy was electric. This was the Coors Classic of the 1980s reborn.

The energy at the USA Pro Challenge made sense. After decades of drought, the cycling hotbed of Colorado once again had a major professional race. Lance Armstrong was a household name after dominating the Tour de France for nearly a decade and Floyd Landis kept the flame burning with an unbelievable attack to win the 2006 Tour de France. Yes, there were doping scandals and history was rewritten multiple times with those Tour victories, but cycling was always in the news and was now very much mainstream. What has received less mention was what it all had been built upon. What sparked America's original fascination with this niche sport?

For roughly a hundred years, road cycling was almost exclusively a European sport. On the old roads of Europe, the sport thrived, giving birth to the Grand Tours of France, Italy and Spain. Epic one day races like Paris-Roubaix, Tour of Flanders, Giro di Lombardia and Liege-Bastogne-Liege stole the hearts and minds of millions and were often front-page news. In America, however, the sport was fringe at best and generally non-existent. Then seemingly out of nowhere, in the 1980s bike racing, often highlighted in Colorado's Coors Classic, exploded in popularity in this country. A spontaneous big bang that gave rise to a rich universe of American racing heroes like Greg Lemond, Davis Phinney, Andy Hampsten and Alexi Grewal.

Saddling Up to in Ride Cowboy Country, is a unique first-person account of the often-radical formation of what became the foundations of modern American cycling. I thoroughly enjoyed the book and the memories it brought back. After all, I still have my signed photo of Greg Lemond in my childhood bedroom! After reading this book, I spent nearly an hour explaining the significance of these formative moments to my four-year-old daughter. I do not know if she absorbed any of the significance, but for me those heroes of the past are as animated as ever, thanks in large part to the pages of this book. This is the true and real story of the American spirit of adventure, grit, and fast paced cultural churn. Buckle your helmet straps and enjoy the ride.

Alex Howes
2019 US Pro National Road Champion
5x Grand Tour Finisher
(2 Tours de France, 1 Giro d'Italia, 2 Vuelta Españas)
The 41st American to ride the Tour de France

CHAPTER ONE:

BICYCLE, BICYCLE…I WANT TO RIDE MY BICYCLE

My lifelong friend, David Milleson, lived just two houses down Buena Vista Street in Lander, Wyoming. Lander is a quiet little mountain town of around 7000 people that sits about a mile high, right at the foot of the Wind River Mountains. Dave was right there with me from kindergarten on, for most of the key moments in my life whether they happened in the schoolyard, on the bus, at church, or in the neighborhood. Before Dave, I entertained myself by dressing up like Tarzan and giving my best ape man calls from high in my leafy fortress. Or at least from the plywood platform my dad had built in an old cottonwood tree in our backyard.

Dave was a little older than me and not quite as studious or outgoing and he often needed some convincing to come along on my adventures. Like a true friend, though, he always did. He joked that I could talk him into anything and ultimately, I usually could. Dave was a shy kid and was a little quiet until you got to know him. With both parents working and his older brothers and sisters out of the house, he was very independent.

While "playing Tarzan" and climbing on rocks above Fiddler's Lake in the summer before second grade I fell and broke my leg. Immobilized in a full cast in the weeks that followed, I became a comic book junkie. I spent hours drawing my heroes, ultimately becoming quite good at it with Tarzan as my prime subject. Perhaps this phase of growing up was really about searching for glimpses of the world beyond my tiny mountain town, being unique, and desiring new adventures. But thanks to Dave, these adventures soon left the realm of imagination and often happened through the freedom and independence brought by riding bikes.

Dave's parents both worked, and unlike mine, who

were both teachers, they worked during summers, too. Lazy unsupervised summer afternoons spent hanging out at his house were sowing the seeds of adolescence for us both. We spoke of things deeper than comic books while listening to rock music, especially the band Kiss, one of his favorites who quickly captured my imagination as well. The music brought us freedom and independence from our parents and sparked anger and frustration as it widened the generation gap. In the coming years my father would regularly tell me to turn down that "bangity-bang crap you're listening to!" Dave and I talked freely about the things that were starting to really seem important-mostly girls, bikes, sports, and music.

Around this time, girls were starting to seem like more than just kick ball teammates at recess. Suddenly, they were becoming much more interesting. I was on the youth swimming team and travelling to away meets with older kids who introduced me to other rock music that resonated like Queen, Boston, and ELO. One very pretty girl in the neighborhood, who was several years older, was Debbie Skorz, and she lived just down the street. She was the one, earlier in the year who had spied a Tarzan comic on me when I boarded the school bus and confronted me. "It's YOU! You are THAT BOY in the neighborhood that makes those MONKEY MAN CALLS!" I can hear it all the way down at my house!" GULP. Instantly recognizing the gravity of the situation, I summoned the deepest and most mature voice I could find and proclaimed "No, that's not me. That must be somebody else." Tarzan was out! My next intense focus was bikes.

Bikes at this point for boys our age meant BMX... bicycle motocross. Bikes were at the heart of childhood freedom, especially in small towns in Wyoming. In fourth grade, Dave and I both still had the typical kids' bikes from the 1970's...the only bikes we had ever owned! They had basic twenty-inch steel wheels, ape hanger bars, sparkly vinyl banana seats, safety flags...at our age, though they were not cool! With some help and supervision from our dads on mechanical matters, we undertook a project to turn them into BMX bikes. This was an exciting project, self-designed and self-guided that would bring more freedom and individual expression.

Dave was the one that got us going on our BMX bike adventure in the fifth grade. More mechanically inclined than me, he showed me how to strip the old bike down and rebuild it…into a new, cooler, and more rugged form better suited to the things we wanted to do. Like jumping or even "freestyle" tricks like the kids in our *BMX Action* magazines. Banana seats were swapped out for perforated nylon saddles. Chromed ape hanger handlebars with basic grooved white hand grips gave way to reinforced matte black handlebars with tacky, soft, yellow-flanged grips like on a motorcycle. And of course, the wheels were shod with fat, knobby tires. Eventually the chrome steel wheels themselves were replaced with heavy and strong yellow nylon "Mag Wheels", the height of cool. We wanted to ride on the motorcycle track out by the High School Field House and go off the big jumps. Several of the coolest kids on the scene had "Team Murrays", which were fully equipped with the parts that we had to add on. Of course, buying a Team Murray or some other BMX bike would be the easy solution…if we had the money! But we didn't, so converting ours bit by bit with what we made from lawn mowing, paper routes, and babysitting was cheaper, and we had a lot of fun doing it.

The trips down Main Street, all nine blocks of it, to the Bike Shop, located near the high school and in a cramped cellar below a hair salon, were magical. The racks lining the walls were packed with shiny new bikes and there were posters of bike riders, adults on road racing bikes and kids jumping and sliding through the dirt on their BMX steeds. The tiny space behind the counter was crammed with the gleaming parts we longed for, and we saved our pennies to buy them. Bit by bit, week by week we made progress. Bob Moon, who owned the shop, was super friendly to all the kids who came in, teaching us how to install the parts we bought, and always treating us like adults. He was the first to guide me on my journey of discovery of all things bicycle. He knew all our names and was happy to loan out an allen wrench or a socket so we could install a new part out in the sunny driveway alongside the shop. When we considered an upgrade, he would note things like "Kenny just got pedals like that, you should ask him how he likes them", effectively teaching us how to network. He trusted us and allowed us to pay for the equipment we needed in installments. Together we built a BMX track across town near the Northside Grade School. We would labor joyously in the dirt with our shovels, out under the hot sun, a dozen kids aged ten to fourteen and Bob, our teacher and mentor. My parents thought he was a hippy, but we just thought he was cool. Our new track was much better suited to the needs of BMX riders than the motocross track. Soon after the track was completed, Bob held races there and Dave and I joined in.

The bikes had to handle all the stress we were going to put on them as well as look the part. As such, the bikes had to be repainted in a bold new color scheme. The color had to be simple, strong, and NOT girly in anyway. Dave's bike was sky blue, mine was purple, and for boys seeking to prove their manhood among their friends while aboard these machines, clearly this would not do. We painted the bikes "bad ass black" and adorned them with yellow foam pads on the top tube, stem, and handlebars. We planned to get "rad", and a guy could hurt himself if he wracked himself on an unpadded gooseneck, so we planned accordingly. Little by little, we converted the bikes...more aggressive and reinforced pedals, sturdier stems so our bars didn't move down on jumps, and finally those critical but expensive yellow nylon mag wheels. We rode those bikes a lot and along with other kids established a large network of jumps and dirt tracks all over town. We would spend hours just riding around, talking to friends, going swimming, catching frogs and crawdads, building and taking jumps, exploring and talking.

I rode that bike so much, and so hard in fact, that its department store core was not up to what I was asking of it. The forks bent and parts started to fail. After about a year, Dave's enthusiasm for bikes began to wane and he wasn't as into it anymore. Christopher Downham, however, was! Chris, who would later go by Topher, was a longtime friend and our fathers worked together at Lander Valley High School. We became good friends through bus trips to Spelling Bees, as he and I both made the fifth-grade team at South Side Grade School. Topher brought BMX bike mags along on the bus trips for us to study together. He was much more of an entrepreneur than me and had a knack for finding good paying jobs to help him support his bike habits.

He had recently purchased a metallic orange Rampar R10 frame and fork from Bob at the Bike Shop for $50, a significant sum for a fifth grader in 1979. After many months we learned that the shop was actually named "The Freewheel" but to us it was just "The Bike Shop" and Bob always made us feel welcome there. The $50 was a relative bargain compared to the price of a complete bike, but still an intimidating figure to eleven-year-old me. Topher's parents soon divorced, and he would start spending the school year in Minnesota, only returning to Wyoming for the summer. Prior to the start of sixth grade, he presented me with an incredible opportunity...his lawn-mowing job at "The River's Edge" apartments, just down the hill from my house. There was still a month of mowing needed in the fall, the pay was great, and I could earn enough to get my own Rampar frame with a reinforced fork like his to upgrade my BMX bike. I couldn't believe my luck!

As sixth grade wound down and the weather warmed, I would often ride my new bike to school. This freed me of the trappings of the school bus and the waiting around before and after school with kids of all ages. It brought more of those elusive things I so longed for: freedom and independence. The bicycle was a dear friend and partner in adventure to every twelve-year-old boy I knew, but for me it was becoming even more. It was becoming part of my identity. Throughout that year, I had built up my new BMX bike and on the first few rides to school was thrilled to find several of my friends and classmates waiting to greet me at the bike racks, eager to check out my new ride.

Topher and I were dedicated pen pals through all those months that he was with his mother in Minnesota with much of the correspondence focused on our biking plans. Our *BMX Action* magazines were full of images of Freestyle riders who could do "tricks". Topher crafted logo note pads emblazoned "C and D Trick Team" and we worked on balancing, jumping, kick outs, and bunny hopping. We dubbed ourselves "Crazy Campbell" and "Downright Radical Downham" and had t-shirts screen-printed. We only tried big jumps once...Topher propped up an old door in his front yard and hit it at full speed. I watched him launch into the air, but his front end was way too high and his weight too far back. He kept it up briefly upon touching down but was quickly on his back and sliding across the lawn. Ouch. We toned it down a bit after that, always practicing for some big performance that never happened. We weren't very brave or very good, but we stayed in touch, encouraged each other, and made plans for more summer adventures together.

Somewhere around seventh grade these BMX bikes became "kid's bikes" and seemed to fade out. As we entered Junior High and got taller, we were now riding "10 speeds". For me, this meant riding not only as transportation, to and from swimming practice but also riding loops on the quiet country roads near our home. During summer vacation, we rode to places to swim or float the river in inner tubes. I rode mine daily on my paper route in the neighborhood down around the city park. We regularly sped around the five mile "Tomato Loop" on Hillcrest/Mortimore Lane. The Squaw/Baldwin Creek Loop was a veritable rollercoaster of climbs and descents. The longest climb along the red cliffs was a huge challenge physically and mentally. It was followed with a fabulous high-speed descent, and the whole thing seemed like a great adventure to a kid. The first ride there required packing a lunch, since it was twelve miles around and took so long to get up that big hill. Lyon's Valley was our biggest challenge, featuring an intimidating climb called Snavelly Lane, that could be seen for miles, looming ominously out on the highway. At nearly seventeen miles, it made for a big day, but we felt brave, strong, and grown up even at accomplishing such a challenge.

Transportation and escape had become the prime

function of the bike...and less jumping and doing tricks. The "10 speeds" afforded us even more even more independence by giving us the ability to ride even further out into the countryside. They were nothing fancy and just came from the local hardware store. "Real cyclists" that we met later would teach us to look down upon them as "department store" bikes. But, for us they meant freedom and adventure. With no helmets and no parents, we rode many miles out on rural Wyoming roads just talking, dreaming, and enjoying the sunshine, the physical exertion, the conversation and our friendship.

About this time, I saw a trailer at the local movie theater for a film called "Breaking Away". It showed high School kids hanging out and swimming in an old quarry and one of them was a bike racer. The imagery and vibe resonated with many of our experiences at the time. I never managed to get to the theater to see the film, but I hoped it would turn up on TV at some point. It did...sort of. The movie became a short-lived TV series starring Shawn Cassidy, who I knew from "The Hardy Boys" and the teen heartthrob magazines that the girls brought on swim trips. This guy was cool! The storyline of the initial shows paralleled the movie and so, in a round-about way I got to see it...and I loved it!

Like all teenagers I was trying to find my niche and my tribe. Swimming was fun but lots of kids in the community did it and while I was competitive, I wasn't one of the best. I liked it, but I didn't love it. I wanted to find a way to stand out and be unique. I wanted to do something that I was truly passionate about. I was inspired by the character Cassidy played, also named "Dave". He not only rode ten speeds, but he went out training because he was a bike RACER. He competed at high speed and in close quarters, breezing down the road in a big PACK! It seemed fast, exciting, and even a little dangerous. In the TV show, Dave would be at the back of the group; then this Italian opera music would come on and he would roar past everyone and into the lead. Digging deep and with great self-belief, he would win! He was REALLY into this sport, and he wore a funny little cycling cap all the time and spoke in Italian.

Saddling up to ride Cowboy Country

Italian? Now bike racing seemed even more exotic. Nobody I knew of in Lander was doing anything like this-it was a European sport! Sensing my interest, my mother explained that her younger brother, Jim, had a real racing bike. She thought it was top-of-the-line and from England, but the parts were Italian. The next time we were in Denver perhaps he could show it to me or even let me ride it.

I was really getting interested in cycling (a much cooler name than bike racing) and so I needed a cycling cap. I needed to look the part...like Dave. I went to see Bob at the Freewheel bike shop, the only place I had to turn. Dave's yellow cap had a multi-colored stripe down the middle and some kind of Italian bike brand logo on it. In cursive. Bob had ONE cap at his shop. One. It said Cicli Colnago and was yellow and blue. He explained that Colnago was an Italian bike and that was all I needed to hear! Since I was going to be a cyclist, I also purchased a pair of yellow vinyl padded cycling gloves. The nicer model had soft leather palms with a knit cotton back, but they were out of my price range. I started wearing my cap everywhere, backwards, and saying "Ciao, Mama! Ciao, Papa!" to my parents, just like Dave did in "Breaking Away". He was the only example I had at that point of what a cyclist was, so I mimicked everything about him. I wanted to be a cyclist!

During the winter of 1980-81, my sixth-grade year, thanks to our Lander Swim Club and our amazing coach Bruce Gresly, I was beginning to really enjoy and understand the rhythms of training and competition. The idea of setting ambitious goals and working hard to achieve them was taking hold, as was going deep for the ultimate effort in competition. Quite simply, I was learning how to push myself. The previous summer I had participated in an "All American Swim Camp" at our local pool. The camp required quite a commitment on my part, getting up early on summer vacation, fixing my own breakfast, and riding my bike to the pool since my parents were busy or working.

Several esteemed coaches with Olympic Experience came from Alaska to not only conduct twice-a-day workouts in the pool but to teach us about visualization, goal setting, and improving every aspect of our swimming.

Only the most serious local youth swimmers took part, as well as many on the high school team, so it really felt like I was in the big-time now…a serious athlete! There were lectures on technique, we were all filmed in the water, had our strokes analyzed, and had improvements suggested. We even took our pulse in between sets to gauge our efforts. The red, white, and blue T-shirt we received on the camp's completion was worn with pride as it displayed my new-found dedication to all my friends. Heady stuff for a twelve-year-old in a small town in Wyoming!

One of my first experiences really giving it everything on a bike happened while riding home from swim practice. A few blocks from the pool lived a kid named Alex Magnus, who always seemed to be out in his yard when I rode past. He would regularly hurl insults at me and since he was bigger, older, and stronger than I was, I ignored him. Somehow, he had gone to Scout Camp with my troop the summer before despite never being involved with any of our other activities. He was one of those creeps we all seemed to face at some point growing up who loved to pick on younger and smaller kids.

He wasn't just a bully; he took it to a new level. He was mean, crude, and nasty. A real psycho. At camp, he had climbed a tree on the path that led to our tents and just hid up there waiting. Then, when my friend Andy Whiting and I walked by, he peed on us! And of course, he then laughed his ass off and bragged about it to everyone. It was so nasty…I hated that guy! One evening, weeks later, riding past his house on the way home from swim practice, I could hear him yelling what a "f#@kin' pussy" I was, and I suddenly lost it and told him where to stick it. And then to top it off, I flipped him off! What was I thinking? He came after me on his bike, like a bat out of hell, intent on beating the crap out of me! It was the fastest I had ever ridden IN MY LIFE!!! I glanced back only once, right at the start of the chase, and he was close, so I dug deeper, and I found another level. I knew if that psychopath caught me, he would kick my ass three ways to Sunday! So, I blasted the length of Cascade Street like my life depended on it, because well, it kind of did. After flying through a half dozen blocks as fast as I could and blowing through a couple stop signs along the way, I looked back, and he was falling behind. Another block and that piece of shit had given up completely. He couldn't catch me, not even close! I sat up, no handed, and coasted an entire block still flying along with momentum and adrenalin, I was going SO fast and feeling SO good…it was my first victory salute!

Lander Youth Swim Team 1978-79. The author is the kid wearing the Tarzan Speedo.

CHAPTER TWO:

DO YOU BELIEVE IN MIRACLES?

On Friday night, February 22nd of 1980, my dad and I sat down to watch the US Hockey team take on the mighty Russians in the Olympic Hockey Semifinals in Lake Placid, New York. The Winter Olympics were something my family would enjoy together on the couch in front of the fire during Wyoming's long, cold and dark season. Mom relaxed her strict rule about only one hour of TV per day since the Olympics were something quite special. My parents emphasized that the Olympics only happened once every four years, only the very best athletes from all over the world competed, and what an honor it was to represent your country and give your best effort. The winner of this game would play for the Gold Medal and the USSR was highly favored.

The Soviets had won several Olympic titles in the previous decades and had dominated international competitions. It was approaching the height of the cold war, and the Russians in those Red CCCP jerseys seemed deadly serious, intense, and scary. My Dad explained how the Olympics were for amateur athletes and the Russians weren't really amateurs. They were soldiers in the Red Army, amateur in name only, and their real job was to play hockey full-time. The US team were college kids, the youngest in the tournament, who went to school, had part-time jobs, AND trained..." just like us." And now they had this incredible OPPORTUNITY...but they would have to rise to the challenge!

Dad and I had followed this "scrappy young team" throughout the tournament, and like many in our community and indeed the entire country, we had embraced these underdogs and their story. They had huge hearts, and had a tough, hard-nosed coach by the name of Herb Brooks who backed them up and believed in them. They had in fact, played the Russians in Madison Square Garden just prior to the Olympics and got shellacked 10-3. Far from breaking their spirit, though, this seemed to mobilize and bond them for their upcoming task. Since then, though, we had watched them go from strength to strength in these Olympics first tying Sweden and then winning four in a row, highlighted by dominating a very strong Czech team 7-3.

The images we saw of the American fans in the stands was nothing short of electric. You could feel the energy, the belief, and the passion pouring out of our tiny black and white television into our living room. No one was seated, everyone was up on their feet and FIRED UP. The stands were packed, flags were waving across the ice arena, fists were pumping...it felt like "US against THEM". The fans were chanting U-S-A, U-S-A! You could sense that something very special was about to happen.

Just nine minutes into the game, the Soviets scored and a sense of dread crept in. Were they in over their heads? Our belief quickly returned, however, as minutes later, Buzz Schneider tied the score. Dad turned to me and said, "now we have a game!". My father got a sparkle in his eye and made life-impacting points to me during the commercials about believing in your teammates, not being intimidated, playing hard, and never giving up. Just three minutes later, the "big red bear" scored again and there was a sense of "Oh, boy here we go...can they hang in there"?

Well, they could! Mark Johnson picked up Davey Christian's slap shot at the very end of the period, and as the Soviets eased up, he put it in the net right as time expired. The score was tied! Dad pointed out what a massive mental error that was on the part of the Russians. They were "not staying focused and playing hard" and "you could never ease up when there was still time left on the clock" ...this was really getting good. Perhaps most importantly he explained that you can never underestimate your opponent!

The second period opened with Tretiak, the Russian goalie who was widely acknowledged as the best in the world, sitting on the bench! The Soviets scored quickly to make it 3-2 while outshooting us 12-2 in the second period. It was at this point that Goalie Jim Craig, a favorite of my mother's, became a focal point. He was "keeping us in it!" Dad said, "that kid is incredible!" His story was well known by now to all American viewers. His mom had been a big supporter of his, driving him to early morning practices, and had died recently. His father was devastated, and Jim would look for him in the stands after each game.

On a power play early in the third period, Mark Johnson scored, and the game was tied at 3-3. Dad and I were going crazy, and Mom and my sister Amy were joining in on a moment that we were beginning to realize could be truly historic. "These kids can win this game!" Dad exclaimed, "We can beat the mighty Russians!" All the athletic teaching and experiences I had been exposed to and thought about up to this time seemed to crystallize in this moment, illustrating that the things that are preached to young athletes actually work. Self-belief, trusting your teammates, hard work and determination, and taking advantage of opportunities... these tools were being successfully applied right in front of my eyes. They were doing it! "We", the USA, were living it!

Just a few moments later, team captain Mike Eruzione scored to give the Americans their first lead with ten minutes left to play. We were going nuts on the couch in Lander, Wyoming! The closing moments of the game seemed to go on forever, as Craig deflected shot after shot. The Russians were clearly a better team, but the US kids were defeating them almost by sheer will. Almost certainly less talented, they simply wanted it more. When the announcer started counting down those final seconds he announced, "Five seconds left, do you believe in miracles-YES!"

The US Hockey team had, against all odds, defeated the Russians and the template for my athletic belief system had been forged. Two days later, Dad and I were allowed to skip church, never an easy feat with my mother, but that didn't stop me from trying EVERY WEEK, to watch the Olympic Hockey Final. The US come from behind again to beat Finland for the Gold Medal! Grit and determination, unbreakable team spirit, unbridled enthusiasm, and tenacity yielded the ultimate prize...Olympic Gold Medals! It was a big moment for our country and a big moment for me, perhaps one of the most inspiring events in my life.

Chapter Three:

GONNA FLY NOW

The Olympics weren't the only time I bonded with my father over athletic moments on television. We watched the movie "Rocky" together around this time one winter evening after swim practice. We both really connected over the underdog story. As a standout three sport high school athlete and former college football player, it was the beginning of him giving me his insights into training and competing. Rocky's best quality was his indomitable spirit, his effort. I sensed that was Dad's hallmark as well, and in coming years it would certainly become mine.

Dad was my prime source of athletic information and guided me through the dynamics of the athletic struggle during the ads. The timing was ideal for me, as I had really started enjoying training and competing. In the movie, an underdog fighter was given a once-in-a-lifetime opportunity to fight for the heavyweight title of the world. His background was humble, but he was determined, committed, and I saw beauty in the way he wholeheartedly chased his dream. Dad told me "You have to be tough and keep pushing despite the difficulties and never stop believing in yourself". Perhaps most importantly, according to my father "If you keep training, your time will come." I was eager, desperate even, for my time and the images constructed in my imagination of mighty battles and worthy victories would drive me through miles of solitary training on lonely Wyoming roads.

By July of 1981, I was nearly 13 years old, and I finally "raced" my first cycling event...a 17-mile "citizens" race on the Lyons Valley course. I rode down to the start line on my "Coast King" department store 10 speed with several of my buddies including Topher. My friends and I had all fully transitioned from our BMX bikes to 10 speeds but were still fresh off the turnip truck in terms of cycling knowledge. None of us even carried a water bottle. We knew the Lyon's Valley loop racecourse well and by that point we rode it often. None of us wore helmets but the race required them and so we rented them for a buck. They were big, heavy, unventilated mountaineering helmets borrowed from the National Outdoor Leadership School, which was based in Lander. I loved riding already, but racing was something else entirely, we went so much faster! The dynamics of being in a race allowed me to go deeper and find so much more inside of me. It inspired me to stretch my mental and physical limits, and I loved that. The dozen or so other riders were much older and stronger than us and we were among the last finishers, but it didn't matter. We battled it out against each other for bragging rights and couldn't wait to do it again.

I enjoyed the connection between myself and my machine, and I loved being outside on the open road and the sensation of the wind rushing over me. Comic books fired up my imagination about flying but on a bike, pedaling furiously down a steep descent, I really was flying! It wasn't just some childish fantasy; it was real life adventure and one that I effectively got to design. The speed and freedom were intoxicating. On the bike I could explore the countryside and also my physical limits. How far could I ride? How fast could I go?

After my first race, I trained even more and sought out all the information I could find about cycling and tried to find others to ride with. Riding for miles and miles, especially on hilly terrain, was difficult and tiring but I loved the sense of accomplishment that washed over me once I had finished. I especially liked the serious nature of going out alone...training. I wasn't just some kid riding; I was a bike racer, and I was training, getting stronger, working towards a goal and preparing for the next race...serious business! As I pumped up my tires and filled my water bottle, I felt like I was setting off on an epic adventure and facing up to a mighty challenge. It was just my machine and I, out on the open road, putting in the miles, riding fast and riding hard. I whistled my Italian song ("Barber of Seville" I was told was the title), just like Dave.

My world and all my experiences growing up in Lander were wonderful, but quite limited. My supportive parents, many great friends, our neighborhood, the local swimming pool, and the mountains. My grandparents and most of my extended family, however, lived seven hours south in Denver, Colorado. Denver and nearby Fort Collins were the places where we could buy and do MANY things that weren't available in tiny little Lander. The trips we made there a couple of times a year were a big deal for all of us and would come to greatly enrich and inspire my cycling experiences.

Later that summer while visiting family in Denver, my Uncle Jim finally came by with his racing bike. A REAL racing bike, a Raleigh Professional, hand built in Nottingham, England. It was painted mink blue and the frame had half-chromed seat stays and forks. The components were all supplied by Campagnolo: the very finest cranks, brakes, and derailleurs from Italy. Jim explained that the bike was equipped with a complete Italian Campagnolo Nuovo Record group set. Or "Campy" as the American riders said-it was the best equipment available and very expensive. Campagnolo! And it finally struck me...that was the Italian name on the sides and brim of Dave's hat in "Breaking Away"...Campagnolo! Jim even taught me how to say it-"Kahm-puhn-yow-low". A few pieces of this foreign puzzle started slowly coming together now.

The saddle was hard and intimidating, a leather Brooks Professional with copper rivets. The shiny aluminum rims were ultra narrow and shod with super skinny tires. There were intimidating toe clips and straps to "lock you into the pedals" so you could provide power all the way around. This bicycle, a real racing bike, was beautiful and SO exotic, featuring intricate details on every bit of the bike. Engraving on the handlebar, textured shift levers, "Brev. Campagnolo" inscriptions on each individual part. Every bolt and dustcover atop the anodized aluminum alloy componentry was brightly polished and gleamed in the sunlight. The bike was unbelievably light; I could lift it with one hand! My folks had always said when Jim "got into something" he always sought out the best equipment and this had been no exception.

Jim had ridden a "metric century" with a club in Greeley, Colorado where he went to college. He told me stories of his visit to the factory in England and how his bike was just one level behind what the professionals rode, and he showed me photos of the team from the color catalog. And then he let me ride it! I only took a lap around the block, but it was incredible, so light and so nimble. I was positioned much lower and further forward than on my clunker. Unlike that heavy and sluggish machine, Jim's bike responded immediately to my steering and pedaling input. Coming back to my grandparents' house, I threw up a victory salute just like the TI-Raleigh pros in the catalog, which really freaked out Jim and my dad. They seemed to think I was on the verge of crashing! But I was fine, I knew how to ride no hands and had already practiced my victory salutes many times. In fact, I was hooked, and I wanted a REAL racing bike...Campy equipped! Alas, but for now I would have to settle for a Campagnolo t-shirt from "Self-Propulsion" a cool bike shop not far from my grandparents in Golden, Colorado. It was the only Campy I could afford. Yellow with Blue, it matched my Colnago cap nicely and gave me a bit of a riding kit, especially when I included those yellow cycling gloves. I loved that no one else in Lander had one, or even knew what it was, let alone could they pronounce it. I would wear it constantly.

My quirky British soccer coach, Dr Peter Jammers Murdoch, owned the local Sporting Goods store and I would often stop by on my bike on my way home from swim practice. I knew that the Tour de France was THE bike race in the sport of cycling. I knew about Greg Lemond, the 1979 Junior World Champion who possessed massive potential, from reading *Bicycling magazine* in the school library, but he was still making his way in the pro ranks. He was young and would not race the Tour de France for a few years yet. I didn't know of any other Americans in the sport's highest levels. I was desperate for any information on cycling, and I had no one to follow in this new sport. "Dr J" got newspapers from the UK and told me of the progress of a young

Saddling up to ride Cowboy Country

Australian, debuting in that year's Tour de France-Phil Anderson.

Frenchman Bernard Hinault had won both the 1978 and 1979 editions and was leading in 1980 when a knee injury forced him to withdraw. In 1981, he was back and at the height of his powers. As reigning World Champion and "the boss" of the peloton, few dared even attack him. Dr. J taught me that "peloton" was the French word for the field or group of riders in the race and that "attack" was the cycling word for accelerating away from the others in an attempt to form a breakaway. In his first Tour, however, this English-Speaking rider had stuck with Hinault on the first Mountain Stage...73 miles over three climbs in the Pyrenees mountains and finishing at the Pla d'Adet Ski Station. Even though he was an outsider, he wasn't intimidated, and he stepped up to the challenge and took on the very best! Like our US Olympic Hockey team and Rocky!

Belgian climbing ace Lucien Van Impe had won the stage and Anderson finished with Hinault just 27 seconds down. Combined with his strong finishes on the earlier stages, Dr. J explained that the 23-year-old Aussie took the yellow jersey which was given to the leader of the race based on overall time. Stage races such as the Tour gave out these jerseys in a podium presentation after each day's race (called a stage) and the race leader then wore it in the following day's stage. As I read the reports and asked Dr. J for clarifications, I became aware of the sheer magnitude of the Tour de France. The challenge and difficulty were almost incomprehensible! The riders competed every day except one for three weeks straight. They circled the entire nation and climbed both the Pyrenees and the Alps, for a total of over 2300 miles in twenty-four stages. Rider's times were added up each day and the overall standings were called the General Classification or GC. The rider with the lowest overall time each day was the race leader.

Anderson had become the first non-European ever to lead the Tour de France! I learned on my next visit, that Phil lost the lead to Hinault in the following days 27 km time trial, but he took over another jersey, the white Neophyte jersey designating "Best Young Rider". He ultimately faded to tenth on GC by Paris behind winner Hinault, but he battled all the while, a guy with a big heart who raced like he had nothing to lose in his first attempt at the biggest race in the world. It was an attitude and racing style I could really get behind! His grit made an enormous impression upon me. Tall, muscular, and aggressive, he embodied what I hoped I could be as a bike racer. He didn't just hang back, he attacked repeatedly! His attitude meshed nicely with what I had learned from my dad and that US Olympic Hockey team.

In the fall of 1981, during my seventh-grade year, my family spent a long weekend in the mountains at a church retreat. Hanging out with a bunch of old people singing terrible hymns and being told how to live my life was nothing short of torture. The one saving grace was that the cabins we stayed at had a "reading room" featuring a stack of *Bicycling magazines*. I devoured them. This was the only publication around at the time that focused on ten speeds. or more accurately road bikes. One issue had a road test of a variety of entry level racing bike...just what I needed to learn about. A basic department store bike at this time was around $100 but decent "bike shop bikes" started at around $300. The bike that had the biggest bang for the buck in their road test of racing bikes was the French Bertin C-70.

I had to be realistic about this to get my parents on board. *Bicycling magazine* claimed this bike was an incredible value at only $275. And unlike others in that price range, it was race ready! I had never heard of this brand before this, but it had the look...exotic and fast but priced (maybe) within my reach. It wasn't Italian unfortunately, they were too expensive, but French, which still seemed cool enough to me! Bertin bicycles were imported from France into New Mexico and Bob at the local shop was confident he could get one. I asked for a Bertin for Christmas in a 52 cm size, carefully determined after Bob sized me up.

It was never going to be easy to get my parents on board with this and they noted that Bob sold Schwinns. They were nice, they assured me. I could "get into racing on a Schwinn." Schwinns? NOT COOL! Not exotic, not racy and not European! They were boring and run of the mill! Sure, Jim told me about the Schwinn Paramount...but that Campy-equipped staple of the American peloton sold for over $1000. Mom and Dad were thinking of Schwinn Le Tour's! Gag! I stayed after them and kept the faith. On Christmas eve, shortly after Dad had noted Bob was having a sale on Schwinn's, we were driving through the snow to the annual Christmas eve candlelight church service. Bob passed us going the other way with a white Schwinn Super Le Tour, with dorky black foam rubber grips in the back of his pickup! Oh, no! He was certainly heading up to our house to leave it in our garage. How could I be a cool bike racer on that thing?

Christmas morning dawned and I put on my treasured Campagnolo T-shirt, my Colnago cap-backwards, sweatpants, and my down slippers and headed to the tree to face my fate. No Schwinn. In fact, no bike at all! Being spoiled or entitled was NOT tolerated at my house, so I put on a brave and grateful face and happily opened packages of socks and sweaters from relatives in the living room. After a while, Dad asked me to help him with the wood stove back in the family room, so I went along. Leaning behind the sofa was a shiny new Bertin C-70 road racing bicycle in a beautiful champagne color. Black cloth handlebar tape with gum rubber brake hoods atop drilled out levers adorned the alloy handlebars that were engraved just like Jims. Thin racing tires were mounted on shiny polished alloy rims and laced to high flange hubs while the crankset had drilled out chainrings just like in the magazine! I was beyond stoked!

It came with the receipt...the price had gone up since the Bicycling magazine road test and Mom and Dad had laid down $350. Gulp. My folks had altered the receipt into an IOU, and I was responsible for $175. Additionally, I was enrolled in Bob's Bicycle Maintenance class that started next month. The class was held Sunday nights in the "warming hut" at the city park where kids rented their ice skates. The adjacent skating rink was just our local baseball diamond flooded every winter to freeze into a rink. Each week we would take apart, clean, and grease a different part: hubs, bottom bracket, headset, etc. Additionally, we would learn to true wheels and adjust shifting. Mom was adamant that if I had a nice bike, I needed to learn how to maintain it. Much to my father's chagrin, she agreed to let me keep the beautiful European machine in my bedroom, leaning against my bookcase.

A local artist who went to our church, Jerry Antolik, was an avid cyclist and had been very supportive of my interest in cycling. He lived in Hudson, about nine miles from Lander. We were having a very mild December with light snow on the sides of the road but clear highways. The temperature was a little above freezing. Cold but clear Wyoming winter weather. I asked if I could ride to Hudson to show Jerry my new bike. My parents agreed, so I bundled up and off I went!

Jerry was surprised to see me and impressed with the new bike. He gave me some tips about taking care of it, which I always appreciated. Not wanting to linger too long and get cold, I set off for home after about an hour. On the final climb past the Wyoming State Training School, rising out of the saddle for more power, I suddenly tumbled to the pavement! The front wheel had folded underneath me. I was devastated! Coming from BMX, somehow, I must have been too rough on this lightweight bike, and I wasn't riding it properly. I thought I ruined it through my ignorance of how to ride these fancy and fragile foreign machines. I thumbed a ride from a guy passing by in a pickup truck. He of course knew my parents and I dragged the bike into the garage with tear-filled eyes. Bob assured us that it wasn't my fault, the spokes in the front wheel must not have been tensioned correctly and he would get it replaced. Whew!

Through the maintenance class I met other local cyclists, all adults. No matter to me...if you rode bikes, I wanted to meet you. I needed people to learn from and ride with! The adults, most of whom I already knew from the community and were primarily interested in bicycle touring embraced "the energetic young kid". They would ultimately form the nucleus of what became our local bike club, The Wind River Wheelers. The club would have weekend rides, host local races, and even go on trips to Yellowstone Park and Thermopolis to ride and camp out. My father got involved by driving "the sag wagon"-his Ford Bronco towing a trailer holding all the camping gear.

One of the riders, Neil Brooks, travelled to Europe every summer to ride. He gave me a "Bike-ology" mail-order catalog that introduced me to yet another exotic European bicycle-Colnago...the name on my cap! They sold these beautiful Italian machines, again with that ubiquitous Campagnolo equipment like Jim's, in a gorgeous red paint scheme with white panels. It was adorned with rainbow stripes because I learned that the World Championships had been won on Colnago's and the rainbow striped jersey designated the World Champion. The multicolored bands were derived from the Olympic rings symbolizing all nations. Only a past or present World Champion could wear those stripes in competition. Ah ha! Like the multicolored stripe down the center of Dave's cap in the movie! More pieces of this cycling puzzle were starting to come together for me. Decoding this exotic European sport was a joy in itself with every discovery inspiring more interest and continuously building my love of the sport of cycling.

My first racing bike Christmas 81

CHAPTER FOUR:

BREAKING AWAY

One winter evening the club had a movie night and showed "Breaking Away", on a video cassette player. Fully fired up, I wore my Colnago cap and my "Campy" t-shirt to celebrate and embrace the occasion. Up until then, I had only watched movies at home on TV and with ads. Most popular culture things happened late for us in Wyoming and thus, over two years after the theater release and following the short-lived TV series, which did give me the basic plot, I finally saw the movie. The movie that would change my life and cement in stone the idea that I wanted to be a bike racer. I wanted to train long and hard out on the open road and compete in races. I wanted to ride and race on beautiful and exotic European bicycles. I wanted to push my physical limits, throw my arms up in victory, and maybe even shave my legs…once I got really serious, of course.

"Breaking Away" resonated with me on so many levels. Dave and his friends spent summer afternoons swimming in the old limestone quarries around Bloomington, Indiana. My friends and I spent lots of summer days at swimming holes in the Popo Agie River that ran below my house, as well as hiking far upstream and floating down on our tubes. His parents were quite conservative, and he often butted heads with his dad. He was a dreamer, and his dad was all about practicality. This was yet to come for me, but it would arrive soon enough!

Cycling made Dave unique and helped him stand out from his peers. It even helped him meet girls! While drying themselves in the sun at the quarry one day Moocher told Dave, "Ever since you won that Italian bike, man you've been acting weird. You're really beginning to think you're Italian, aren't ya?" To which Cyrille responds "I wouldn't mind thinking I was somebody myself!" It was as if they were speaking right to me. As a small fish in a tiny pond, I had a burning desire to really achieve something, especially something unique. I wanted to stand out and be somebody.

Dave and his buddies also grew up in a small town, and they mirrored many of the fears that my friends and I had. Some of the charms the small town offers during childhood become suffocating in adolescence. In Lander, everyone knew Dave, he was Bruce and Carol's boy. After graduating high school, it seemed easy to get trapped by these charms and be stuck in a rut, never going anywhere or achieving anything big. The movie showed me how the accomplishments of youth could be quickly forgotten as the monotony and anonymity of adulthood took hold. Mike, formerly the High School quarterback, ranted, "You know what really gets me, though? I mean here I am, I gotta live in this stinkin' town and I gotta read in the newspapers about some hot shot kid, new star of the college team. And every year it's gonna be a new one…and every year it's never gonna be me! I'm just gonna be Mike. Twenty-year-old Mike, thirty-year-old Mike, old mean old man Mike!" I had seen that happen to many Lander kids and I swore that would never be me. Cycling would be my way out of that rut.

I think another reason the movie resonated with me and so many other aspiring cyclists of the time was because it was not "an American movie about bike racing", but rather it used bike racing to make a movie about America. It was about growing up in middle America and trying to figure out what to do with your life after high school. Of course, it was also about one guy embracing a European sport that was so peculiar to most Americans. The movie even referenced Wyoming, basically painting it as "Cowboy Country". One day while hanging out at a pizza joint, Mike noted a Marlboro ad in a magazine. "Hey, now look at this! That's the place to be, right there…Wyoming! Nothing but prairies and mountains and nobody around. All you need is a bed roll and a good horse!" Many of the Marlboro ads at that time just so happened to be shot a few miles from my house on our friends, Margie and Jared Nesset's ranch.

While this line cracked up my club mates, it emphasized something I was feeling strongly...I didn't want to be a Cowboy! My family lived just down the road from the town Rodeo Grounds, but I was the only kid I knew of who had never been to a rodeo. I had, in fact, never ridden a horse! I was horribly allergic, and I couldn't even get within a city block of that place without my eyes swelling, my nose running, and going into a sneezing fit. On family summer trips to the "Bar Lazy J", a Colorado dude ranch, I spent all day in the pool while the rest of my family went on horse-packing trips in the mountains. I knew real cowboys from the swim team and saw how hard their lives were. I had seen ranch kids like Jack Kennah, drag themselves into swim practice utterly exhausted in the spring, after getting up early every day to help deliver calves. The very romance that appealed to Mike had never been there for me. It became clear to me that when my time came, perhaps because of cycling, I would go far from Cowboy Country!

While in Denver at my Grandparents for Easter of 1982 we stopped into a bike shop. The Boulder/Denver area of Colorado was a rich source of cycling culture with one of the most active racing scenes in this country. Now that I was riding a lot, my mom insisted I get a helmet. I, of course, wanted a leather hairnet, like the racers wore, but she insisted on a hard shell. Luckily, a cool Italian one, a Brancale Cortina was available. I also purchased the Velo-News book "Ten Years of Championship Racing: 1972-1981" that detailed the biggest races in the World, including National and World Championships, with a special focus on the progress of American riders. I was trying to learn as much as I could about this exotic sport...and there was SO much to learn! As a proud American, I studied that book intensively to see where my compatriots were placing in the biggest events. How were "we" doing?

The 1978 Junior World Championships, held in Washington, DC, jumped out at me. The home country significantly earned one medal: Bronze in the Team Time Trial. It was the first men's Worlds medal (women's sprinters Sheila Young & Sue Novara had taken track medals earlier) in decades, indeed in modern US Cycling history. This was a sign of hope for the new US cycling programs put in place by Polish immigrant Edward Borysewicz. "Eddie B" I learned, had defected to the US following the 1976 Olympics in Montreal to become the first US National Coaching Director. By 1978, he was holding "camps" at the Olympic Training Center in Colorado Springs and organizing National team trips to compete in major European amateur events to help develop riders. The hopes were high that he could prepare a competitive team for the home 1984 Olympics in Los Angeles.

Yes, in fact this historic result was very much a sign that our riders could compete on the World stage. When you look now at those fresh young faces, just consider what they went on to accomplish: Ron Kiefel (1984 Olympic Bronze Medal, First American Grand Tour Stage win- 1985 Giro d'Italia, six consecutive Tour de France starts & finishes), Greg Demgen (stalwart member of dominant domestic 7-Eleven & later Levi's-Raleigh teams and the 1982 National Road Champion), and Jeff Bradley (fourth in the Junior Worlds Road race in 1979 and part of the pioneering 7-Eleven pro team that took on Europe in 1985, culminating with riding the 1987 Tour de France). Then there was Greg Lemond who was ninth in that 1978 Junior Worlds Road race. He won three medals the following year including gold in the road race, later two pro world road race titles, & oh those three Tour de France wins! When Eddie B. met him in 1977, he called him "a diamond", he just needed polishing. At the time, I remember wondering, just like the editors of the book, how far could we Americans could go? Well, the answer was FAR! But as of early 1982, "we", both the elite American riders and I, still needed some time to learn and develop.

It was clear as I studied this treasured "Ten Years" book, that in the World Championships the women were carrying us. Sheila Young and Sue Novara in the Match Sprint on the Track and Connie Carpenter and Beth Heiden on the Road had all won medals, even titles at the World Championships. The top American stage race, The Coors Classic, formerly known as the Red Zinger, had become the biggest women's race in the world and the Americans were right up front. With its weeklong format and tough climbs in the Rockies, the Colorado race was one of the few events in the US that was as hard as European races. The current American women were already consistently the top in the world and additionally young Rebecca Twigg was up and coming, both on the road and the track.

The men's amateur side was developing, and we were still searching for a star. George Mount's gritty sixth place in the 1976 Montreal Olympics was very promising. By 1978 he achieved the best finish by a US rider at a major international amateur stage race, by finishing fourth in Britain's prestigious Milk Race. That same year he won the Red Zinger Classic in Colorado. In 1979 he won the Tour d'Auvergne in France and the Pan Am team time trial with the national team but then went on to race the rest of the season in Italy on his own.

Immediately after the 1980 Olympic boycott, I learned that "Smiling George", the original "rugged, salty, independent, and pioneering" American bike racer turned professional. Following Eddy Merckx's advice of "if you want to win some bike races, go to France…but to LEARN bike racing, go to Italy". He "made some calls" and "got a contract" as soon as the Olympics were out due to the boycott. He raced in support of star riders Roberto Visentini, a future Giro winner and Moreno Argentin, future Ardennes Classics star and World Champion on the Benotto team. With almost zero fanfare, he finished 25th in the 2416-mile long 1981 Giro d'Italia, the Tour of Italy, which I learned was second in prestige only to the Tour de France. He was 39 minutes and 20 seconds behind Italian winner Giovanni Battaglin and a remarkable third in the Young Rider Category. Thus, he became the FIRST AMERICAN to ride and finish a Grand Tour. Mount ultimately was the kind of "never had any money, so I didn't need to be coddled" maverick that inspired my foray into the "alternative" and free-spirited world of bicycle racing in the 1980s. George was a true pioneer!

1979 Junior World Champion Greg Lemond, now a second-year professional, was featured prominently in the book. He seemed to ultimately hold the most promise, but he was still very young. That promise, however, meant he was quickly becoming my new hero, and inspiring my own growth and development as I learned this sport. I desperately needed an American to follow and Greg was it. Mount and Lemond, along with Jonathan Boyer (who became the first American to ride the Tour de France in 1981, finishing 32nd) seemed to be right on the cusp of really achieving something at the professional level. One photo showed them all together in the 1981 Worlds in Prague, Czechoslovakia. The race was ultimately won by Freddy Maertens in front of Italian Giuseppe Saronni, and Hinault while the three Americans finished "together well back in the pack"...46th, 47th, and 48th.

Earlier that winter I was given a gift that absolutely lit me up! A Campagnolo finish line poster of that very 1981 Worlds, from Bob and Drew Leemon, two of the senior riders in my cycling community. They must have gotten it from the annual bicycle trade show in California. They raced on the local scene and would later regularly take me along. I was only 13 in the early winter of 1982, when they presented it to me.

It was the coolest thing I had ever seen. All those Campy logos on the banners lining the fencing and a huge crowd in bleachers on both sides of the road at the finish line. I could see they were passionate fans who were really into it.

My parents had it immediately framed for me that Christmas and it was soon front and center on my bedroom wall. I knew of Hinault from his Tour wins and would shortly learn about Saronni. He rode a red Colnago...they had even called it Saronni Red in the Bike-ology catalog. I would have to read up on Maertens, but he was on a Colnago too. I studied this poster relentlessly and tried to piece together other details about this complex sport in general and this race in particular, from what I had read about racing. The Italian in the second wave, Francesco Moser I decided, and the Frenchman alongside him (later identified as Gilbert Du-clos-Lasalle) must have been lead-out men. I had recently learned the benefits of drafting and how riders would sacrifice themselves by leading into the wind in front of their faster teammates. The defending World Champ Hinault had fought his way into third place. I later decided this took a lot of heart and pride from the defending champion because I had read he wasn't really a sprinter like the other two.

I later learned that Saronni went on to win in 1982 ahead of young Lemond. I would hope for the same from my hero Greg in the 1983 race. I really studied that poster. That woman in the crowd right on the finish line, socking her fist and overcome with joy...was she Maerten's mother? And the huge crowd there in Prague...so many people, all riveted on the riders thundering down the homestretch. This must be what races are like in Europe. When did Maertens take the lead? It seemed as if he punched through just at the end, driving all the way to the line. Why was Saronni up on his brake hoods? Everyone else was down in the dropped part of their handlebars. The top two riders were both on Colnago's, this brand just kept popping up...they must be some of the very best bikes around. Part of my attraction to cycling was that it really felt like it was MINE. The work I put into learning about this sport gave me ownership since I had to study it, figure it out, decode it, and then try to live it. Particularly in Cowboy Country where there were only a few other cyclists and so little information to be found.

This veritable quest for information on my new sport took a lot of effort. I had to really search and then reach out and connect with anyone else who was a past or present cyclist in my community. But that was part of the fun and made this sport REALLY MINE. Like Dave, it made me unique and gave me an identity. Cycling in America at this time was almost a cult: very few members and so many rituals, nuances, and traditions. My Dad brought that poster out to me in Oregon decades later, in 2007, and I joyously put it up on the wall. I had just returned from Italy where I visited the Colnago factory in Cambiago and met with Signore Ernesto Colnago himself! I had met his grandson, Alessandro, a few years earlier while riding in the Dolomites, and he set up a meeting for me with his grandfather in Cortina d'Ampezzo, where an invitation was extended. Ernesto's daughter gave my mother and I a tour of their museum, filled with

Saddling up to ride Cowboy Country

the race-winning bikes of the sport's great champions. I had a photo taken alongside Saronni's famous red world beating Colnago. Just like the one on my poster, that I had stared at for all those years. My many ensuing years in the sport of cycling would be FULL of serendipitous moments like this in the closely knit cycling fraternity. Many other Americans had similar experiences as significant numbers of us found this sport during a truly golden era. Connections made in this magical sport would keep coming around full circle for me and continue to deepen my love of the sport of cycling and its rich culture.

1981 saw a record 3 stars-and-stripes-jerseys in the pro road championship. Finishing together well back the pack in Prague were from left, George Mount, Greg LeMond, and Jacques Boyer.
Photo credit Cor Vos

US Cycling Team, first camp at OTC. Greg Lemond front 3rd from left, Kiefel center back, Eddy B. far right.
Photo credit Road Bike Action

Ron Kiefel, Greg Demgen, Greg Lemond, & Jeff Bradley make history at the 1978 Junior World Championships.
Photo credit Piet Kessels

July 2007 arriving at the Promised Lan
Photo Credit Carol Campbell

July 200
Cambia-
go, Italy
in the of-
fice of th
master
Ernesto
Colnago.
Photo
Credit
Carol
Campbel

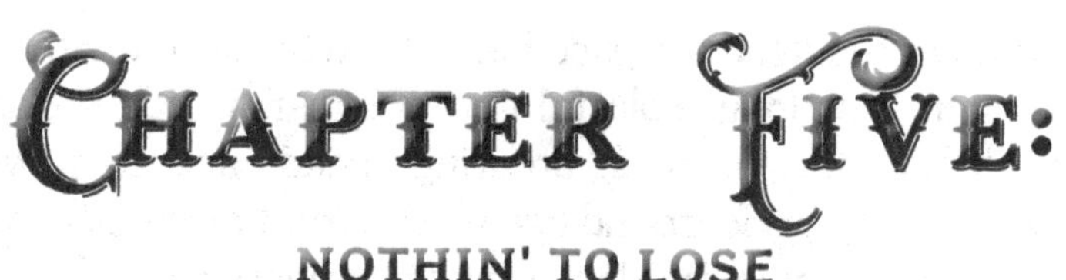

CHAPTER FIVE:

NOTHIN' TO LOSE

In June 1982, just after my seventh-grade year, my aunt Mary was getting married in Denver. I had been riding more and was gaining interest in racing, but there was precious little information available, let alone events or riders in my home state. *Bicycling* magazine, available in the Junior High Library, was a source but only had a minimal amount of racing content. It did have a monthly racing column written by a rider on the National Team that was always insightful and helpful. The guys at the local shop (Owner Bob & mechanic Drew-a former NOLS instructor) were also generous in sharing knowledge but they were nearly as new to the sport as me. As my dad read Denver's morning paper, he noticed the final stage, a criterium, of "The Rocky Mountain News Classic" was nearby that day. A criterium is a multi-lap race held on a short, flat downtown circuit and they are very spectator friendly. Each lap is usually less than a mile. Dad noted that if the wedding got over in time, we could go watch the race!

We got to the start just as the elite men, both professionals and category 1/2 amateurs, took to the course. I couldn't believe the speed, color, and intensity. The energy of the whole scene was electric. The course was packed with spectators. I had never seen anything quite like it! We felt a rush of wind as the riders blew by us, only inches from one another, accompanied by the soft yet powerful "whir" of their wheels. Rock music thumped out of the speakers, as an announcer kept us updated on what was happening in the race and explained some of the tactics like conserving energy by drafting.

The pack, the American term for peloton, was large and there were precious few breaks in the action on the .7-mile circuit. Periodically, small groups would "break away", gaining a gap over the field and then trade off the lead. We came to understand that this gave each rider a brief rest from the wind in the dead airspace behind the leader but kept the pace high. This long, colorful line of super fit riders blazed through the start/finish at amazing speeds and then were quickly coming back around again. The front of the pack was constantly changing as riders attacked or were chased down. Periodically the officials would ring the bell (I learned this was called a prime, pronounced 'preem') for cash or prizes on a given lap, and they would go even faster...a race within the race!

Two amateur riders from a powerhouse new team called 7-Eleven ended up lapping the field. They were Ron Kiefel and Andy Weaver-both destined to be part of the 1984 Olympic Team Time Trial bronze medal squad. This guy who was a pro-John Patterson won the sprint for third. As we stood near the podium studying his super tan and amazingly well-developed legs, my dad decided he had "an extra muscle" behind his knee. I later learned it was the popliteus, maybe that was from pulling up in those big gears I heard the pros used? Whatever it was, I thought his legs looked awesome-and I better start training harder and get stronger!

Kiefel, part of that historic 1978 Team Time Trial I had read about, won the race. But his 7-Eleven teammate, Florida native Weaver, impressed me as well. Once Kiefel was well off the front, Weaver attacked, and then time trialed up to his teammate. Time trialing was the art of riding fast alone without the benefit of a draft, so you had to be fast and efficient and mentally strong to focus through the pain since you never got the relief of drafting. I knew his name from my "Ten Years" book that I had been studying intensely. He was a nine-time National Champion and a regular member of Worlds Track and Road teams, especially for the Team Time Trial. On that day, he just FLEW away from the field, sleek and smooth...the quintessential image of a great time trialist. They had traded off the lead, helping each other, while distancing the rest. They were clearly always giving maximum effort when on the front, but that rest in the slipstream was clearly key to their efficiency...this sport was quite complex!

As we walked back to the car, I was rapidly recounting all the exciting details of the event, and my dad was right there with me. He really enjoyed the race too. We passed a table piled high with T-shirts and my dad, normally not sentimental at all (and damn cheap to boot) offered to buy me one. The guy said "Ah, the event's over, just take one!" We couldn't believe our luck, so dad got a blue one and mine was yellow. Like other prized t-shirts before, I would wear it thread-bare, and it was effectively my first "racing jersey" since it fit relatively snugly and had bike logos on it. Good enough for me!

Shortly after getting our shirts, dad pointed out that we would need to come up with a way to put my bike on the car to get me to races. Wow, my father was really buying into this! He was looking at the racks on the rider's cars and so we asked a guy who had just raced about his rack. The rider was a Schwinn team member named Thomas Prehn. Prehn was a long-time US National Team member, future US Pro Champion, and ultimately became the ONLY rider to compete in every edition of the Red Zinger/Coors Classic.

We could not have met a better ambassador for the sport. Tom, the first elite racer I met, was super friendly and very helpful in advising my dad about racks. This was 1982 and cycling was truly a fringe sport. Our humble shop in our tiny town didn't sell racks, there was very little written information, and of course there was no internet...you had to talk to people and figure this stuff out on your own. After the rack advice ended, Tom introduced himself and told me he wrote a monthly column for *Bicycling* magazine and had I read his articles? Of course, I had! His columns were about racing in Europe with the National Team! He wished us well and gave me an important lesson about promoting yourself and the sport of cycling. It was not the last I would hear from Tom Prehn...

A couple weeks later I would wear that shirt in my third ever race, again in my hometown of Lander. After watching the Colorado race, I had been practicing standing up out of the saddle and accelerating by rocking the bike back and forth beneath me, something I had seen the racers doing. It took me a little while to get the hang of it, but once I did, I loved the rhythm and connection to my bike it gave. I also love the powerful burst I felt as I accelerated. The local event was again a "citizen's race" which was open to anyone, it was promoted by Bob from the local shop and riders could do one (12 miles) or four (48 miles) laps of the hilly Squaw/Baldwin Creek loop.

He called it "The Red Dog", because he had a beautiful copper colored golden retriever, the hillsides along the road were red, and well that long climb "was a real bitch!"

Topher and Dave (I talked him into it!) both did the short race of 12 miles, but I stepped up to the 48-mile distance now that I had a "real racing bike" and my own helmet. I had even purchased a pair of Italian wool cycling shorts with a leather chamois. I got ahold of some special "chamois cream" (with fish oil?) to prevent chafing on long rides. I was the only "kid" and lagging behind most of the adults I didn't get to use my sprint, but I had been training often and riding with our local club and made it through the hilly course in 2 hours and 48 minutes.

My dad pointed out that my cycling hobby would entail expenses…the gas to travel to races, entry fees, tires, and the like. He had an idea for us to finance my new sport. We would often "hunt nightcrawlers" (large earthworms) in our backyard for fishing trips. Dad suggested we start selling them. Our house was on the way to Sinks Canyon, a popular fishing destination and so Dad made a wooden sign for the front yard, and I painted it up…" Nightcrawlers FOR SALE, $1.00 a dozen". We purchased small Pepsi cups and lids from the local Dairy Queen and Dad brought home some Styrofoam boxes and worm bedding from his friends who taught Biology at the high school. Our expenses were minimal, and we would hunt for the worms most evenings after watering the lawn and watching "Mash" together on television. The plan was to split the proceeds 50/50 and if one of us was out of town the other was in charge. Over time, we would provide worms to our local sporting goods store and a local drug store as well as the sales made from our house. Eventually, we would sell 500 dozen worms a summer!

Throughout my small community I was finding support and other money-making opportunities to support my cycling. Our neighbors, the Langs hired me to cut their grass all summer while they traveled to Europe. Upon learning about my newfound interest in cycling, Gary had regaled me with tales of riding his Italian road bicycle down the California Coast right after college. He understood the sport and was very supportive. Gary and Sue were my parents' closest friends, Gary was my pediatrician, and I grew up with their twins Corby and Amy at school. When they returned from Italy, they brought me a genuine wool Italian team jersey, covered in sponsor logos and a matching cap that I promptly wore in another small citizen's race in Casper.

Shortly after that race, my National Geographic "World" magazine arrived in the mail with a kid in a cockeyed helmet racing his bike on the cover...he looked just like me! Topher got the magazine too and it detailed a race in Colorado called the Red Zinger Mini Classic. It was organized by four 14-year-old kids and was modelled after the Red Zinger (now known as the Coors) Classic adult race that the kids had watched pass through their neighborhood. Red Zinger was a brand of tea made by the Boulder-based tea company Celestial Seasoning, the race sponsor. This event lasted ten days and raced on many of the same famous courses as the adult event in and around Boulder, but with shorter distances for riders from ages 10 to 18. I knew about "the big race", mainly from my Uncle Jim in Denver, who had watched stages, and I knew it was the biggest race in America. I had also seen footage of the 1980 edition won by Jonathan Boyer at Bike Club movie night. But this was a "Junior version" ...still long and hard, with a big field of participants, and it was held just south of us in Boulder, Colorado! All this meant it was very, very interesting. Topher was fired up too...we had to figure out a way to do this race.

August 1982, 14th birthday, proudly displaying my Italian jersey from the Lang family.
Photo credit Sue Lang

CHAPTER SIX:

SOMETIMES I FEEL I'VE GOT TO RUN AWAY

I'VE GOT TO GET AWAY

Cycling events of ANY SORT were very hard to find in Cowboy Country and my parent's church (First United Methodist) had a "bike camp" for young people in July, a few weeks after the local race. My family went to church every Sunday, and I hated it. I found it boring and unimportant, and I was always looking for a way to dodge any events happening there. Perhaps I could tolerate the church thing if cycling was involved. Our minister's wife Mrs. Donkle and the youth pastor Dwan were the hosts. Most of my interactions with Mrs. D involved her rolling her eyes at me as if to say "Lord, give me strength". Her expression was always stern, and smiles were rare. An exasperated puff of air usually followed her eye rolls, as if to signal the frustration she felt in my presence.

Realistically, they both meant well and worked hard to plan and chaperone a fun trip. In hindsight, Dwan was very enthusiastic just not very athletic. Mrs. D was the mother of two mellow bookworm daughters so maybe hyperactive teen boys were just more than she could handle. She certainly wanted the kids in the church to have a nice bike trip or "bike hike" as she called it. She drove her Ford pick-up, which carried the camping gear, and our duffle bags and Dwan rode along with the kids. The route began in Buffalo, Wyoming and headed south to Lander...covering 230 miles over five days. We would cross the Powder River Pass at 9,666 feet, as we rode through the Big Horn Mountains, a challenge at any age.

By this point, Topher had become my chief companion in all things bicycle, so he was in. He was also becoming interested in music, although we were still mainly confined to the Top 40 of the local FM radio station. His winters in Minnesota, however, were broadening his musical horizons and he had begun sharing the new tunes he was finding with me. I was becoming increasingly difficult to communicate my feelings to my parents, but both Topher and I were finding an outlet and an emotional connection from "our music". Often the lyrics and even the spirit of the music we enjoyed seemed to resonate with what we were feeling or experiencing at the time. We frequently took to quoting lyrics that seemed to address the situations we found ourselves in.

He rode an older French Peugeot bicycle that used to be his dad's and much like mine, was a racy upgrade from our peers run of the mill ten speeds. Dave, who still cites this ride as the ultimate proof that I can "talk him into anything", came along on board his "Huffy" department store bike. He was athletic and played basketball and football and ran track. I helped him tune his bike up and reassured him that he was up to the task. My folks drove us up to the Methodist Church in Buffalo that would host us for our first night. We met the other kids from the area and sat down to a group meal together, kicked off by a long prayer. Topher ripped a giant fart during the prayer, an inauspicious start, but in many ways an appropriate one.

As it turned out, Topher and I were the only kids in the group who had done much cycling. We were much faster and stronger than the other campers, including Dwan. We would leave the others far behind and then Mrs. D would force us to stop for mandatory rest breaks. These occurred much too frequently for our taste. She had prepared many trays of homemade granola bars, which we would wolf down while anxiously awaiting the arrival of the other kids. Many times, especially in the mountainous terrain, thirty minutes of riding was followed by thirty minutes of waiting. For adolescent boys who wanted to ride fast and push themselves it felt like torture. After each day's ride of around fifty miles, we would sleep in the local church or occasionally camp out. Evenings often involved some sort of Bible readings or even little skits, which we saw as even more torturous than waiting idly on the roadside. I had a hard time taking these things seriously, and my perceived rebellion irritated Mrs. D. Topher let another one fly during one of these interminable evenings, and Mrs. D. took me aside to ask if Topher had "some sort of a gas problem". Maybe it was all those granola bars.

The climb up Powder River Pass was the real deal and many of the other kids were walking their bikes for long stretches. The wait periods at the rest stops seemed interminable to Topher and I who stuck together and rode hard. While we didn't exactly fly up the mountain, we at least managed to stay on our bikes! I got a flat tire at one point and none of us carried pumps and spares. While Topher rode on to the designated rest point only a few miles ahead, I did what I had always done back home when I flatted…I hitched a ride! It was Wyoming and almost everyone drove a pick-up, so I just stuck out my thumb. Mrs. D was furious and regaled me with tales of all the horrible things that could have happened to me. Tired of what we perceived as her tyranny, Topher and I began to hatch a plan to ride the final day from Thermopolis to Lander, the longest day at 70 miles, straight through and hard…blowing right through all those rest stops! Topher came up with the perfect song for our little escapade and we sang a couple key lines to each other as we rode, eagerly anticipating our great escape…

TAINTED LOVE-Soft Cell from "Non-Stop Erotic Cabinet" (1981)
"Sometimes I feel I've got to
Run Away I've got to
Get away"

On day three, we camped near the summit of Powder River Pass, cooking out for dinner and breakfast, which was a rare treat. The descent off the Pass was a blast, long and fast, dropping down into the town of Worland. By the time we left the tree-lined roads of the mountains and hit the open, shade-less highway below it was nearly 100 degrees. The tar on the road started to melt and Dave hit a soft patch and launched over the handlebars. Almost no one wore helmets in those days and Dave landed face first and really tore himself up. Mrs. D took him to the church in the back of the truck and he called his folks to come and pick him up. The heat in the church's basement that night was awful, so Topher and I, "always the rebels" in the words of Mrs D., drug our sleeping bags through the side door to sleep on the cool grass outside.

We awoke to Jim Milleson and Bruce Campbell walking up to the church from Jim's truck as they had come to take Dave home. Dad had big news; I had won a drawing for $100 at the local Ford dealership! He didn't know that I had maximized my chances by throwing my name into the bucket at least ten times, but no matter...I had won! I still owed about $80 on my beloved French Bertin racing bike so now I could pay it off. I told Topher I would take him out for lunch and video games with the rest when we got back to celebrate. Dad got a kick out of us sleeping outside to cool off, but Mrs. D, of course, was upset with us "rule-breakers" yet again, which was, according to her, "a now predictable pattern". We knew we had only one more day of enforced rest stops before we would make our big break. The final night involved no bible readings or skits since "some of us were such unenthusiastic participants". We kept repeating those new wave lyrics that night as we settled into our sleeping bags...

"Now I know I've got to
Run Away I've got to
Get Away"

The final day's ride had some long and fast downhill stretches out of Thermopolis, driven by a tailwind along Wind River Canyon. We made the first few rest-stops so as not to show our hand too early. By the town of Riverton, as if on cue, dark angry clouds were forming overhead, and it was clear that we would have afternoon thundershowers to deal with. Just twenty-five miles separated us from home, and we were tired of all the stops. It was time for two skinny adolescents to make their stand, so we charged! Mrs. D squawked at us to stop, but not only were we enacting our rebellious plan, we were racing the incoming weather system and wanted to get home before it dumped on us! She passed us in her old pickup and stopped again and this time her pleas were more frantic and desperate but whatever she was saying we didn't listen, and we raced onward with everything we had. We hit Lander just as the wind started howling and the first drops of rain started to fall. Everyone else arrived wet and cold, while we were home free, warm and dry! We thought it was awesome...we did it!

That evening there was a pizza party downtown to celebrate the conclusion of the trip. Dave was there, already healing nicely, with all the parents beholding the miracles of youth and good health. Many of the kids were still soaking wet and shivering but Topher and I had showered up and changed into dry clothes. Mrs. Donkle was so mad, she practically had steam coming out of her ears and she didn't even speak to Topher and me. She did, however, speak to our parents. It turns out she had a flat tire in the truck and was yelling at us to stop and help her, but to be fair we couldn't hear. Whether there was an ass-chewing or not, I don't remember but I feel like Mom and Dad let this one slide. They were probably amazed that their little church dodger made it that far before going rogue!

July 1982 arriving home from bike tour from Buffalo to Lander.
Photo Credit
Carol Campbell

CHAPTER SEVEN:

THE EYE OF THE TIGER

My dad and I watched the second "Rocky" movie at home on television. As an aspiring bicycle racer in the isolation of a small Wyoming town the underdog story and the training sequences really resonated. The images of the determined fighter running the streets of Philly and doing one armed push-ups in a dingy gym inspired me to train and train hard! The music helped too. I now truly believed deep in my soul that with enough effort and determination, any athletic challenge could be conquered. I fully embraced this "Rocky style" approach in my own athletic quest. The vibe with my father was similar to watching that seminal 1980 Olympic hockey game. He used the teachable moments the film provided to reinforce important concepts of training, competition, and mental preparation. One of his key messages was always "keep training and your day will come".

In my training rides outside of town, two recurring fantasies drove me on: that I was training to represent the US in International competition or better yet that I was the National Champion. Both evoked images of proudly wearing the stars and stripes jersey. I adopted a new training routine on the Squaw/Baldwin Creek loop, which I rode often. As an adrenaline junkie, I loved the long descent back into town and always pedaled it furiously to achieve maximum speed. After flying past the sagebrush in the sandstone canyon nearly spun out in my highest gear, I faced one last climb before a short and twisting final descent down into the Lander valley. I would time the Rocky theme song in my mind as I started the climb and then stand up and stomp on as big a gear as possible, resisting the urge to downshift, so that right as I hit the summit the climactic "Ba-ba-BUH! Ba-ba-BUH!" of the music would ring out as my hometown came into view below. I would keep pushing to carry maximum momentum over the top and then plunge down onto the flat outskirts of town. Without shifting from my highest gear, I would unleash the biggest and most fierce sprint I could muster for an imaginary finish in front of the High School field house and a huge crowd. Always hoping, of course, that friends and neighbors would see me and realize how hard I was training and how fast I was getting. Many years later I realized that my imagination fueled quest for an adrenaline rush was an excellent training method for developing power.

The third installment of the Rocky movies was highly anticipated amongst all the kids at my school in the spring of 1982. Even rumors of the training that Sylvester Stallone had done to prepare for the role circulated amongst my friends. The ads promised great music, high intensity, and Mr. T as Rocky's ultimate rival. The hype was huge. By this point, movies like this were not just entertainment for me... they were fuel. Inspirational and motivational fuel for training and racing. Movies in a small town were a huge social event and a small breath of freedom and independence for my age group. In perhaps a final hoorah before I fully embraced the "with friends all the time" state of adolescence, my dad, whose coaching advice from the first two Rocky's had meant so much, accompanied me.

At age 13, "Rocky III" was the most incredible movie I had ever seen. Rocky was on top of the world until a mighty opponent came along. He had to find a new level, new training methods, even a new coach, and rise to the challenge yet again. It fired me up! All through the movie, I kept thinking of those photos and stories from my National Geographic "World" magazine of the Red Zinger Mini Classic (RZMC). One thing kept going through my head throughout the movie... "I have to do that race". It was my opportunity for a big athletic challenge, and I wanted to step up. Dad loved the movie as well and when we left the theater, I shared my revelation..." Dad, I have to race the Mini Zinger in Colorado!" Dad's response was a little lukewarm and he encouraged me to find some races to do "around here". Huh. Mom might see things differently, so I kept the faith. RZMC seemed like MY ultimate challenge, and so I kept training, hoping my day would come.

The seat post on my French bike, meanwhile, was at maximum extension as I shot up over six inches in height during junior high school. Bob sold Japanese Miyata's at his shop, which were very well made and reasonably priced. I got the "Pro" model, a special order, as racing machines like that were not kept in stock in Cowboy Country. It was just one notch below the "Team" version that Drew rode. Both high-end Miyata's looked the part of a full-on racing machine. They had a blue paint job which seemed to be applied over chrome, which really shone through in the sunlight. The fork tips and dropouts were chromed, a racing touch for sliding wheels in and out without damaging the paint. Unlike my Bertin, there were braze-ons for the down tube shift levers, an elegant head badge, and the catalog showed that their pro team in Europe had raced the Tour de France!

As was the custom of the time, I bought the frameset and all the parts separately to suit my needs. That bright blue beauty sat idly in my room all winter in anticipation of the spring thaw, while I saved my pennies to purchase the componentry needed to equip a not only bigger, but much-improved racing bike. After the "Breaking Away" influence, I had to have some Italian stuff on the bike and so Bob found an Italian "economy group" with Modolo brakes, Campy (YES!) derailleurs, and Miche hubs, cranks, and pedals. The components came individually boxed in colorful packaging (later repurposed to hold my cassette tapes) adorned with the all-important words "Made in Italy". There were now six cogs on the back, meaning my new machine was a twelve speed. Building it up, particularly cabling the brakes and derailleurs, was a long slow process for me as a novice mechanic. But I learned a lot from my maintenance class and enjoyed the process. Bob generously let me use his work stand after hours to slowly bring my beautiful machine to life in a ritualistic labor of cycling love that so many of us performed in those days.

In early 1983, Bob and Drew advised me to take out a racing license with the United States Cycling Federation (USCF) so I could do bigger and more challenging races against better riders, like the RZMC. Through USCF racing, I could also compete in State Championships with a chance to qualify for and compete in the National Championships! It was an exciting next step. The rulebook that came in the mail noted that Juniors (riders under 18) were to ride on restricted gearing, so I would need to figure that out at some point.

Bob hand built the wheels for me on dark anodized Mavic G40 clincher rims, since I also learned from my new rule book that Intermediate (age 12-14) aged riders were prohibited from racing on tubulars, known as sew ups in the parlance of racers. The tires, usually Italian, were sewn up at the base around a tube that was held inside and then cemented onto the rim as a single unit. Unfortunately, I had recently acquired a nice set of sew ups: gold anodized Super Champions rims with beautiful Campy hubs for use as my racing wheels. They were going to look great with the blue bike which had gold decals. I bought them from a very cool former racer named Kevin Hildebrand who lived down the street.

I think this rule was about the difficulty of mounting the tires correctly as well as the expense. Gluing on tires for a rookie like me was quite a challenge and I distinctly remember my friend Wade Doidge helping me one day. We managed to get that terrible Red Clement cement on our hands, our clothes, and all over the side of the rim. I think Wade even got some in his hair! The nuances of tubular tires were yet another part of the bike racing mystique I would need to study and unravel. Regardless, as per USCF rules, they would have to wait for the following season. Kevin was suffering from cancer and couldn't ride anymore but readily shared stories of racing in Wisconsin from a rocker on his front porch. Our close family friends, Gary and Sue Lang thought Gary's sister Judy could ride the Bertin and so I sold it to her.

After another winter of swimming, I was excited to get out on the road on my new bike as soon as the snow melted. Especially after being cooped up in the pool all winter, it felt great to be outside. Spring in Wyoming can still be very cold and windy so dressing well was key. Cold weather cycling gear in general at that time was mediocre at best but in Cowboy Country it was even worse. The best piece of kit I had were my blue Italian Sidi insulated vinyl shoe covers that my mom purchased for me on a trip to Denver. My trusty poly-propylene long underwear top that was also used for camping and skiing was good too. After that options were sparse and based on the teachings of NOLS, whose lore loomed large in our home.

NOLS is the National Outdoor Leadership School, based in Lander and founded by Paul Petzoldt, a world-famous mountaineer back in 1965, just three years before my parents moved to town. Paul climbed the nearby Grand Teton at age 16, in 1924, among the first to do so, and he did it in football cleats! He lived just down the street from us and dad had worked summers for the school, driving a bus. He taught his students (known locally as NOLSies or GraNOLS) to dress in wool, which would insulate even when wet and breathe when it was warm. We would see the old character out in his yard, always in his wool long-underwear, with a wool cap on his head, hanging his laundry, mostly wool, up to dry on his clothesline.

Fishing, hiking, backpacking, cross-country and downhill skiing, camping, and hunting were all deeply woven into our family culture. It wasn't until I was about ten years old, in fact, that I learned you could buy meat at the store! All of my family's protein came from the deer, elk, antelope, and moose that my dad and later I harvested. We loved being outside and enjoying "our" beautiful Wyoming mountains, the Wind Rivers. Given the rugged weather of our mile high mountain town, we had outdoor clothing, mainly wool, for most conditions. "There is no such thing as bad weather, only bad clothing choices" was a mantra from both my parents, as was "always wear your wool socks".

Thus, in the absence of any other teaching or availability of gear, I leaned on those NOLS and family philosophies for my early cold weather cycling outings. A short sleeve jersey, the only one I owned, went over the poly-pro. Luckily, our club's Orange Italian Cinelli jersey was wool but for a jacket I only had this baggy orange sweat tent from my time in the Boy Scouts. Wool liner gloves went underneath my knit-backed leather palmed cycling gloves. Thanks to the night crawler business, I could finally afford them! Wool leg warmers were SAFETY PINNED to my wool shorts and a wool ear band beneath the helmet was all I had. When the temperature really dropped and the wind howled, I had a wool neck and face warmer normally reserved for skiing... and I certainly always wore my wool socks!

As the weather warmed, my mileage increased, and my eighth-grade year wrapped up, I took another step in becoming a serious cyclist...I shaved my legs! Much to my amusement, the moment went down a bit like the "Breaking Away" movie, with my father coming into the bathroom and shaking his head and wondering "why in the world would any guy do such a thing"? My mother came next telling me how "strong and masculine" my legs were starting to look and why would I do this? Wasn't I worried about being teased by the other boys in the locker room? Although that never happened, one of the most popular girls in school did ask me once in the stands at a football game if the rumors were true...did I shave my legs? This was followed by giggles and whispering to her friends when I told her that yes, I did!

None of this bothered me, serious bike racers shaved their legs. I wanted to be a serious bike racer, so I shaved my legs...the end! Besides, it looked super cool, just like those riders in the magazine or the elite riders I had seen in Colorado. The rituals of bicycle racing were almost cult-like...and I wanted to belong to this cult!

I now had a job at Freewheel Sports, which had re-located to a larger location on the other end of Main Street and just down the hill from my house. I was "Flat Tire Boy"and would stop in every day to take care of all the flat tires in the repair area. I was given one dollar in credit per tire change to support my cycling habit. It wasn't much (even my dad thought it was cheap), but it was something...and I got to hang around the shop. I would save up my tire credits to buy gear I needed at wholesale pricing, which proved to be a huge help in equipping myself for my new sport.

When the schedule of Wyoming bike racing arrived in the mail from our USCF District Representative in Laramie, I was thrilled to see that there were several races in Lander including the State Championship in early June. The winners of their respective categories would qualify to compete at the Nationals to be held in San Diego in August. The guys at the shop told me about a kid from Casper that was fast and surely there would be riders from Jackson and Laramie. I trained hard in anticipation of a big battle on my home roads, in fact the course was that same Lyon's Valley loop where I did my first race nearly two years earlier. It would be two laps, 34 miles, and last year I had ridden 48, so I was confident I could go the distance but how fast would these other kids be?

The day of the big race arrived cold and clear, and I had on most of that wool winter training gear when I rode down to the start line, located only about a mile from my house. There I met a kid from Jackson named John Griber. I remembered seeing him that spring at the Mother's Day Road Race in Hoback Canyon outside Jackson the previous year. We had spoken briefly before the start of the 40-mile race as we were the only young riders in a field of grown men. We raced the B's (there were only two categories) and while I was dropped almost instantly, John hung on until just after the turn around. He was a couple of years older and had a Teledyne Titan Titanium (!) bike, but he raced in the JUNIOR category for ages 15 to 18, and I was in the younger INTERMEDIATE group. He was a friendly, cool guy and he was as new to this bike-racing thing as I was, but ...where was everyone else?

As it turns out John was the ONLY JUNIOR, and I was the ONLY INTERMEDIATE who had shown up for the Wyoming State Championship in 1983. The USCF official from Laramie told us it was pointless for us to go out there since we had no one else to race. He would just give us our medals, and we could go home. WHAT? We suggested racing each other or just going for a training ride but no, he wasn't having it. He told us we would just be in the way. I was so disappointed! Later when the Lander newspaper, "The Wyoming State Journal", known as "The Urinal" to many locals, printed the results, it was noted that "given that no other riders in his age group attended, Campbell was awarded the title". How humiliating! What would the kids at school say? John and I spoke, our parents met, and we agreed we had to find some bigger races to do. This Red Zinger Mini Classic thing was still on my mind, I told John about it, and he seemed interested.

The best thing about the State Roads debacle in 1983 was meeting other Wyoming cyclists. The best rider in the State was Danny Birkholz from Laramie, Wyoming's University town. The home of our ONLY four-year University in fact. Danny was deeply tanned with well-defined leg muscles and wore a shiny lycra jersey and shorts, unlike my old-world wool. He was everything that was cool about cycling. He drove a Volkswagen van, had a beautiful yellow Italian Masi (with so many clear coats that you couldn't even feel the decals!) with full Campagnolo equipment, and his style on the bike was smooth and fluid. Most Wyoming riders were Category 4 (new to the sport) or Category 3 (several years' experience) but he was a Category 2! He was, in fact, our state's only "Cat 2" rider, just one level below the National team. Everyone seemed to have a story about him... "I heard he has fifty pairs of wheels! And most of them have Campy hubs" was one. He went on training rides from Laramie all the way to Walden, Colorado (where my parents first lived after getting married) and back, which was 135 miles! He had ridden across the country on his bike and had even lived in South America. During one race he had initiated the break then started speaking Spanish to the other riders... and then quit!?!? Supposedly it was a race he had won before, and he wanted to give a new guy a chance. One of his friends and travelling companions Charles Pelkey (more on him later) referred to him as a "Government Funds Redistributor" ...meaning he was often on unemployment. This guy was a unique and eccentric individual, in many ways the prototypical American bike racer of that era. He became a friend of mine and someone I admired and looked up to.

I also met a cool older guy, Bill Wade, who raced in the "Veteran category" meaning age 35 and older, known today as Masters. He lived in Casper, Wyoming's biggest city with around 40,000 people. He had a Winnebago, known amongst the riders as the "Wade-abago" and was racing a two-day stage race the next weekend in Utah. He was coming through town to pick up Clay Hendrix. Clay was a strong but eccentric older guy with a long ponytail and one of the racers in my local club, but Bill offered to take me as well. Somehow, my parents agreed, including hosting these guys for lunch on the Friday before we left. My mom sent along several loaves of fresh home-baked Honey Whole Wheat bread, a real hit with the guys. The race was the "Vaughn Angell Memorial" consisting of three stages held over two days at the ski resort in Park City. Away from home, sleeping in an RV, and competing in a multi-day stage race with a large prize list...this was a real adventure!

Also on the trip was Brian Davis, known as "Fuzzy" to his friends because of his curly hair. He was one of the first "real" bike racers I had ever met. He raced in a leather hairnet helmet and had lapped me the year prior in the downtown Laramie criterium, my first ever attempt at America's favorite style of road racing. Brian had raced at the Junior Nationals the previous year in Milwaukee. Originally from Cheyenne, he was now attending Central Wyoming College in nearby Riverton and studying broadcasting while DJ'ing on the College Radio Station there. We quickly bonded and he set about educating me about music, another topic I was interested in and desperate to learn about.

Growing up in Cowboy Country had left me woefully lacking in rock and roll knowledge. Most of what I knew came from the radio and swimming bus trips. He started me with the Rush album "2112" on the long trip down which was exciting and interesting. It was honestly a little over my head, though, as a 14-year-old currently listening mostly to Asia, Journey, and Michael Jackson. Later that year, Brian would give me one of the coolest gifts ever. Upon leaving town for several weeks, he left me his stereo and record collection to help continue my rock and roll education. Led Zeppelin, The Who, U2, Pink Floyd, Rush, The Police, INXS, and many others spun on his turntable and continued to expand my horizons...and inspire my training rides! Over the next few years, he would ride with and coach both Topher and me. Even though I was taller than him, he christened me "Little Davey".

I was thrilled to have two riders my age to race against in Utah. One was younger than me and not very strong, but the other kid was a solid rider. The first stage was a hill-climb time trial up the access road to the top of the ski lift. The French call time trials "the race of truth" and riders start at intervals, racing alone and against the clock. I had never done a race like that. I certainly didn't do a proper warm up since I had no concept of what one might entail. I charged off the line at a pace that I couldn't maintain and was soon huffing and puffing and searching for a lower gear. I barely struggled across the line, but the results said I was a few seconds faster than my rival. That afternoon there was a criterium in the ski resort parking lot and the final day was a tough, hilly little circuit race and I won them both. As such, I won the overall and was THRILLED at my prizes…a long sleeve wool jersey, a Campagnolo logo (!) water bottle, and a tubular tire spare bag for under my saddle. All items were red, all were things I needed, and all were pressed into service immediately. I had learned I could compete successfully against riders my age and perhaps more importantly you could win cool gear!

Shortly after the Utah trip, Topher was back in town, so I now had a regular training partner as well as someone to race against. We practiced drafting, riding closely behind one another to shelter from the wind and always finished our rides with an all-out sprint. We pushed each other hard. The older riders on the Utah trip had taught me about the basics of cycling tactics: riders only have a fixed amount of energy so it must be used judiciously. Race to save energy whenever you can. When the intense moments came like breaking away on a climb or sprinting, though, you had to go deep! I shared these insights with Topher, and we also talked a lot about music.

His interest in music continued and was deepening as well. We were both absolutely intrigued by a new format called "music videos". The imagery and energy took us far from our mundane and predictable little world. We watched them on the USA channel late at night during a program called "Night Flight". When we travelled to bigger towns or stayed in a hotel, we could watch loads of music videos non-stop on MTV, 24 hours a day! Occasionally it was just seeing the artists performing on stage but other times, artists like Duran Duran, Tom Petty, or Michael Jackson made mini movies that created a story that went along with the song. Billy Idol, who also had great videos, had attitude and style, and his songs rocked! Watching the videos as well as talking with Brian really expanded our musical horizons. Expanding them well beyond the standard fare of mostly terrible Country music swill being served up throughout Cowboy Country!

By 1983, Lander's local race, The Red Dog, was in its third year and became a stage race with a time trial and criterium on Saturday and a road race on Sunday. Bob got the local Chamber of Commerce on board and put together a solid prize list that drew all the Wyoming riders as well as some from Utah, Idaho, and Montana. Nearly a hundred cyclists came to our little town but in the Intermediate category it was just me and Topher. Danny and his buddy Charles stayed at my house, crashing out on the carpet in our front room. Charles was about ten years older and a student at the University. He was irrepressibly enthusiastic about the sport, much like me, and he was also super into music and introduced me to exciting new artists outside the mainstream like the Dead Kennedy's and the B-52s, which were among his pre-race favorites.

I found that most if not all of the members of my "cycling cult" were really into music and many were into music that was not on the pop charts. Part of this was certainly due to listening to and sharing music while travelling to races, and with the long distances between towns in our state you always needed "tunes for road trips". Additionally, we all needed to find inspiration for the long miles and intense efforts of training. Perhaps most importantly though the sport of cycling in America was outside the mainstream and filled with unique and oddball characters who desired a similarly unique and oddball soundtrack to their activities. Whatever the case, I had many great friends from my childhood, but as I met other cyclists, on many different levels I was "finding my tribe!"

Getting up early to help my mom fix breakfast, Charles was an immediate hit with my parents. He would faithfully call us every Christmas morning for many years to wish us well. Charles, more than anyone perhaps, would typify the heady cycling times we were living in 1980s Wyoming. The newness of the sport presented immense opportunities for enterprising and energetic people like Charles. He became a commentator on NPR and hosted a cycling program. He would later work for *Velo-News* covering the biggest races in the World and he ultimately became one of the foremost journalists on cycling's doping problems, helping to bring down Lance Armstrong. Many years later, he got a law degree and even served in the Wyoming legislature.

Since Topher and I were both now licensed racers with the USCF, we were receiving a *Cycling USA newspaper* in the mail, which helped us learn about our new sport. American amateur cycling was really coming on and we were avidly following it all. The carrot of the upcoming 1984 Olympics in LA and all the developments in coaching and sponsorship were continuing to bring "our" riders up to a higher level. US riders, particularly the men were starting to win internationally while US women had already been among the best in the world for years. On June 6, 1983, Matt Eaton, made history by winning the British "Milk Race", then one of the most competitive and prestigious amateur races in the world. He joined two American legends as only the third US winner of a major international amateur stage race: George Mount had won 1979 Tour d'Auvergne and Greg Lemond took the 1980 Circuit de la Sarthe, both in France.

Eaton was supported by an all-star cast of riders, many of whom we were starting to know of and others we would soon meet: Alexi Grewal (One of the few Americans to challenge the Colombians on the climbs of the 1982 Coors Classic), Raleigh team riders Andy Hampsten and Steve Tilford, Chris Carmichael, and Steve Speaks. Their teamwork was noted in the press as a key to their success and they were second behind mighty Czechoslovakia in the team competition. Of note was that this was a National "B team" as American cycling had grown so deep that we could now field TWO highly competitive teams. Thurlow Rogers, Davis Phinney, Doug Shapiro, Weaver, and Kiefel were also competing in Europe as an "A" squad. That spring, Rogers had won stages in both big Italian amateur stage races: the Settimana Bergamasca and the Giro delle Regioni, enroute to second and third place GC finishes. Perhaps more significantly, he was fourth against all the best Eastern Europeans in the prestigious Peace Race. Phinney had even won a stage of the prestigious Circuit des Ardennes in France! Both groups were now strong enough to win against the Europeans, an exciting development. All the cyclists in the US felt we were riding this building wave of growth and competence in the sport together and "our" prospects were looking promising for the upcoming Olympics.

The Coors Classic, held in Colorado, would feature prominently in my formative experiences as well as helping to launch the careers of the best American riders of the era. Not only was it the biggest race in America but it was accessible to me due to its proximity and my family in Denver. 1983 was significant with the Classics final stage starting outside Colorado, a first. The 106-mile Capital to Capital Road Race would travel from Cheyenne, Wyoming to Denver, Colorado and there was a criterium after the start for the rest of us. I would get to see some of the riders from my magazines in person. The course was hot, windy and fast since it was on mainly flat roads. A local shop, where everyone knew Fuzzy, sponsored the "crit" right after the Coors stage start, so the Wyoming cycling crowd (and some party crashers from Fort Collins who schooled Topher and me in the Junior race, giving us a taste of what we would be up against at the RZMC) watched the start, cheered our heroes, and then did our own race.

Prior to the start, we spoke with the friendly and affable Phinney of 7-Eleven who had won nearly all the criterium stages that year and got his autograph in our *Cycling USA newspaper*. A skinny Raleigh rider we had read about, Andy Hampsten, was wearing the Best Young Rider's jersey and had stayed close to the Colombians on the climbs. He was shy but gladly took time to talk with us. He spoke in detail about supporting Eaton's historic win in Britain. Steve Speaks, another of the riders on the US team with Eaton in Britain, reinforced the idea that American cycling was starting to really come on and talked to us about how "we" had beaten some of the best riders in the world, even the Eastern Europeans. We...the Americans!

In the overall standings at the Coors, Colombian Lucho Herrera held a commanding seven-minute lead over Canadian Steve Bauer coming into the final stage. Bauer was Phinney's fiercest rival in the North American criteriums that dominated the US calendar at the time. It was the second year in a row that "The Colombians" had schooled the American riders in the mountains and they were none too happy about it. My dad and I stood on the barriers right by the tiny race leader in his baggy and oversized red race leader's jersey. He was visibly nervous. As the start approached, it was clear he needed to pee and my dad, always willing to lend a hand, offered to hold his bike so he could. The clearly suspicious Colombian made it clear he wanted no help from some gringo in cowboy country!

Out on the road, he would get no help either...a break went clear early in the crosswinds, and the Americans ripped the Jersey right off his back! The locomotives of the escape were the 7-Eleven riders and the East Germans. Dale Stetina, the 1979 Classic Champion and one of America's very few professional riders, had been consistent all race and was the main beneficiary when he hopped on board this train. His temperamental teammate Grewal, hampered by his asthma for much of the race, did a great job blocking the chase group behind, which also contained Bauer. Alexi had won a dramatic stage earlier in the race on the Morgul-Bismark course. He was true to his surly reputation when Topher and I tried to get his autograph that morning, which really disappointed us.

The break gained enough time for Stetina to claim the overall win on the final day and without having won a stage. An ecstatic and exhausted Kiefel (who later swept the 1983 Nationals, winning the time trial, the road race, and the team time trial) outsprinted his 7-Eleven teammate Ron Hayman of Canada in downtown Denver to win the stage. The break had averaged over 30 mph and put over nine minutes into Herrera. The East Germans, who placed their three best riders into the move took the team classification as a result.

Back in Cheyenne, we local Wyoming riders heard

these stories from race officials and then, as was always the case in the pre-internet era, read about the details much later. After the race we crowded into the local shop for awards and Charles was ecstatic about winning a new kind of bike called a mountain bike in a raffle. We also watched some clips of the Tour de France on ABC's "Wide World of Sports", wincing when Dutchman Henk Lubberding forced Frenchman Michel Laurent into the barriers in a sprint for the finish. Laurent went down hard in a terrifying crash and Lubberding was relegated, providing further education for me in the nuances of cycling. In the final 200 meters of a race, you had to "hold your line" to give others a fair chance. You couldn't cut them off like the Dutchman had done. This was the first time I had seen the Tour on TV. Herrera may have lost the Coors, but he would be prominent on our TV screens the following summer, though…dropping European legends Laurent Fignon and Hinault to win the Alpe d'Huez stage in the Tour de France!

By now Topher and I had both somehow convinced our mothers to drive us around the Boulder/Denver area so we could take on the ten-day, twelve-stage Red Zinger Mini Classic in August. Realizing we needed to step up our game, Topher's dad and stepmom agreed to take us to the Steamboat Resorts Stage Race a couple of weeks ahead of our big goal. The format was a Saturday morning road race and afternoon time trial, and a criterium on Sunday. The field was by far the largest we had raced in, with over thirty riders, all of whom were strong and savvy. The racing was relentless, fast, and aggressive and we struggled to finish in the middle of the field. We whined back at the shop that the riders seemed to sprint up every hill and Brian laughed at us, remarking, "That's called attacking!" We clearly needed to learn more…and get stronger.

To that end, Drew and Bob took us up to Togwotee Pass outside of Dubois, an hour's drive from Lander, for "mountain training". It was very generous of them and very challenging for us. Dubois sits at just below 7000 feet elevation but then rises to nearly 10,000 up on the Continental Divide at the summit of the Pass. Usually enroute to skiing in Jackson Hole, we had sat in our parent's cars over this brute

Saddling up to ride Cowboy Country

many times over the years but riding it? And while trying to keep up with fully grown and strong men? It was a daunting task.

Tightening our toe straps in the parking lot of a local coffee shop, we crammed our pockets with bananas and my mother's chocolate chip cookies, excited but a little scared of what would be our longest and hardest ride yet. We rode several miles on the flat before the earliest slopes of the pass reared up, but once they did, it seemed like we were out there climbing forever. There were many false summits, and it seemed like we would never reach the top. Drew and Bob were great, giving us tips about keeping our breathing under control and alternating standing and sitting down on long stretches. The descent back to the car, of course, was a blast!

Our races to that point were all well under two hours but we had just slogged through four hours of the hardest riding we had ever done. We were starting to discover the undeniable positive feedback loop of endorphins that came from pushing deep into your physical capacities. Despite the suffering, we learned how great it felt afterwards to bask in the glow of your achievement. There was also something about riding hard amidst the rugged and majestic beauty of the mountains that just felt right. It inspired us and allowed us to dig deeper. Before falling asleep for the car ride home, we thanked Bob and Drew for pushing us as we really felt ready now to take on the Mini Zinger!

This was 1980s Wyoming bike racing. My friends from Laramie-Rex Burke, Danny Birkholz, and Charles Pelkey.
Photo credit Charles Pelkey

CHAPTER EIGHT:

SWEET DREAMS (ARE MADE OF THIS)

My mom purchased a Swedish Thule roof rack from Bob for our 1968 Ford Mustang to carry my bike all over Colorado. Dan Lander, a nurse, and member of the local club generously loaned me a pair of wheels for spares. I only had the one set on my bike and would need to put wheels in the follow car or the pit zone in criteriums in case I had a flat tire. My sew-ups had to stay behind in the garage, as they were "illegal" for Intermediate racing in 1983. We planned the race "on the cheap" with Grandma and Grandpa Boxell's home in Golden as a frequent place to crash and minimal hotel stays. We coordinated with Topher and his mom, Barb whenever we could, as well as John and his stepdad OJ.

Junior gears were "restricted" in those days and unlike in Wyoming where officials never checked our gears, every day after our RZMC stages we would have to do a "roll out". The bike was placed in its highest gear and the pedal aligned with a piece of tape and then rolled backwards to another tape mark marking the allowed distance. For Intermediates it was a few inches beyond 22 feet. Gears were spoken of by the number of teeth on the chainrings (front sprockets) and on the cogs (rear sprockets). In an era when most every bike came stock with 42/52 chainrings and freewheels with a 13 or 14 (or rarely a 12) highest cog, meeting this requirement wasn't easy and often required special modifications. Since my basic freewheel was a 14-24 six speed (up from five cogs on the Bertin), the cheapest and easiest way to make my gears junior legal was to remove my 52 tooth chainring and replace it with a smaller 45. I had to get this odd-sized chainring from a mail order catalog since Bob only stocked standard sizes. My front chainring combination was a somewhat ridiculously closely spaced 45/42, meaning I was usually riding in the big ring. Some riders my age just used a single chainring. The logic was to encourage young riders to spin and not ruin their knees stomping on big gears. In practicality it meant on a descent of any steepness we were spun out and coasting while in flat, fast races we were in top gear the whole time and spinning like crazy!

We picked up our race packets with hundreds of other kids on August 11th at the University of Colorado in the American cycling mecca of Boulder. The Intermediate category would feature 65 riders, far and away the largest peloton Topher and I had ever raced in. In fact, it doubled our previous biggest field experience in Steamboat! John was racing too, and the Junior field had nearly 100 competitors, including several riders like Craig Schommer, Tim Hinz, Roy Knickman, James Urbonas and David Farmer who were permanent residents at the Olympic Training Center. Knickman, on the same Raleigh team as Hampsten, Tilford, and Rogers, especially had a buzz about him, being dubbed "the next Lemond" by the cycling press. Many thought he was in with a chance of making the Olympic Team the following year. He would go on to place top five in five different events, including two medals, the following month at the Junior Worlds in New Zealand.

The race was extremely well organized, and everyone received a musette bag with a race logo t-shirt, cap, poster, water bottle, and the all-important race bible upon check-in. In Wyoming, the races rarely even gave out a t-shirt! In addition to stage details and directions, the Race Bible listed each of our hometowns and our best race results, mine of course being "Wyoming State Champion". Given the circumstances, it felt like a dubious distinction. I hadn't really earned it after all. There were lots of REAL state champions at this race. I immediately met Colorado, California, Arizona, and east coast riders, and there were many unknown quantities from across the country including the national champion in my age group, Andrew Gellatly from Virginia.

The ten days featured twelve stages: A street sprint prologue, four criteriums that had famously featured in the

Coors Classic (North Boulder Park, The Boulder Mall, Vail Village, and Washington Park in Denver), four road races, two hill climb time trials, and a concluding circuit race. I got stung in the eye by a bee warming up for the sprints and could hardly see and ended up getting smoked and eliminated immediately. Everything at this race was bigger, harder, and faster than in Wyoming. There were team vans with high-end matching machines on top, and riders getting their legs oiled up and massaged by soigneurs! * Topher and I were some of the few lacking any team logos or sponsors on our jerseys. It was all a little intimidating but exciting and I loved it...this was where I wanted to be!

The afternoon's criterium was even worse than the Street Sprints as I was dropped quickly and got lapped, nearly twice! The following day's road race, which featured a long climb, was better, but I was dropped again. My Aunt Mary and Uncle Lyle came to the next race, a criterium at the Boulder Mall, to take photos and I vowed I would do better. I scored a personal victory when, although once again off the back, I was determined to NOT get lapped. When the bell rang signaling one lap to go, the pack was bearing down on me, and I had a Rocky moment, deciding I would not go down without a fight! I basically sprinted the whole last lap as if I was in a solo breakaway and not some wanker out the back and I just managed to make it to line without being caught...progress!

Coming from a tiny rural area, the Red Zinger Mini Classic was as much a social and cultural experience for me as an athletic one. I was very interested in the music played over the PA before and after the stages. Two songs that I really loved were The Eurythmics "Sweet Dreams (Are Made of This)" and Duran Duran's "Rio". I had seen the videos for both at our hotel the night before the first stage. The imagery, the fashion, and the color were all mesmerizing! We all had dinner that night at the Hotel Boulderado alongside the Mall after the fourth stage, eating outside right across the street from a record store. Kids would roller skate through the mall and right into the re-

*A soigneur is a team helper who cares for riders during a race by giving massage, preparing food, and handing up bottles and musettes.

cord shop.

And it was a "real record store" stocked full of so much music I had never even heard of. Music in my hometown of Lander, Wyoming was quite limited: we had KOVE, a country western station and KDLY, which played the top 40 on the pop charts…and we didn't even have a record store! We could only purchase records and cassettes at a couple of department stores and the choices were very limited. It seemed we heard and could buy only the very worst and cheesiest of the Top 40. We were still well over a year away from having the current revolution in modern music, MTV in Wyoming. Many of my other friends were into heavy metal and although I did like the way that got me pumped up for training and racing, I longed for something deeper and more meaningful. Music that lifted me, much like cycling did, above what I saw as the mundane, boring, and predictable ways of life in "small town, Wyoming". I began to find it during my time racing in Colorado in the form of Punk/New Wave and the music that was played on college radio stations.

One of the best riders competing in the RZMC was Erik Bennett from Fort Collins. We quickly became friends and hung out after the races, even though during the races he was regularly leaving me behind. He wore the Green King of the Mountains jersey throughout the race, ultimately winning that category. In bigger stage races, officials awarded points to the first few riders to the top of the major climbs and the more difficult the climb, the more points were earned. Patterned after the Tour de France, there was a separate prize list for this category as well as a points jersey competition for the most consistent daily finisher to reward the sprinters. In this race, the biggest in the country, the winner of each competition got a new bike! Erik had spikey hair with a "tail" in the back. On the chrome forks of his Italian Benotto racing bike he had affixed big blue stickers that said SEX on one leg and PISTOLS on the other. I had no idea what this was all about, so he explained that it was a punk rock band and played some of their songs for me on his Walkman. Now, THIS was a new world…wild, raw, exciting, and rebellious, and like nothing I had been hearing back in Cowboy Country! In the time after the races, I continued to pay attention to what the other riders were listening to and browsed in the numerous record stores throughout the college town of Boulder after our daily races.

My last stop, not coincidentally, prior to driving back home to Lander was the Record Store near my grandmother's house where I went to find some punk rock to bring home. I will always remember what the clerk told me when I asked for a Sex Pistols cassette..." This is the coolest punk from when punk was cool." I bought "Never Mind the Bollocks", playing it on my Walkman on the drive home. It was angry, it was rebellious, and nobody else I knew in Lander had it or had ever heard anything like it. In what I perceived as the sometimes shallow and occasionally repressive world of Wyoming, rock and roll and cycling both meant freedom. They were both places where you could spread your wings and express your individuality. The Sex Pistols cassette was the perfect soundtrack for my continued journey into the world of bicycle racing.

For Stage five we left the Boulder/Denver area and drove up through a dramatic thunderstorm to the mountains. Topher's mom's friend had a condo in Copper Mountain and we crashed on his floor. In the morning, we faced a four-mile hill climb time trial on the bike path from Copper Mountain to Vail pass. I was hoping to improve my overall standings with a good ride here and was going well when I approached a pedestrian. I yelled out "on your left" and that is exactly where she moved... to her her left! We clipped shoulders, which sent me over the handlebars... and pretzeled my front wheel. I couldn't continue and there was still nearly a week's worth of racing ahead! I was totally screwed.

I limped back down to the start-line, distraught and angry. My mom convinced me to plead my case to the race officials, and they agreed to let me continue in the race, but I would be given the last placed riders time on the day. The Intermediate class included riders from age 12 through 14 and hence there was a wide range of physical development among us. Some kids were muscular and shaving, most like

Saddling up to ride Cowboy Country

Topher and I were just skinny kids who were either amid, or had just gone through, their growth spurt. And some like the guy in last place were still just little boys! Shortly after negotiating our deal to continue, this rider was just setting off, so mom and I cheered him off the line. The time of this little guy who placed last every day would keep me in the race.

Fortunately, I had those spare wheels from my Lander clubmate for the afternoons race. We found a shop in the village at the foot of the ski lift that could rebuild my wheel with a new rim before we left the next morning. The afternoon criterium consisted of 25 laps through Vail Village for twenty miles total. It was right at the foot of the ski mountain and was a route regularly used in the Coors Classic. I had seen that race on TV and in magazines with Davis Phinney having won the last few editions. The village was styled to look European with little chalets and shops, and the start/finish banner was adorned with national flags from all over the world. The course was packed with spectators and there was a little climb shortly after the finish. I felt like I was racing in Europe! Thoroughly inspired, I didn't get dropped and recorded my first pack finish, an important lesson in letting the race inspire rather than intimidate and rising to the occasion. After days of floundering behind, in Vail I was finally IN the race!

I had been doing all the races in my Wind River Wheelers wool club jersey but most of the cool kids had spandex jerseys or even skinsuits. I had only recently upgraded to "skin shorts" (Lycra spandex) which were a massive improvement over wool in every way. Cycling gear was very hard to come by in Lander, usually requiring a special order. I had found a cool Italian spandex jersey, made by Sergal, in a supplier catalog at Bob's shop in the weeks prior to my big race and cashed in all my tire credits to order it. It hadn't arrived in time, but Dad mailed it to Grandmas when it did. As such, I got my bright shiny teal, yellow, and purple Italian jersey just in time for the Stage seven Washington Park Criterium in downtown Denver. I thought it looked "new wave", but my father thought it was girly and hated it! The tight fitting, brightly colored clothing that became the norm among racing cyclists during the 1980s would elicit many comments and insults out on the roads of Cowboy Country over the coming years.

The Denver stage was another I had seen in the Coors Classic and it only had one 90-degree corner with the rest being just sweeping bends. The whole thing circled around a big pond amidst large flower gardens. My Grandmother and Grandfather Campbell lived nearby and came to watch, joining Mary and Lyle, while Aunt Bev was there too, having driven out from Illinois. Between my new jersey, more family to cheer me on and the morale from my improved results in Vail I was fired up! The race was 25 laps for eighteen miles and with around ten laps to go, I was not only still in the pack, I was also feeling great...so, I moved up! Before I knew it, I was near the front and when I saw all my relatives approaching, I charged! Right onto the very front of the peloton! A classic rookie ego-move. My family, who by now had grown accustomed to seeing me either dropped or hanging on for dear life, went crazy! "He's leading the pack!" I could hear my Aunt Bev exclaim!

It seems every bike racer goes through this phase of development. After a period of struggle and adjustment, once they are finally "in" the race, the excitement inspires them to drive hard on the front of the group and just tow everyone else along. And that is exactly what I did, lap after lap and right when I passed my family...I got on the front and threw down! I knew about the benefits of drafting and how much harder it was to just ride on the front with everyone in my slipstream, but I couldn't resist. I was drunk on my newfound power and confidence! Bike racing, however, as I would learn in the coming years, is all about conserving your energy and making a move when it can really count, like breaking away from the field, or winning a final sprint. Riding hard on the front just gives your competitors a free ride and wastes valuable energy. And, of course, with a few laps to go, I started running out of steam and fell back. I still managed to get into the top twenty in the final sprint, which was my best result yet. I had to endure some humiliation when my Aunt Mary, very proud of my improvement, had me sit on the #1 step of the podium after the race for a photo. No rider wants a picture on the top step unless it is earned! I moved quickly, didn't smile, and hoped none of my competitors would see me.

For Stage eight we had to drive back up into the mountains, this time to Estes Park. My mom was fired up as she had worked summers here in college and on the beautiful drive up there told me story after story of her days there. It was only our second night in a hotel, and I was stoked to find MTV once again. In the morning, we had a tough road race called "Devil's Gulch" which started by hurtling down Big Thompson Canyon. This was both exciting and terrifying, as 65 gung-ho kids blazed along at 40-50 miles an hour bunched tightly together and completely spun out on our tiny top gear.

After the fast descent, we turned left and climbed back to Estes Park through Devil's Gulch Canyon, a long and steady climb. Brimming with newly found confidence in my abilities and no longer in awe of my competition, I was hanging tough as we approached the last steep switchbacks before the descent back down into Estes Park. Just as I was imagining going with a break over the top or contesting the final sprint, the pack compacted and the rider behind rammed into me. I didn't go down, but his front wheel had hit my rear quick release skewer, and it was now flipped straight out! It was on the verge of opening all the way which would cause my wheel to fall out enroute to an almost certain crash. Yikes!

Back in Bob's bike maintenance class, we were taught to put the skewers parallel to a frame tube to prevent them being forced open. I had seen pictures in magazines of top riders with both skewers pointing straight back and this looked cool to me...aerodynamic and sleek. Being very in tune with the visual aspects of the sport, I mounted my skewers like this. Now in the heat of battle, I was paying the price for choosing cool over practical. I had to stop and close that skewer or risk the wheel pulling loose on the descent and causing certain doom. I tried to pass as many riders as I could, but I finished off the back and was angry at myself for missing an opportunity for a much better result.

As I waited to watch John finish, the Junior women came in. Well, one Junior woman…Ruthie Matthes, a ski racer from Sun Valley, Idaho and a virtual unknown. She wore a grey jersey with no team logos or sponsors… stealthy! She had attacked on the long climb and left behind a field of strong women, several of whom lived at the Olympic Training Center. She arrived over four minutes clear and took the overall lead. She made quite an impression on me and over time she would make quite an impression on the sport. In her ensuing nineteen-year cycling career she would win three National Road championships, five National Mountain bike championships, the Mountain Bike World Cup, a silver medal in the World Road Championships, represent the USA in the 2000 Olympics, and win the 1991 World Mountain Bike Championship!

Just like at the Coors Classic, the penultimate stage was on the barren roads of the Morgul-Bismark outside of Boulder. A tough, hilly circuit that finished with a couple of very steep climbs, the last of which was known as "The Wall". And just like at the Coors, there were officials on hand to help catch exhausted riders on the line and even medics with oxygen masks! My Uncle Jim, one of my first cycling tutors, came for this one and I hoped for a solid performance to move me up on the GC. I secretly wanted to move ahead of Topher, and I was getting close. Alas, I was dropped near the end but still managed to distance Topher. Our long odyssey was nearing its end. That evening we blasted up the 1.2-mile NCAR climb outside of Boulder and then raced a twenty-mile circuit race around the National Bureau of Standards on the final day.

I was 33rd and Topher was 34th on the final General Classification. In just over two months, I had come a long way with my cycling, from merely hoping I would have someone to race against to racing for ten days straight against sixty-five of the best riders in the country my age! All the riders gathered at the awards ceremony in a Colorado University auditorium, cheering our newfound friends and basking in the glow of our collective accomplishment of finishing a ten-day long race. The organizers gave out some incredible prizes. Erik won a new Trek racing bicy-

Saddling up to ride Cowboy Country

cle for being King of the Mountains. Back in Golden, my grandfather told me how proud he was of me for "racing against all those more experienced kids' day after day and hanging in there." I had learned a lot and was proud of my improvement over the course of the race. I overcame some setbacks, but I desperately wanted to really compete and be up front in a big race and score a solid result. I wanted to be up on that podium for real!

Vail Village Crit RZMC 1983, finally staying with the pack!
Photo credit Carol Campbell

Boulder Mall, 1983 Red Zinger Mini Classic. Only three days in, exhausted and still in wool jerseys!
Photo credit Mary Gallivan

Chapter Nine:

IN TOUCH WITH THE GROUND,

I'M ON THE HUNT

I'M AFTER YOU

My head was spinning with cycling mania from my ten-day long RZMC immersion into bike racing nirvana. Colorado in the 1980s was the beating heart of American cycling…loads of talented riders, a well-organized state association, a full race schedule, the Olympic Training Center in Colorado Springs, and the Coors Classic. Most of the riders at the Mini Zinger were light years ahead of Topher and I in terms of racing experience and tactical sense, particularly in a large field. My new buddy Dan Berger even told me that he and some of the Boulder guys went out training on a weekly basis with my 7-Eleven heroes Kiefel and Phinney!

The bike shops, and they were everywhere, really catered to racers. There always seemed to be a bright blue decal on the door framed in the world champion's rainbow stripes to greet you: "Campagnolo spoken here!" Once you saw that, you knew it was a shop for racers! They were jam-packed with the equipment I treasured but was only available to me through mail-order catalogs. It was also gear I mostly couldn't afford: hand-made Italian frames, Campagnolo components, tubular tires and wheels, glossy photo books of the Coors Classic, and pro team jerseys and shorts. Posters of European champions in the world's biggest races adorned the walls and everyone knew the sport well. They spoke the language of bicycle racing and one of the mechanics noted that cycling in this country was getting so big that Colorado might even host the World Championships, a first ever for the US, in a few years!

They also had a BRAND-NEW magazine: *Winning*

Bicycle Racing Illustrated. I bought the inaugural issue at the shop in Vail that rebuilt my wheel. It primarily detailed the career of Belgian Eddy Merckx, the greatest cyclist of all time and at the finish in Boulder at a shop called "The Spoke", I grabbed the current issue that was just out. Boulder rider Davis Phinney was on the cover, his muscular physique nearly busting out of his stars and stripes skinsuit as he led the breakaway at the recent US PRO Championship in Baltimore. It turns out this US AMATEUR had defeated a bunch of European professional riders to win that race! It was only a few weeks before I met him at the Coors and the article said the crowd numbered 80,000 people! One of OUR guys beat the best in the world including two future Tour de France winners in Laurent Fignon and Stephen Roche! He and Canadian Steve Bauer, who dominated most North American Criteriums took the big money away from the pros! And it was big, Phinney won $25,000 of the $100,000 purse. As an amateur targeting the Olympics, he was only allowed to keep $1000 but the USCF banked the rest for him until he turned pro…WHOA!

The cover also detailed "Boyer and Lemond Success Abroad" with a special focus on the 1982 Worlds Road Race in England. This would be the first detailed accounting I had ever read of a professional road race, and it lit me up. The magazine detailed the final exciting moments of the race blow by blow. Greg Lemond, only 21 years old and in his second year as a pro, had won the silver medal! The rider that beat him was Italian Giuseppe Saronni, the runner-up on that 1981 race poster that now hung front and center in my bedroom. On that red Colnago! The short Italian who had muscular legs that appeared to have been carved out of solid mahogany, was already an established star in the European peloton, but Greg was best of all the rest including Irishman Sean Kelly, a name I knew from the Tour de France. More importantly, WE, the United States, had two riders who were RIGHT there at the end of the WORLD CHAMPIONSHIP going for the win! And this young guy, only 21 years old and in his second year as a professional finished second! Could he win it next year and become the first ever US World Road Cycling Champion? And what about his prospects in the Tour de France? The magazine explained that he had the best coach around, Frenchman Cyrille Guimard, who was carefully grooming him for the Tour. THIS COULD BE OUR GUY!

Upon returning home to Lander from my ten-day long adventure I learned there would be a triathlon at the Lander Swimming Pool, at the end of August right before I started High School. The promoter of the event was my swimming coach Bruce Gresly. Bruce was super enthusiastic, and a fabulous and beloved coach and he was all about this new phenomenon of triathlon. He raved about the benefits of cross-training. He had approached me earlier that spring about an elite summer swim team program that would also incorporate running and cycling training. I was too focused on bike racing by this point and so I passed. The Apple Festival Triathlon began with a thirteen-mile bike course around my familiar Squaw/Baldwin Creek Loop, followed by a 500-meter swim at the pool, and a five-mile run on my mom's morning walking route on Hillcrest Drive and Mortimore Lane. The pool parking lot formed the transition zone and there were both team and individual categories. Lander's bike racers, including Bob and Drew, who was our strongest local guy, were all forming teams.

Recruiting Bruce's son, Glen, an ace swimmer just back from an elite camp in Florida, and my neighbor Phil Gilbertson, who had recently qualified for the Boston Marathon, I formed my team. On the opening rolling climbs, Drew attacked, and I followed as did Bill Scott, a tough veteran racer from Jackson. It was my first lesson on the training benefits of extensive racing. These riders were twice my age and much more developed and muscular than me, but despite their strength and experience, I "hung tough" on the longest climb. Brian had taught me this concept and coined the phrase, which basically meant "stay in the draft, ignore the pain, and be mentally strong". At one point, Drew remarked at how strong I had gotten just since the Togwotee ride and asked how many days of racing did I do in Colorado? "Ten!" I replied and he seemed impressed. The long descent back to town posed a problem, however, because I had forgotten about my junior gears! Drew, however, was acutely aware, and he really pushed the descent in a much larger gear to try to drop me. Spinning like an eggbeater, often tucked and "spun out" I frantically clung to his wheel. The Lander endurance sports people assembled at the pool were impressed that the skinny fourteen-year-old kid had come in with the leaders. Glen and Phil rocked their respective swim and run legs, and our team won, significantly boosting my confidence in my abilities.

After reading about Lemond in those *Winning* Magazines I brought home from Colorado and his 1982 Worlds medal, I became desperate to learn more about my new hero. The coverage of that historic silver medal didn't come to me until about eleven months after the fact, so as usual with information in Cowboy Country, I was playing catch up. I turned to...where else, but my Lander Valley High School Library, mining for bike racing gold on the very first day of high school. While my classmates stood in line for burgers and shakes at the local Dairy Queen, I ate my rice cakes and yogurt (I was a serious cyclist now after all) in the library, a student of my sport. I educated myself on my new hero Greg Lemond, and how he was taking on the world.

There was not much to be found EXCEPT...a July 13, 1981, issue of *Sports Illustrated* with an article entitled "Goldilocks 1, Bears 0". Young Greg vs the Big Soviet Bear!!! I was loosely familiar with the story of Greg defeating the Soviet Olympic Team (Professional riders for all intents and purposes), as the older members of my cycling club (several who "went down to Colorado to follow the Classic") regaled us with tales at the shop. Now I wanted ALL the details! In the early 1980s of Ronald Reagan's America, and particularly in Cowboy Country, the Soviet Union was "the evil empire". They loomed as a threat to our western way of life and so when an American kicked their asses? Hell yeah!

SI wrote "Now the Soviet Union has something else to worry about. It ran into Greg Lemond! The dimple-chinned, blonde-haired, rosy-cheeked Yankee Doodle Dandy from Washoe County, Nevada took on the older, more seasoned Soviet stars in the torturous nine-day stage race in the Rockies!" What a script! Race promoter Michael Aisner had a flair for the dramatic and so, following the American boycott of the 1980 Olympics (where the Soviets dominated) he invited them to race America's premier event.

The Pro-Am event, now in its seventh year, featured eleven stages in Colorado in July with a mixture of high-altitude road races with big climbs, downtown criteriums, and time trials. In the excellent Drake/ Ochowicz book on Team 7-Eleven, Aisner recounted: "I got letters from racers, who were friends, who said the Russians will come and take all the prize money away! Why would you do this? It will ruin the race!" He noted his unwritten response was "Get off your asses and beat them!" One racer who responded positively? Greg Lemond! He said "Bring 'em on! I'll show them which wheel to get on!"

Lemond, who was barely twenty years old when the Coors started, was in his first year as a Professional with the Renault-Gitane team led by Bernard Hinault. His astute director Guimard only wanted his protege to gain experience that year and focus on a few races including the Dauphine and The Coors. He helped Hinault win Paris-Roubaix in April, finished third behind his team captain in June's Dauphine, and then headed to America with a young French team to race the Coors.

Coors promoter Aisner noted that the Russians brought their very best riders and were "supremely confident" of winning the 538-mile event and the lion's share of the $50,000 purse. "They came not just to win, but to embarrass!" Greg Lemond explained "Facing Sergei Soukouroutchenkov and Yuri Barinov, The Olympic Gold and Bronze Medalists, was for me a real test of who would have been Olympic Champion. This was my real revenge on missing the Olympics because of the boycott." Lemond had been a favorite for an Olympic Gold medal following a strong spring campaign with the US National team in Europe. It included an historic American first-victory in a major European Pro-Am Stage Race, France's Circuit de la Sarthe, and ultimately helped land him that 1981 pro contract.

Lemond won the Prologue Time Trial and then Olympic Champion "Soukho" broke away early in the 83-mile-long Bob Cook Memorial Vail Pass Road Race in a supposed show of strength. He fell apart in the high altitude, however, losing nearly ten minutes by the finish and never fully recovered. Meanwhile, his teammate Yuri Kashirin took over the Red Leader's Jersey from Lemond, who was miffed at how intimidated his countrymen were by the Russians. Keen to race on all terrains, the irrepressible Lemond was even earning bonus seconds in field sprints in the criteriums!

Stage seven was the "Suicide Hill" circuit race in Snowmass, a torturous up/down affair akin to Lemond's beloved Nevada City event...18 laps, just 32 miles but with a nasty steep climb every lap. Just three laps in, "LeMonster" broke clear with Colombian Norberto Caceres, ultimately winning the stage and putting four minutes into the Russians. Later in that afternoon's time trial, his second place allowed him to pull on the leader's jersey. Stage ten (of eleven) would be the Morgul-Bismark road race, a hot barren 92-mile test that typically decided the race. Lemond took on the Russians on the very roads I had raced on the month before in the RZMC! The final miles featured those two nasty climbs, first "The Hump", then the 18% grade grind to the finish on "The Wall", famously spray-painted "Beam me up Scottie" at its steepest point. The Soviets had been training there since arriving in Colorado. They would hit our young American hero with everything they had in a final effort to take the leaders jersey back!

Early on, the entire Soviet team broke clear with only Lemond and Italian Alessandro Pozzi able to follow. Pozzi flatted and with 53 miles remaining and in 90-degree heat, SI reported "Lemond was alone with the Soviet juggernaut". Lemond recalls "We went head-to-head, me against four Russians on the Morgul Bismark course. They tried every which way to drop me and every time they'd attack, I'd chase one guy down. I would slow just before I caught him and then as the other group caught up, just before they caught, I'd attack and drop everyone. Then I'd slow down and when they caught me, they'd send somebody off and I would go after him. I just played this game with them, four against one, and they couldn't drop me." With one 13-mile lap to go, early breakaway Alan McCormack of Ireland was caught, and he jumped on the train. Lemond showed his cards early by scorching up "The Wall" to earn a $325 prime at the bell. On the last lap, the Soviets continued to do everything they could to work over the young American but to no avail. McCormack made a do-or-die attack on the hump but faded. Again, from SI "On the final sprint up the wall, the Russians weaved and blocked, while Lemond sprinted for victory from 150 meters out." He went a bit early and Barinov, the Olympic Bronze medalist caught his wheel and came around in the final 25 meters to win the stage. It mattered little, though, as Lemond finished in the same time and retained his overall lead.

Greg was reportedly a bit irked about the weaving bikes in the final sprint and "verbal harassment" to which Soukho responded "He needs to learn respect for his competitors. He is only 20 and I am 25 and I have a lot more time in this than him". Bad blood aside, with only the North Boulder Park Criterium remaining, Greg had a nearly five minutes overall lead, while the Russians lay 2nd-5th on GC and would have to be content with the team prize. 40,000 spectators gathered in Boulder's cycling mecca, and even a last lap crash ("I over-cooked the last corner") couldn't keep Lemond from joining Connie Carpenter on the podium as 1981 Coors Classic Champion. And that, I found out, was the story of how Greg Lemond defeated the mighty Russians or as SI wrote: "Goldilocks slayed the FOUR Bears!" It was an All-American success story not unlike "The Miracle on Ice", only in this exotic sport that I was falling in love with. My sport! And this was my guy!

Perhaps more importantly for America as a fledgling cycling power, this could be OUR guy! According to those *Winning* magazines I was studying intensely, Boyer had improved on his historic 1981 Tour ride, finishing 23rd the following year, and was 12th in 1983. Solid, yes but nothing indicated he could ever really contend for the win. Lemond, on the other hand, had a brilliant and calculating coach whose riders had triumphed in five of the previous seven Tours up to that point and was carefully building him up for his debut in 1984. What could "Lemonster" do in the Tour de France? I had to think he could be a contender. This could really be our guy!

While racing in Colorado at the RZMC & visiting those "Cool" bike shops, I had purchased a Renault headband, just like the one Greg had on in the '82 Worlds. It was a thick, colorful band with the Yellow/Black/White design that matched the Renault team jersey. To be like Greg. Well, Bernard Hinault & Laurent Fignon were cool too... but they were French! I wanted to be like the All-American Greg. My mom paid for the headband and reiterated how it needed to be worn with a helmet. "Always wear your helmet" ...yeah, yeah, of course!

Now that I was really following the sport, it became my role to inform the guys in the shop about the things Mr. Lemond was achieving in Europe. I talked fast and spoke with great enthusiasm, especially about my main man Greg. I mean this guy...he could really be OUR guy! A US rider capable of winning the world's biggest races! So, they mocked me, especially Brian, now working there as a mechanic. "Greg Your Mom won what Dave?" he asked? "Greg Lemond!" I replied... "Come on guys!"

Well, my mom would dramatically intersect my drive to be like Greg, via the headband at least, soon enough. Eager to impress the area's older riders with my Euro look, I made it out of the house in my new headband only and headed for our Tuesday evening time trial. I was in direct violation of my parents "always wear your helmet" rule. After all, how could my clubmates see the headband if it was beneath a helmet? Such an item was real physical evidence that I had been racing outside of Wyoming "in the big time!" It had to be done. Mom was working out back in the garden, so I got up and bolted out the door.

It was five miles out to the start of the weekly training series on the edge of town. Somehow via a neighbor's sighting or just plain intuition, Mom sniffed out my indiscretion. I had just arrived at the group meeting point with my cool new headband, prepared to bask in the admiring glow of the older riders when my mother pulled up in her car hanging my helmet (by now I was wearing a "Skid Lid") out the window and admonishing me "David Campbell, you put your damn helmet on"! Laughter all around as I sheepishly accepted my brain bucket. It was tough to be a big cool "euro style" man at age fourteen and still stay under your mom's rules!

As it turns out, Bob had travelled to Europe that summer and watched the World Road Championships in Alterhein, Switzerland. When he returned home in early September, he brought the news...Greg Lemond was World Champion! WORLD CHAMPION! An American! He went in a break with a couple of laps to go and by the final lap he was solo! He won alone by over a minute! He was now racing the fall Classics in the rainbow jersey and would proudly wear it next season in his debut Tour de France. He had dominated the Worlds by a margin not seen since the days of Eddy Merckx, the greatest cyclist in the history of the sport! Months later, when the *Winning* magazine covering the event finally arrived at the shop, the cover said it all: "A Star is Born". "We" beat the Europeans at their own game, and "I" would never be the same again. I was dreaming big and continuing to study and learn about this incredible European sport that I was falling in love with. My sport!

Greg Lemond on Winning Magazine Cover.
Wnning Bicycle Racing Illustrated November 1983 Cover

CHAPTER TEN:

ACHIN' TO BE

By the spring of 1984, I was out on the road training more than ever. I began to transcend the boundaries between man and machine. The bike and I became like one as together we conquered the countryside that unfurled beneath our wheels. Together we witnessed the transition of the seasons, as the snow melted and we could finally get up to the top of Sinks Canyon, or later get in that one last ride in the golden glow of autumn before the winter weather returned. Training felt like venturing out on an adventure, my partner and I on our own quest against the road and the elements. I was beginning to truly love those private moments with their challenges and sense of accomplishment. It was as if there was a grandstand full of people and an entire orchestra playing for me when I completed a difficult set of hill repeats or was still able to uncork a blistering sprint after an especially long, hard ride.

I was growing taller, becoming more muscular, and I was hungry all the time. I had worked like never before during my freshman year on the swim team, regularly doing two practices a day (lifting and swimming), sometimes logging up to six miles a day in the pool. I earned my Varsity Letter, the "Freshman of the Year" trophy, and the respect of my older teammates. My mind, however, was always dreaming of cycling. On our trips to swimming meets, I was always reading my cycling magazines and dreaming of the upcoming cycling season.

My Dad noted one day that my "butt was getting big! Like an NFL player...that's where your power is!" Huh, OK...cool! My friend John attended the December Junior Camp over Christmas break at the Olympic Training Center (OTC) in Colorado Springs. When we met up at Teton Village in Jackson Hole while skiing, his message was clear...I had to go! The coaching, the training, and everything provided at the OTC was HUGE. In the days long before the internet and with limited and very delayed print media, interacting with more experienced riders like him was the prime way we all learned. It also instilled in me a desire to share the knowledge and experience I gained to help other riders. Growing the sport in America seemed a universal goal for all riders at this time and we all wanted to not only get better ourselves but help everyone else get better as well. There was still a lot to learn!

John was fired up and riding more than ever and I would be eligible the following year. He also had this crazy notion, from the National Coaching director Eddie B, that cycling training started December First! Given the rugged weather of Wyoming winters and the snowy roads, I struggled to understand just how to do this. Topher and I mostly didn't ride in really cold weather. I swam and lifted weights all winter and only got out on the road to start riding once things warmed up in the spring. Topher, in Minnesota, had a similar athletic existence, except he played hockey instead of swimming.

You could even buy cool cycling gear at the OTC, used and on the cheap (which was a big deal for a kid, especially a Wyoming kid) from the permanent residents. At the Mother's Day Road Race that spring, John rocked a super cool skinsuit he had scored at the OTC swap meet. Unlike the previous year, John was a major player in the Senior A race, and I was on the front and in contention with the Senior B's. We both had come a long way in a year!

If riders performed well enough at December Camp, John explained, they could return in April for a more intensive camp from which the US National team was selected. He was also adamant about racing more frequently and in bigger events out of state. There was some skepticism from my parents, particularly my dad, about missing school and all the travel and expenses. However, they were always supportive (within reason) and given how much I wanted to do it and how hard I was training, they promised to help me check it out. On our annual trip to Denver for Easter to see family, we did just that, driving the extra hour south to Colorado Springs to have a look around the US Olympic Training Center!

Some background on the USOTC…President Jimmy Carter had signed the Olympic and Amateur Sports Act back in 1978, after the US Olympic Committee (USOC) wrested control of everything related to the Olympics from the Amateur Athletic Union. The USOC mandated the creation of National Governing Bodies (like the USCF which issued our racing licenses) for each Olympic Sport. Additionally, a permanent Olympic Training Center was to be developed. "When Eddie learned that the OTC could provide free lodging and food for up to 120 riders (numbers he anticipated for future camps) he jumped on it!"

The first USOC offices ("Olympic House" as it came to be known) had been the office of the commanding air general of the North American Air Defense Command (NORAD). NORAD's prime role was to monitor the skies for intercontinental missiles and nuclear warheads. The epicenter for monitoring Cold War activities had now become the center of the American Olympic Movement. Ironically, the first US coach to have an office there had, decades earlier been a Polish machine gunner stationed on a missile base in East Germany!

Eddie used the OTC for his February winter training camp in 1978, becoming the first coach of the first federation to do so. The junior riders I had read about (Lemond, Demgen, Bradley, and Kiefel) who won that historic Worlds medal in the 1978 Worlds Team Time Trial were among the attendees. The OTC administrators were delighted as the training camps justified the OTC's existence. Camp riders and staff arrived to try out the new accommodations and were greeted with a banner that read "Welcome U.S. Cycling!" Upon his retirement from coaching, Eddie B. noted that the enormous progress and international success of American cycling in the 1980s would have been impossible without the meals, lodging, and facilities made available to he and his coaching staff at the USOTC."

It was the first time I had ever seen a velodrome, which alone was something to behold with its smooth surface, steep banking, and all those bleachers! On the track you could see the WHOLE race! We walked around the training center, poked our noses into the cafeteria and some of the facilities and then finally visited the USA Cycling office. We asked about December camp, April camp, and even how it worked with permanent residents like Roy Knickman, "the next Lemond" who I had seen at the RZMC in 1983. We were assured they could "take some classes at the local high school" but dad saw it differently. "Those cycling coaches just think school is your problem and that's not right!" It was an inauspicious start for my ambition to get to a cycling camp at the OTC. But I kept training and dreaming, hoping that soon day my day would come!

My first challenge in the spring of 1984 was a cold and windy road race in Sheridan sponsored by the local Budweiser distributor. The winners got engraved pewter beer mugs with glass bottoms. Sheridan is a beautiful little mountain town, like Lander in many ways. Just south of the Montana border in the northern part of the state, it lies at the foot of the Big Horn mountains, just North of Buffalo where our church trip started. Dad liked the scenic drive and the area in general and agreed to take me.

While my father was supportive of cycling, when it came to the races, we did things on his terms...so we camped out. Eating instant oatmeal, hot cocoa, and my mom's homemade bread in our fleece jackets and wool hats around the campfire was not how elite riders prepared for their races, but I was fine. I liked racing, I liked camping, and I just wanted a chance to do my thing.

There was a new category for 1984, Junior 14-15, giving me, as a 15-year-old, one more year as a "Junior-Junior" in the words of the guys at the shop. I got to have a little bigger top gear: 50/15, necessitating some more equipment modifications, which at this point I was fairly capable of. The older riders were now on seven speed freewheels, but I had to carefully file the threads of a second position cog, a 15 tooth in order to make my junior gearing work, so I was stuck with a six-speed cluster for now but at least I could finally race on my sew-ups!

In Sheridan, however, with half a dozen riders aged 14-18 we all raced together as Juniors. Trying to be just like my main man Greg, I attacked on a hard climb about 2/3 of the way through the 40-mile race and went clear. The thrill of being in the lead and knowing my rivals weren't far behind allowed me to dig deeper and find a new level of inspiration during what I saw as my first great escape. I channeled all the imagery and race commentary I had soaked up over the previous year, riding faster than ever before. I soloed in and raised my arms, giving my first real victory salute in a race. It was just like they did in *Winning* magazine…even though the fans at the finish line were just my dad and a few other riders and their families gathered by a parking lot.

Topher got back to Wyoming just in time for a super tough road race outside of Jackson Hole in mid-June. We stayed in an older friend's dumpy little trailer which was in an alley off the main street in what was then a town for ski bums. "Teton county has the most people on welfare in the state" my father frequently said. It is, of course, now the most expensive place to live in the entire country. The Coal Creek Road Race was 40 miles, about the longest we had raced at that point, and loaded with climbing. The race started outside of town about midway down the fearsome Teton Pass, at around 7500 feet of elevation. We would then descend into Idaho and the little town of Victor at 6200 feet and turn left to climb up Pine Creek Pass, at a little over 6700 feet high. The course then descended again before turning around, climbing, and descending back to Victor and then slogging back up the opening grades of Teton Pass to the finish. It was the toughest single-day race we had yet faced. And that would have been if it was sunny and warm…but it was wet and cold in town and SNOWING when we got to the start.

As a Wyoming kid brought up with outdoor activities I was taught to "be prepared" and I still had those wool liner gloves purchased from NOLS that I wore underneath my leather palmed cycling gloves. The SIDI shoe covers had been critical as I got out training more frequently and in colder weather and of course, I had wool socks! I had my wool ear-band under my helmet, my trusty poly-pro long underwear top beneath my standard wool cycling jersey, and wool leg warmers to tuck (no more safety pins!) under my lycra "skin shorts". My jacket was still that terrible bright orange, baggy non-breathable thing that had been issued to everyone in my scout troop and I knew it wasn't very cool, but it was all I had. Scared that it wasn't enough, I even put on my fleece jacket underneath the raincoat. Topher dressed similarly, but he had forgotten his gloves. Ever the gamer, he just put thick wool socks on over his hands, and we rolled up to the start line, both a bit intimidated but ready to tough it out...Wyoming tough!

The only other young riders decided it was too cold to race, and so Topher and I lined up with the Women and Veterans in a field of maybe ten riders. We had both seen images in our *Winning* magazines of the euro pros toughing it out in foul weather, with these races called "epic" and "classic" so we knew that suffering in the elements was part of the sport and to persevere was part of the glory. In that regard, we felt like we were doing something really cool too. Mark Ward, our beloved Wyoming state USCF representative, explained what we were in for, and then it got scary! He told us our gears would freeze up and not work and our hands would become so numb that braking would be difficult. GULP.

On the initial freezing descent off Teton Pass, I flatted. The guy in the follow car was quick to bring me a rear wheel and assured me "It has a 12 cog! You can catch!" I was both encouraged and confused by this as in USCF junior racing a 15 cog was the largest allowed gear. A bigger gear would be a huge advantage on the long descent. I decided that given the misfortune of a flat tire it was fair to use it. I rode as hard as I could and passed a couple of frozen women and vets. My effort was about catching up but perhaps even more about trying to stay warm. As I rolled across the state line and through Victor, Idaho, my fingers were so cold I was whimpering and trying not to cry.

At the base of the next climb, I caught the field, which as this point was Topher, a couple of vets, and Vini Scott from Tetonia, Idaho. Vini was a former NOLS instructor and the toughest women's racer around. She went head-to-head with Ruthie a few weeks later at Lander's

Red Dog race. Topher, always astute about bike equipment, looked down at my wheel and said "That has a 12! You didn't use it, did you?" In this ethical dilemma, I decided it was best to own up so I said yes, I did. "OK" my good friend responded, "But just promise not to use it again, OK?" I agreed and we carried on suffering together. The two men dropped us on the climb, but Vini, as sweet as she was tough, stuck with us and encouraged us. The cold and wet was made even more difficult by the distance and the constant up and down. Sweating up the climbs and then freezing down them was torturous, but we stuck together, and we stayed with Vini. The finish would be the first of many photo finishes between Topher and I, and I just nudged ahead.

The result didn't matter. Once we got to the cars and out of all that wet, heavy gear and into warm, dry clothes we started to feel the magnitude of our accomplishment. We made it. We didn't quit! We suffered through the cold and the snow just like those Euro-Pros in our *Winning* magazines and we finished the race. Wyoming tough, our own Rocky moment! All the finishers got a T-shirt, and we wore those things like a badge of honor back home. At the awards presentations at a local restaurant at the foot of the pass, both these "tough young riders" received prizes and applause. We basked in the glow of our accomplishment long after, feeling like big, strong men who could handle anything and not just the skinny, insecure adolescent boys that we really were. Decades later, we still talk about how important and formative that experience was in shaping both of us to move forward and face even greater challenges.

CHAPTER ELEVEN:

IF YOU WILL DARE, I MIGHT DARE...

The 1984 State Championship Road Race was held a few weeks later in Buffalo. I was keenly aware that the winner of each division qualified for Nationals, slated for Mid-August in New Hampshire. A long way from Cowboy Country, but one of my mom's good friends had recently moved to neighboring Vermont, a point I hoped to leverage if I could win the race. Unlike the previous year, there were four other riders I would need to beat. Mom and I drove the course in advance, on the advice of Bob and Drew, bringing a new level of seriousness to my racing strategy. I noted a tough hill after the halfway point and planned to attack there.

My mom had driven Topher, Brian, and I to the race in the Mustang. We planned to camp out and I was charged with packing the camping gear, normally Dad's area of expertise. Brian, just twenty years old and living on his own, had begun coaching Topher and me. One day it came up that my mom cut my hair and Brian asked if she would cut his too? Having finished college, Brian was now Bob's mechanic at the Freewheel and money was tight. I observed his eating habits at the shop, which consisted of a Snickers bar and a soda for lunch. In fact, he drank soda constantly. I was starting to pay attention to my diet, and I knew he ate a lot of junk, which certainly wasn't good, but my mother was mortified. When she cut our hair each month, she noted how brittle his hair was and that it hadn't grown nearly as much as mine, likely due to his diet. It was a powerful lesson that I took to heart, and I started paying closer attention to what I ate.

After previewing the course, the race organizers had a "pasta feed" for all the riders at a local church with camping nearby. My mom had made it her mission to make sure Brian ate well, because as a Senior rider, he had to race 100 miles. Topher and I faced around 35 as Junior 14-15's. Shortly after dinner we discovered that we had no tent. My mom was furious! I realized that, while I made sure my bike was cleaned and lubed, I had neglected my new responsibilities in packing! We scrambled to find a cheap motel and Topher and I rolled out our sleeping bags on the floor while my mom shared the bed with Brian, which Topher and I thought was hilarious. We made our instant oatmeal meant for camping using the hotel coffee pot, while mom took Brian out to breakfast to "make sure he ate something healthy and substantial".

Junior racing in Wyoming at this point tended to be very reactive and the riders were all nervous and tentative. Self-conscious teenagers with little experience in a new sport was a recipe for apathy. The first part of the race passed without attacks of any sort and five kids just riding along looking at each other. This situation did favor someone who was willing to take the initiative and when my chosen hill came, I gave it absolutely everything and slowly pulled away from the others for another solo victory. I was thrilled to learn I won by 1:13, almost exactly the margin that Greg triumphed by at the Worlds, Topher was second and with the temperature in the 90s, Mom took us all to an outdoor swimming pool before the long drive home in the Mustang with no air conditioning. An example of classic Wyoming mountain weather of late spring and early summer...the previous weekend we had raced in the snow and now we were getting sun burned!

Throughout this time, *Cycling USA*, *Velo News*, *Winning*, and even *Bicycling magazine* were hyping the American's chances for the upcoming Olympics. I felt like not only MY cycling was taking off, but so was American cycling, OUR cycling ...on the world level. All my cycling friends and competitors would read with great delight at the enormous success "our" riders had in Europe in the spring racing against the best. In the Circuit des Ardennes in Belgium, the team dominated, winning three stages and the team competition while placing Phinney third and Doug Shapiro fifth on GC. Shapiro, riding much stronger in 1984 told *Winning* magazine that he attributed his success to "going on really tough training rides with Greg Lemond this winter in California" Our pro World Champion was helping the amateurs bring up their level! In that same *Winning* magazine, Phinney noted that "Eddie B. has coordinated our efforts in a focused, international program. Before we were much more scattered."

Next, Thurlow Rogers won the important Italian amateur classic Milan-Mendrisio, ably supported by Shapiro in the break. In the team time trial prologue of Italy's Settimana Bergamasca, where Rogers was so successful the previous year, the American team of Rogers, Kiefel, Phinney, Shapiro, and Grewal BEAT the East Germans to win! The East Germans were like gods in amateur cycling at that time, especially in team time trials and had dominated recent World Championships. Shapiro and Kiefel both won stages, and the Americans took the team title, placing three riders in the top ten overall. Were we on track for an Olympic medal? It certainly seemed like it to me!

American's progress in the European Professional Peloton, excepting my main man Greg, was still very much like my own quest to compete on the National level…slow and with a steep learning curve. Our riders were largely overwhelmed with a few occasional glimmers of hope and progress. But I couched it all into my "Rocky" mentality of taking your lumps and rising to the challenge. After all, if you keep training hard, your day will come! That summer, *Velo News* magazine brought our bike shop the story of the history making American Gianni Motta-Linea MD Italia squad who had competed in the Giro d'Italia, becoming the first ever American team to contest a major Grand Tour. Additionally, Boyer was CAPTAIN of an Italian squad Supermercati Brianzoli-Willier Trestina and despite illness and injury, finished 43rd overall.

The American team with Italian sponsors had taken on the second biggest professional stage race in the world. Six of the nine riders were Americans, all were neo-pros, and cue the "Rocky" music, ALL the Americans (National pro champion John Eustice, Karl Maxon, Daniel Franger, Michael Carter, Tim Rutledge, and Greg Saunders) finished the race! After the historic and groundbreaking bits, though the story became more like my own…their best finisher was Californian Franger in 78th overall at nearly two hours down on Italian winner Francesco Moser. Of the 171 starters, 143 riders made it to the finish in Verona and the last placed man was American Saunders. He was in this position from stage nine through to stage twenty-two but, again in mind ala "Rocky", he didn't quit! He hung tough! The team finished last of the nineteen teams in the team competition, over five hours behind, but they finished.

The team was the brainchild of two members of the Pennsylvania Bike Club, Robin Morton and John Eustice. It was another "do it yourself" maverick American story. Eustice was the US Pro champion in 1982 and 1983 (earned at the criterium in Baltimore, by placing 15th place behind Phinney, Bauer, and the euros, but the top US Pro). He was a bit burnt out on racing in Europe but was interested in racing with an American team. Morton's husband was a club member, and she had been actively involved and the two put together a team for the 1983 Tour of America, a short stage race around the Washington, D.C. area. There they met Italian bicycle maker Gianni Motta, a past Giro d'Italia and Tour de Suisse winner.

Morton explained, "The charismatic and gregarious Italian was very outgoing, and he had a lot of connections. At that point the 7-Eleven team wasn't over in Europe yet and we were a much different organization. Race director Vincezo Torriani wanted to have an American team in the Giro. And certainly, I was something totally unique to get them publicity, an American team with a woman as a manager. So, they wanted the team! At that point, there were a lot of free agent pros and also a lot of guys who wanted to turn pro. The first race we did in 1984 as the Gianni Motta team was the Tour of Texas and then we went and did the Tour Willamette and the Cascade Classic, both in Oregon, and then headed to Italy."

Morton added, "We were the outliers. We were a blip on the radar screen, because a lot of people don't have the historical information, they don't even know about the team because we did it a little bit differently. We didn't go through USA cycling, it wasn't a national team, we didn't have a big budget and a lot of money for promotion like 7-Eleven did. We did it on our own…a very small team with a very small budget. It was definitely an adventure and an experience and something that wasn't done by the book. It was just something that John wanted to do, it was his vision, and I bought into that, and we just said "hey, let's do it!" It was a really wonderful experience, and we had teams for eight years and the next year we did the Vuelta (Tour of Spain). For me it led to a lot of other things, and I went on to work for the company that put on the Philadelphia race and the San Francisco race, (future major American events) and I worked for them for fifteen years. But when we did it, it was not something that a lot of people were aware of. We did not find the sponsors, that was controlled by the European management and there were some issues as there often is. All the riders were given an incentive, a bonus to finish the Giro. Well, apparently, we found out afterwards that one of the European mechanics was told to tighten the rider's bottom brackets. So that every day when he worked on the bikes, he tightened the bottom brackets, so it made it a little harder to pedal! So, the fact that they finished the Giro is pretty incredible because it was like they were riding through quicksand!"

But, despite the challenges and "extra resistance", a major bright spot had been Karl Maxon, of Eugene, Oregon. The 24-year-old distance runner turned cyclist broke away alone on Stage four from Bologna to Numana on the Adriatic Coast, nearly from the start. Amassing a lead of 22 minutes at one point, Maxon was off the front for 217 of the 238-kilometers! Until recently, it was the longest solo breakaway in Giro history. He was even the virtual race leader at one point! *Velo News* reported that he likely would have stayed away but crashes by two favorites (Laurent Fignon and Johan Van de Velde) prompted Italian favorite Saronni's team to attack, putting paid to the Americans chances. Maxon rallied to finish a very respectable twelfth in the final time trial into Verona, enroute to 127th overall. Morton noted that his TT result was achieved without any aero equipment, not even a disc wheel. It was noted how much promise he had shown, and I would note that for me personally, he would later become a mentor and ultimately a rival when I moved to Eugene to go to college and race in Oregon. Cycling, especially my experience, was full of these wonderfully serendipitous moments.

1984 also marked the highly anticipated Tour de France debut of "Lemonster" …wearing the rainbow bands of World Champion no less! Greg was billed as a pre-race favorite alongside past winners Laurent Fignon and Bernard Hinault of France. I loved Greg's attitude, who told *The New York Times* on the eve of the race, "I want to do the best that's possible. If I don't succeed this year, I've got five or six more tries".

Lemond showed his rookie stripes, and his nerves, when he forgot to sign in for the prologue and then was still tightening his toe straps when his time started. His powerful team triumphed in the team time trial and won four of the opening eight stages but by the end of the first week, my hero had contracted bronchitis and was struggling. By the end of the second week, he now had blistered feet in addition to breathing problems and was lying in eighth overall. Wheezing, he was being dropped on long climbs and chasing back on with the help of teammates. Fortunately, in Cyrille Guimard, he had a calm and patient director. *Bicycling magazine* reported, "His youthful features were hardening, his bright eyes were drawn, his short blond hair looked lank and limp". Such were the tortures of the Tour.

However, I again saw the fighting spirit and grit I first witnessed from the US Hockey team and the "Rocky" movies, as I watched Lemond tackle the final week on CBS Sports. Although he conceded that Fignon was the strongest, he started to feel better and in the mountainous final week; after languishing in eighth place, he began climbing up the overall standing. By stage 18 at LaPlagne, he had taken over the white "neophyte" jersey as best young rider and moved up to third overall. In the ensuing mountain stage, he was threatening Hinault's second place, ultimately finishing a little over a minute behind his former mentor in third place and securing the white jersey. It was an impressive debut and quite remarkable given his illness and problems with his feet. Guimard stated Greg "rode the Tour on one leg". Surely, he was going to win cycling's biggest race…and soon!

There were in fact two Americans on the podium! American women were still the best in the world and Marianne Martin of Boulder, Colorado triumphed in the inaugural 18-stage Women's Tour de France ahead of thirty-five other women on six national teams. The women's Tour would run concurrently alongside the Men's through 1989 before being fully and properly given its own place on the calendar in 2022.

As the Olympics approached, the US was coming on. Winning Bicycle Racing Illustrated, August 1984

May, 1984. The first American team to ride a Grand Tour-Gianni Motta. Photo courtesy Robin Morton

CHAPTER TWELVE:

WE ARE THE CHAMPIONS

There were more races throughout the summer for me in Wyoming, but I was focused on NATIONALS. I wanted to race the best kids my age in the country. Finally, I struck a deal with my mom, much to the chagrin of my father. At the time, I just could not understand him and felt he was always holding me down. It took me years to understand that his resistance against travel and big events was his way of keeping us from being "spoiled". He knew, all too well, from his job at the High School about how entitled kids could get when you "gave them everything" and so he worked hard to keep us grounded and humble. My mother took a much more sensible approach and one that I would adopt when I parented my daughter Gabriella decades later…help your kids take advantage of opportunities when they show drive and initiative, but make sure they have some skin in the game!

So, my mom laid out the offer. She first noted how I trained every day, rain or shine and really pushed myself. She admired my drive and commitment and then noted that opportunities like Nationals "don't happen every day". She asked me to pay for my own plane ticket to New Hampshire from my summer jobs and then she would accompany me as well as covering the hotel costs. It was a deal!

1980's Wyoming bike racing was nothing if not "do it yourself" and Bob asked all club members at that year's Red Dog to only race one stage and help with the others. Topher and I raced the downtown criterium but hauled hay bales, swept corners, and worked as corner marshals during the road race and time trial. Although disappointed not to race more, we learned valuable lessons about the enormous tasks involved in promoting a bicycle race.

The last event before Nationals was the inaugural "Dead Dog Classic" in Laramie. The name came from Danny and Charles. They held a weekly time trial on the highway outside of town and a dog had been hit by a car and perished right on their start line. Additionally, the Laramie guys loved the Lander race and thought their name made a funny parallel. Their event t-shirts over the years, from goofy punk rock inspired squashed dogs beneath wheels to Grateful Dead like celestial skeletons reflected their humor and character. It was a great race that featured a flat ten-mile time trial on Saturday morning followed by a road race that afternoon. Sunday was a downtown criterium.

My dad drove me down but as was his way, he made sure there was something in it for him. The reigning state champion in high-powered rifle shooting, he found a nearby rifle match that same weekend. Charles had a tiny apartment near the campus where my father and I rolled out our sleeping bags on literally the only open floor space Charles had in his living room. John and another rider were "crashing" with Charles too and they had gone record shopping in the University town the day before. We awoke to Jimi Hendrix's "Purple Haze" playing loudly, which I thought was awesome. Dad, on the other hand, bolted for the rifle range lickety-split!

There was a new phenom on the Wyoming Junior circuit named Mike Stieb who had triumphed in our absence in Lander. He was a speed roller-skater from Casper that came along with Bill in the "Wade-a-bago". He was goofy, hyper, and very fast and had us racing for second place in every event. As was becoming the norm, the juniors got to race with the Masters and Women in the criterium, which really helped Topher and I develop our skills and tactics for racing in a pack. Even though we had only eight juniors, the criterium field numbered more like twenty.

Most races seemed to end in a sprint, and I constantly worked on mine. It was becoming "my thing" and I had confidence I could win most sprints. I had learned to push and pull on the handlebars with the upper body I had developed from swimming while forcing the bike side to side. Topher regularly beat me in time trials but thanks to my sprint I was better in road races and criteriums and we ended up second and third overall behind Stieb. My Wyoming cycling hero Danny was second in the Cat 1/2 men's events behind some Colorado hot shot. Remember the legend that he owned 50 pairs of wheels and most of them had Campy hubs? I had won hubs at our local Red Dog race and wanted to build up a second set of race wheels. Brian would generously build them for free, I just had to pay the cost of the spokes, so I just needed some rims. Danny had won a pair of Gold-Anodized Mavic tubular rims (OR 10s) and was walking around the parking lot after the awards saying to anyone who would listen "What do I need a pair of rims for? I have 50 pairs of wheels!" It turns out, he really did! I asked him if he would trade, and he quickly agreed. A big smile quickly came across his face, and he carried on through the parking lot saying "What do I need a pair of hubs for? I have 50 pairs of wheels." That guy!

The most significant event, however, was not our race nor my trade with Danny. It was the Olympics! After all the press, excitement, and speculation it was finally here! America had not won a medal in cycling since 1912! Eddie B, the OTC, the 7-Eleven team, amateurs training with Greg Lemond, the Coors Classic…all of this was pushing towards the LA Olympics. Our HOME Olympics! All the progress and preparation had been detailed in the months leading up in my beloved *Winning* magazine as well as in *Cycling USA*.

The cycling road races were on the opening weekend of the 1984 LA Games and as such had enormous crowds and unprecedented TV coverage. Immediately after "our" crit, I huddled into the "Wade-a-bago" with my friends and competitors to watch the Women's Road Race. American cycling was still such a small world at the time and there was great comradery amongst all the riders. On the local level "we" were doing our thing…getting better, learning, and racing more. "Our" calendar grew because, in many cases "we" put on the races. We had ownership. And on an International level, "we" were competing at higher levels and doing better against the Europeans and this all culminated in "our" Olympics. All American cyclists at that time felt like we were part of the growth and success of the sport, our sport!

The Women's Olympic Road Race was being held for the first time ever. I favored the young and talented Rebecca Twigg, whom Eddie B. had christened "The Golden Girl". A world pursuit champion in 1982, she was second at last year's World Road Championship and a permanent resident at the Olympic Training Center. Bill's wife favored Connie Carpenter. Connie was the undisputed queen of Women's cycling and an incredible athlete. She had already competed in the Olympics, in speed skating back in 1972 at the tender age of just fourteen. After an injury kept her out of the 1976 Winter Olympics, she took up cycling, ultimately winning twelve National titles and a silver medal at the Worlds. She went to college at the University of California-Berkeley where she then won a National Rowing Championship. She won the premier American race (and the biggest race in the world for women) the Coors Classic three times and was the reigning World Pursuit Champion on the track. She had recently married Phinney, who would compete later in the Men's race.

By the time we tuned in on the tiny black and white in the RV, a breakaway had formed with six riders, including both Carpenter and Twigg. The Americans main rivals were Maria Canins of Italy, a strong climber and all-rounder Jeannie Longo of France. At the finish, Twigg jumped first and Carpenter, normally an ace sprinter, appeared to be too far back. At the line Carpenter got the gold with a perfectly timed bike throw and the video of the two Americans in their Stars and Stripes jersey riding alongside each other hugging was an incredible image with which to begin the Games.

Since dad was still at the Rifle Range, I left the race with Charles and several other riders after the Senior men raced. We watched the Olympic men's race at a neighborhood barbeque on another small TV set. The scene was incredible and not like any we had ever seen at other events in American cycling. Thousands upon thousands of people, many of whom had camped out overnight, crowded every inch of the course. American flags were waving everywhere under brilliant sunshine and "our" riders were delivering!

My "studying" of the US men had me favoring Thurlow "Turbo" Rogers. I listed off his results, particularly those in top international stage races over the past year, to Charles and anyone else who would listen. When the break formed, Rogers was indeed there as was Phinney, a big favorite due to his sprint, and the enigmatic Alexi Grewal. Even I knew from experience how difficult he could be! Grewal was dominating the Coors Classic a couple of weeks earlier before being kicked out for a positive doping test that presumably would keep him out of the Olympics. All of that had been resolved at the last minute, however, and here he was! Perennial strongman Steve Bauer from Canada was there as well as Nestor Mora, a Colombian we knew from the Coors, and two unknown Norwegians.

With Grewal there always seemed to be drama of some sort and this day was no exception. Perhaps the ultimate example in fact! Never a darling of the National Coaching staff, he attacked solo on the big climb with two laps to go. He looked strong, he looked smooth, and with a lap to go, he looked every inch like an Olympic Gold medalist. Until he didn't. On the last time up the climb he seemed to fall apart...bobbing, weaving, and gasping. He was coming undone! Bauer, now a complete all-around road rider (also thanks to training with Lemond) and not just the criterium specialist of years past, shot out of the field and blew right past him! Grewal suddenly, as if hit by lightning, got himself together and rallied to grab the Canadian's wheel just over the top. Just. He looked like he could blow up at any minute. Bauer confidently did most of the work (and not for the first or the last time) as they approached the finish, and we were all plagued with doubts as Bauer was a much better sprinter than Grewal. Bauer thought so too, and led it out only to have Alexi charge past, effectively beating him in the first ten explosive pedal strokes of the sprint. Mouth agape and arms flung high and wide, Alexi crossed the line in victorious glory...the most incredible and inspirational finish I had yet seen in cycling.

He had won America's first Men's Olympic Road (and as of this writing only) cycling gold medal. In the coming days, the Americans would take six more medals, including a bronze in the team time trial (Kiefel, Phinney, Weaver, and Knickman) and gold and bronze in Pursuit (Steve Hegg and Leonard Harvey Nitz), silver in team pursuit (Hegg, Nitz, Brent Emery, and Pat McDonough), and gold and silver in the Match Sprints (Mark Gorski and Nelson Vails).

Back home in Lander and on my own quest to be successful at the highest level of cycling for me, my training was going well. Bob, Drew, and Brian not only offered frequent training advice but were often out on the road pushing me. They were generous and very helpful and of course, Topher was there as well. On my last big training ride before flying out to New Hampshire, the older guys orchestrated an attack and chase game with Topher and I out on the Lyon's Valley Loop. First Topher attacked and the rest of us eased off and then we organized a chase. Upon capture, it was then my job to attack. I was feeling strong and when I attacked, I was really flying up the road with only about five miles to go. Suddenly a storm blew in, thunder cracked, and the rain came dumping down. I only went harder. To my great satisfaction, they never caught me. I left behind four guys including one of the best Senior men in the state! My confidence went through the roof!

The next day mom and I drove down to Denver and my Uncle Jim helped me pack my bike in a cardboard shipping box Bob had given me from his shop. I had never flown with my bike before. The departure gate in Denver was loaded with other bike racers. Of note, I met and spoke with Kelly Kittredge, future Mountain bike star Cindy Whitehead, and Sterling McBride. But the rider I was most thrilled to see was Thomas Prehn. He remembered me from a couple years prior and was super friendly again and so stoked that I too was going to Nationals. We talked about the Olympics, and he was just in awe of what "our riders" had accomplished. He noted that we placed the entire team in the first ten as Phinney and Rogers were fifth and sixth and Kiefel won the field sprint for ninth, an incredible overall team performance behind Grewal's emphatic victory. I would later learn that Tom had won one of the selection races for the Olympics himself and was very nearly an automatic qualifier for the team but was not named as a coach's selection. He mentioned none of this personal information, however, instead focusing on the incredible progress "we" had made. He would earn the silver medal a few days later in Sunapee behind Milk Race winner Matt Eaton. Again, an incredible example to me and a genuine ambassador of our sport. He would later become Nike's first employee in their cycling division and I would often race Oregon events with him.

These were the days when travel agents made reservations for you, and we had one particularly tight layover in Boston. We were advised to gather our own baggage and transfer it ourselves to make sure our bags made it. The clock was ticking, and my mother was freaking out while I was trying to drag both my cardboard bike box and my big duffle bag across the airport to the next gate. With only minutes to spare, we were told to take the bike down into the basement and leave it by a door, which I did. No one was there to meet me, and I raced back up the stairs to board the plane with my mom. We were the last passengers to board and the plane took off immediately. I was almost certain I would never see my bike again.

I was both thrilled and amazed when we arrived at the tiny airport in New Hampshire and my bike was the first item off the plane and onto the carousel. Mom had booked us a room at a beautiful hotel right on Lake Sunapee, a place with a summer camp vibe straight out of the movies. John was there with OJ and helped me assemble my bike. He too had found punk rock and was listening to The Cramps "Bad Music for Bad People" ...pretty wild stuff! We rode around the fourteen-mile circuit together and found it to our liking. It had a lot of short, steep climbs including one to the finish right in the center of the town. I regularly sprinted to the Lander city limit sign on a finishing climb that was similar. I was sure I was going to be right in there.

Cycling was absolutely booming in 1984 and pretty much every rider that had qualified from their State Road

Race made the trip to race the Nationals. The club system in America was strong and there was great support for Juniors. We all wanted to be part of this incredible new sport as public interest after the Olympics and Greg Lemond's World title and impressive Tour debut surged to an all-time high. 145 kids (!) lined up for the Junior Men's 14–15-year-old title race. The USCF rule book stated our maximum race distance was 38 miles and so with a fourteen-mile circuit we would race only two laps, 28 miles, for our Championship. As a state champion, I lined up right near the front. Derin Stockton, a big strong guy from Santa Barbara was right next to me and future 2x US Pro National Criterium Champion Frankie McCormack, the Massachusetts state champion was right in front of me.

The course was well suited to me with lots of short, steep climbs but the field was easily double the size of anything I had ever ridden in before. I worked hard to stay near the front of the field and out of trouble. This was a significant evolution from the year before when I was just trying to keep up with a mob of riders! The short hilly course created a race of attrition with all the best riders scrambling to maintain the status quo and stay near the front. Unlike at the Mini Zinger, I was staying in the pack and fully believed I could be there at the end to use my sprint.

On the long and straight backstretch that preceded the steep climb to the finish, with only four miles remaining, the inevitable finally happened…a screeching of brakes followed by yelling riders, and then that terrible sound of metal sliding across the pavement. I veered to the right, just avoiding the mayhem as riders piled up, but I went off the road and into the ditch. Somehow, I stayed upright despite riding through the mud along the side of the road. When I did get back onto the course, fifty riders were disappearing up the road. The few of us who had survived the chaos, rode as hard as we could to get back into the action. We basically caught the tail end of the lead group on the final corner with just a few hundred meters left to race. I charged up the hill, passing as many riders as I could, eventually finishing 43rd. I was proud of my recovery but left wondering what could have been. Despite the intimidating field size, I had come a long way and was much more competent and competitive.

To my great joy, there was a new race on the Wyoming calendar for the weekend before school started in late August. I had gone through a tremendous growth spurt in the previous couple years, and after riding a 52 cm bike in 1982, I was now on a 57. As my sophomore year approached, though, I needed a 60! A criterium in Thermopolis promised a huge payout, even to the Junior field which would greatly help me buy the new frame. I had my eye on an Italian one (finally!), an Atala Professional with all the cool chrome bits and the official pro team paint job. Bob would give me wholesale pricing since I worked at the shop.

The Junior field raced with the vets once again in a circuit around the mineral spring's hot pools in the little tourist town at the mouth of Wind River Canyon. The city planner had recently moved from Colorado and was a savvy bike race promoter but seemed disappointed at the realities of the bike racing scene in Cowboy Country. All the area riders turned out but there just weren't that many of us and our "blow in and blow out" approach did little for the local economy.

Bicycle racing has an undeniably dangerous side, and on this day, I narrowly avoided a very scary last lap crash that took out my buddy Bill Wade. It shook me up to see how bloodied and battered the old warrior was and his injuries required a trip to the hospital. As second placed junior, I claimed a $100 "value prize". Huh? My "big money" was a t-shirt, a beer cooler, a gift certificate for breakfast at a placed called "The Greasy Spoon", a ball cap, a steak dinner for two at the Holiday Inn, and...$7 in cash! The value of all these things totaled $100! It would not be my last encounter with the "big money delusions of small-time cycling." Dad, for his part, made sure we had the steak dinner before we headed home. Sadly, it was the last time I ever saw Bill, whose cheerful invitation to climb on board his RV had been instrumental in my development as a bike racer.

Now that cycling wasn't my full focus, I went back

to being a normal teenager in my sophomore year, got my driver's license, and started borrowing the car. I took a Lifeguarding class for my PE credit and like many of my swimming teammates, got a job at the pool. I found the College Radio Charts in the back of Dave Milleson's *Rolling Stone* magazine and realized this was a great source for that "new music" I had gotten turned on to in Colorado. Finding the actual albums in Cowboy Country, however, would require quite a bit of creativity and collaboration. Still lacking a record store, we could occasionally find cassettes of interest in the two department stores we had, but mostly we enlightened few shared with each other.

Swimming, once my main sport, now only got my attention once bike racing was finished for the year. Dave and I lifted weights together in the fall to prepare but I now rarely swam outside of the season. The actual start of swimming season that December gave me a staunch reminder on the value of off-season training. Kevin Butler, a neighbor and a friend as well as a soccer teammate, was a rookie on the previous year's team and not very good. He had trained extensively since then, though, and was now faster than me. Much faster! It bothered me but not enough to refocus me on swimming year-round. In fact, I now saw swimming as a winter bridge for year-round cycling, which had been recently enhanced with an indoor trainer (A "Racer Mate") my parents got me for Christmas so I could ride in my bedroom in the dead of winter. During the season, however, I gave everything in the pool and became one of thirteen on our team to qualify for the state meet, no small feat for a sophomore. Swimming is still very popular and enormously successful in Lander, and the High School team won their 30th consecutive state title in 2026! But the sport I loved now was cycling. It made me stand out as unique in what I saw as the homogenized and overly bland world of Cowboy Country that I was currently stuck in.

The increased freedom brought on by my driver's license, chasing girls, drinking beer and partying with friends, and perhaps most importantly the arrival (finally!) of MTV to my television screen provided some significant distractions over the school year. Brian was by now the DJ at our local radio station but was prohibited from straying from the top 40 playlist. He was also our de facto buyer of beer and a continuing source of musical information, providing albums for us to tape! For the first time I earned some Bs on my report card and my parents noted my tendency to arrive straight home from school and turn on the music videos. Being able to hear and now see new music was a dream come true and could really "pull me down the rabbit hole!" I reluctantly realized the truth in my parents' words and that my music obsession and social life was taking my focus away from training and schoolwork.

1984 Nationals, 145 riders. The kid from Wyoming is now in pink Spandex.
Photo courtesy Classic New England Cycling

1984 Junior 14-15 National Road Championship, Sunapee, NH. Number 137 far left center is Wyoming's representative in the field.
William Harting credit

CHAPTER THIRTEEN:

OUR BAND COULD BE YOUR LIFE

At the State Championship Road race, held in Jackson in mid-June of 1985, I was a little short on training and got it handed to me. Instead of getting directly onto my bike upon arriving home from school, I was watching MTV. I would get sucked into the exciting vortex of music and energy and end up shortchanging my ride. The winner was the same rider who had won the State Time Trial the week before and smoked me last summer, Mike Stieb. He was irrepressibly energetic on and off the bike, had super well-developed legs, and just never seemed to struggle. He could climb, sprint, and time trial without any real weak points. He had followed in John's footsteps and spent December at the OTC and was now even faster. David Lingle from Jackson was another new rider on the scene and the three of us broke away from the field. Both riders were hurting me on the climbs until I flatted. I took a spare wheel from the follow car and limped in for third. Despite the flat I was struggling against stronger riders and third would likely have been my result anyway. Topher, still in the younger age group based on his date of birth, had won his race and was stoked to qualify for Nationals. They were scheduled to be held in Milwaukee, Wisconsin that year which he could pull off since he had family nearby.

I had travelled to the race with Topher's family in their station wagon and the real highlight was the drive home and all the musical updates my friend had to offer after his year living in a big city. He was "spiking" his hair now and his musical knowledge, and subsequently his record collection, had exploded! I had read in *Rolling Stone* about a band called The Replacements and their latest album "Let it Be", which was atop the College Radio Charts. They just raved about it…great songwriting and an exciting and raw sound. In my last letter to Topher, I had asked him to buy it for me if he could. Could

Saddling up to ride Cowboy Country

he? He had the cassette for me and explained that they were a local band! He referred to them as "The Matts" and told me they were great. They had played at a high school dance not long ago! However, they had put my beloved MTV in the bull-seye in one of their tunes. These weren't just songs about girls and cars, there was introspection as well as strong opinions and fiery emotions here!

SEEN YOUR VIDEO-The Replacements from "Let it Be" (1984)
"All day, all night, all music video. Seen your video, that phony rock 'n' roll! We don't want to know, seen your video! Your phony rock 'n' roll! We don't want to know!"

He also introduced me to another intense Minnesota band…Hüsker Dü, who had opened for the Dead Kennedy's at a show Topher had seen that winter. That show was quite a revelation for him. We were entering new territory with this music that in many cases was not merely outside of the mainstream but actively hated the mainstream! As I learned more about Punk and New Wave music it became clear that this music scene was "do it yourself" …much like bike racing in Wyoming, or for that matter, in America at that point. This music was breaking new ground and didn't stick to the predictable styles and topics that dominated the pop charts. These artists forged their own path, often on small or independent record labels, booking their own tours, travelling in their own vans to play small clubs, often doing their own album art and posters, and in many cases learning as they went along. This was quite similar to how most Americans approached bike racing in the 1980s. Additionally, this new music was exciting, different, and wildly creative. It was not just a reworking of what everyone else was doing or mimicking what was popular or had come before. This music was the precursor and in many cases the inspiration to the alternative rock movement that would sweep America in the early 90s, but the term "Alternative" wasn't used yet.

When I last saw him, we were both into Billy Idol, but now he had albums by Generation X, the PUNK band that Billy was in back in the 1970's in England, in the same scene as the Sex Pistols! The other thing he had were two albums by R.E.M.- "Murmur" and their "Chronic Town" EP. They were complex and intellectual and so esoteric and I loved them. They were mysterious and yet evocative, tapping into and stimulating a deep introspection that seemed to characterize my teenage years. The drive flew by, the disappointment of my race abated, as I listened to these and many others (The Minutemen, The Suburbs, Suicidal Tendencies, Black Flag and more) on the headphones of his Walkman, which in those days had two headphone ports. This music had diverse styles, approaches, and subject matter and seemed to offer so much more to offer than what was played on the radio in Lander! Much like bike racing, it felt like it was ours. We chose it, rather than just getting stuck with it. It spoke volumes to us but required great effort to find it in Cowboy Country. Only a very few locally were into this scene and truly appreciated it. Thus, a musical partnership was born. A partnership of seeking out and finding new artists and albums and sharing them. In addition to cycling, together we celebrated meaningful music that was off the beaten path.

Years later, in an excellent BBC documentary called "The Seven Ages of Rock", during the segment "Alternative Rock: Left of the Dial", *Rolling Stone* Senior Editor, David Fricke explained this new music of the 1980s nicely: "It was that separate world of what is now called Alternative Rock. And what at the time was actually just called College Rock because the only place you heard it on the radio was on college stations. It's the classic Replacements song "Left of the Dial". It's a song about where you tuned...you know manually, you turned the little knob to the left of the dial, the 88.9s and the 90.1s, all the stuff that was below the commercial band. You had to look for it. People who really wanted something more out of music, wanted something more out of life, who wanted something more out of their guitars...that's where you went." A song we listened to on the way home that day encapsulated this vibe perfectly...

HISTORY LESSON, PART II-The Minutemen from "Double Nickels on the Dime" 1984
"Our band could be your life

Saddling up to ride Cowboy Country

Real names'd be proof
Me and Mike Watt, we played for years
Punk Rock changed our lives

We Learned Punk Rock in Hollywood
Drove up from Pedro
We were fucking corndogs
We'd go drink and pogo

Mr. Narrator
This is Bob Dylan to me
My story could be his songs
I'm his soldier child
Our band is scientist rock
But I was E. Bloom, Richard Hell
Joe Strummer and John Doe
Me and Mike Watt, playing guitar"

My training goal throughout the summer of 1985 was to get in 200 miles per week. After the Sunday State Championship, I was a bit short of this goal and clearly behind my rivals. The pros always seemed to do these long cool downs (a friend in Oregon would later call it "bonus miles"), so after Topher's folks dropped me off, I suited up and headed out again. Kevin, my swimming teammate who lived down the street hollered at me on my way back home. Eric Heiden had won the Core States USPRO Championship in Philadelphia, had I heard? He ran out with his *Sports Illustrated* magazine detailing the race. The victory salute and Heiden's physique were awesome! Better yet, I realized other people in my little town in Cowboy Country were paying attention to bike racing!

Prior to this, I honestly thought Heiden as a bike racer was a bit of a joke, and more of a publicity stunt for the 7-Eleven squad. With his monstrous legs and five Olympic Golds in speed skating, he drew crowds to races. I knew he was friendly and outgoing, but not a REAL pro road racer... maybe a track rider? He just seemed too big and bulky for the road. He had too many other interests (broadcasting, medical school) I thought ...but he showed me, and many others, we were wrong. Eric was a fierce competitor and an amazing athlete. He had just finished the Giro d'Italia where he won the intermediate sprint competition, which received little publicity. His teammates described his strategy as basically "hit the front hard with 500 meters to go" …and no one could come around him! They had little success getting him to adopt a more tactically astute approach, but it didn't matter, he just got it done. Eric Heiden was a true force of nature!

After sticking with the leaders for ten trips up the steep Manayunk wall over 156 miles of racing, he appeared to be riding a similar finale. This time, however, it initially appeared to be for the benefit of 7-Eleven stalwart Tom Schuler, sitting on the back of the leading quintet. As Schuler began to launch his sprint, he pulled his foot out and was immediately a non-factor. He actually ripped his entire shoe as he wasn't using the traditional clips and straps but rather a new pedal that worked like a ski binding. Heiden, however, kept charging on the front while Danes Jesper Worre and future "Slurpee" Jens Veggerby couldn't come around.

Sports Illustrated covered that first-year race and it gave the young, burgeoning American professional cycling scene a real lift. Would it even have made the magazine if Heiden didn't win? Suddenly friends of mine who didn't know boo about bike racing were asking about cycling and commenting on Heiden's historic victory. It helped put our sport on the nation's radar and that event would thrive for decades to come. Eric Heiden as a bike racer, made a huge contribution to American cycling. The big man would be back on our TV screens in July, commentating on the Tour de France and in 1986, he would race it!

Eric Heiden wins the 1985 Core States US Pro Championship in Philadelphia.
Photo credit John Pierce

By the summer of 1985, thanks largely to the 7-Eleven team, the US cycling team's nine medal haul in Los Angeles, and Greg Lemond's world-beating exploits in Europe (fourth in Paris-Roubaix, third in the Giro), cycling was becoming much more popular and visible. Cycling was even becoming more present in American culture, and it was seen as a new, exciting, colorful, and healthy sport. Bike racing even appeared in mainstream ads on TV! More races were being held, prize lists kept growing, bike sales were booming, and more people were riding and competing. Americans, even in Wyoming, were following the Tour de France on CBS Sports now that we had an American contender. One example in Lander was my friend Derrick Ross, who was several years older than me and had served as an assistant swim coach for our High School team. He had purchased a Trek racing bike from the local shop and had been riding with Topher and me. He drove us to a new criterium around the Casper Events Center, right next to the Casper Hilton Inn on the Fourth of July. Casper had been in an economic downturn since its oil boom in the mid-1970s. The events center was the town's big draw now and a bicycle race was seen as a way to "bring people to town" and "stimulate the economy". The prize list was the likes of which we had never seen…$5000 in cash and merchandise, so we were happy to come to town and race!

Since he was new to the sport, the athletic Derrick scrapped it out in the Citizen's category, finishing third and having a blast. Topher and I competed well in a nice sized Junior field but were powerless against Stieb…again. However, I won a cash prime in another photo-finish with Topher, and we ended second and third. Sprinting had become my forte and I was rarely beaten in the final two hundred meters. I seemed able to build an internal cauldron deep within and then unleash it with a veritable fury as I barreled for the line in an all-encompassing quest for maximum speed. Our prizes were unheard of in Cowboy Country…I won a Campagnolo Super Record headset, worth around $50! Topher took home a new gizmo on the market, a cyclometer. It was made by Cat-Eye, battery powered and mounted on the handlebars to tell you speed, distance, and time. We were psyched!

Topher then decided we should race against the Senior Men. Why not? Only about twenty-five riders were signed up and the prize list went ten deep. I was skeptical but he talked me into it, as he was sure we could make the top ten and score more schwag. The University of Wyoming team, or four of them at least, were among the starters but we lined up near the front and "hung tough". Soon the field split and we were on the right side of things. I was in a good spot when the bell rang for a prime sprint and in my THIRD tight finish of the day, I just held off…Topher! We ended up lapping the field including all the UW guys, which did not go unnoticed by us. At the finish we were seventh and eighth among the men and collected more goodies and this time I got a cyclometer. It was big and heavy, but I thought it would be good for training, and I took $30 cash in prime money as well.

This was another of many "delusional days" that bike racing would provide. "Look, Mom and Dad I won all this stuff and some money too!" I joyfully exclaimed upon arriving home a little late for the neighborhood cook out and fireworks party. "But what about all the money you put into your bike and the entry fees and gas money" says Dad, not going in for this delusion at all. "You'll be lucky if you break even!" But his attempt at a buzz kill was for naught! I would be deluded again and again as this sport was incredible. Doing the training out on the open road with a head full of dreams and then competing and winning prizes, especially cash against other riders in an adrenaline rush of high speed, tight proximity, and ultimate effort? My swollen ego felt as if was soaring high above the world of Cowboy Country…

Saddling up to ride Cowboy Country

A DAY WITHOUT ME-U2 from "Boy" (1980)
"Starting a landslide in my ego
Look from the outside
To the world I left behind
I'm dreaming…"

Immediately after the Casper Criterium, my folks had a two-week trip to the Pacific Northwest planned. Much to my father's chagrin, I insisted on bringing my bike to keep up my training. I even found a race in Beaverton, Oregon from an Oregon racing calendar that was chock-full of events from spring through autumn. Cycling seemed quite well developed there with many well-stocked bike shops and lots of riders out on the roads. One day on the beach, a guy even looked at me and said, "You're a bike racer, aren't you?" What? This had never happened in Wyoming! I said "Yeah! How'd you know?" He said "Shaved legs, tan lines, and scars on your knees. I raced quite a bit back in the 1970's myself". Hmmm…

During the trip my mother, always my biggest supporter, found me a landmark book for all American bicycle racers: "Bicycle Road Racing: Complete Program for Training and Competition" by Edward Borysewicz. The architect of America's rise to international prominence and "our" unprecedented success in the 1984 Olympics, had now published the details that riders like me were so desperate for. I devoured the book in the backseat of our Ford Bronco and at night in the hotels and campgrounds throughout the trip.

Cycling equipment was starting to evolve and I test rode a bike in Seattle with Japanese Shimano SIS shifting, which was an enormous improvement over the standard Italian "friction" shifting where you had to carefully "feel" for the gear…"rattle-rattle thunk". With this system the chain went perfectly and immediately onto the next cog and a positive "click" was all you heard. The chain slipping or over or under shifting, which sometimes happened with the old system were effectively eliminated. It was an expensive upgrade requiring several new components, but I hoped to be able to join this revolution soon.

My ever-organized mother arranged some college visits on the trip including the University of Oregon and Oregon State University, both of which appealed to me. My first thought was that it was too early to visit colleges. It was only the summer after my sophomore year, but this place was intriguing, and I quickly got on board. Oregon was a beautiful state that seemingly had everything: tall trees, beaches, mountains, high plains, and a mild climate conducive to year-round riding. Unfortunately, the race outside of Portland had no Junior field and the Senior men's field was much larger and stronger than I had encountered in Casper. Several crashes shook me up and I ended up limping in off the back. Undeterred, I continued studying my new book and training for the upcoming Dead Dog Stage race being held again in Laramie, with the idea that college in Oregon could be pretty cool.

I was again lack-luster in the time trial but rallied to use what was now clearly my best weapon, my sprint in a wet and windswept road race. In an attacking and aggressive finale, I won ahead of Colorado junior phenom Keith Harper and a tough new rider from Nebraska. Unfortunately, the very skilled Harper, smoked both Topher and I in the criterium. The wheels Brian built with the rims I traded Danny for back in 1984 at the Laramie race were in the pit, a luxury I finally enjoyed in 1985. Danny had won the opening time trial in the Senior 1/2s by thirty seconds and finished with the lead group in the Snowy Range Road Race. He was about to start the criterium with Colorado rider Randy Whicker of the Dia-Compe/Denver Spoke Team, second on GC and one of the best criterium riders in the country, ready to challenge him with everything he had. In fact, Whicker had been ON THE COVER of *Winning* earlier in the year after breaking away with none other than Davis Phinney at a big Mayor's Cup race. He was the real deal with some quality teammates, and Danny would have his hands full hanging on to his lead. The Wyoming riders were fired up to cheer on our hero to what could be a tremendous upset.

My buddy Topher and I got our spare wheels out of

the pit and then sat down on a curb to see "the big-boys race". We watched Danny cover every move Whicker made during the 40-lap race in downtown Laramie. Brian, working as the announcer as he often did, called out "10 laps to go, no more free laps!" and as the pack rolled by, Whicker was driving on the front...but Danny was off the back! He had flatted! He saw me there with my spare wheels, so skidding to a halt, he yells at me "Give me a rear wheel, Dave!" My Junior freewheel only had a 15-tooth high gear, and I knew he'd need more on the course's long straightaways, so I yelped "But Danny..." He was in a panic and cut me off, "C'mon, Dave!" He grabbed the wheel out of my hands, put it in quickly, and tore off in pursuit as I gave him the best push-off I could muster, certain that I had doomed my hero. The next lap, he was 25 seconds behind, nose on the stem, fluidly spinning that 15 cog and Whicker and his teammates were hammering. It didn't look good for our hero! It seemed impossible he would keep his GC lead.

Mark Ward grabbed the microphone from Brian. He was our USCF District Representative and one of Danny's good friends and sometimes boss when Danny worked for him at his "Wheel Fixit" shop. He implored the crowd to get behind their local hero. "And chant his name like the French do for Hinault on the roads of France. Only our hero here in Wyoming is not Bernard Hinault, it is Danny Birkholz!" The crowd started chanting "Danny, Danny!" and he kept spinning that junior gear and the gap kept coming down. And down. It seemed possible but realistically it could go either way. The bell-lap arrived and there he was...sitting on the back, his lead safe and grinning ear-to-ear! He had closed nearly 30 seconds on a tough rival in around five miles...on a junior gear. After the race, he gave me back my wheel, thanked me, and acknowledged no handicap from the gear. "Actually, it was perfect!" he said, "I never had to shift, I just had a good gear for the whole course". Then he took a closer look at the 10 unique gold anodized rims. "Wait, Dave...are these the wheels? Those rims from last year?" Yes, Danny, these were THE WHEELS. And he was THAT rider. A legend. Our Hero.

Danny would go on to become a US Cycling Federation National Team Coach, but he would be lost in a plane crash over Colorado Springs on March 3, 1991. Upon hearing of the tragedy, I wrote this very story and sent it off to *Velo-News*. It would be my first ever published piece, entitled "Tribute to a Friend". Brian, working for the US National Team as a mechanic at The Milk Race in Britain at that time, came across a copy of the magazine in the team car. Upon seeing the tribute, he burst into tears, which was quite confusing to the other staff members. The community we formed in Cowboy country was small, but it was very strong, and it bonded many of us for life.

It was after the 1985 Tour, and shortly after the Dead Dog race, that I met my biggest hero and inspiration in person...Greg Lemond! Just 16 years old, Topher and I drove down to Boulder, Colorado to watch the final two stages of the Coors Classic. The last two days were nearly always the same and very spectator friendly...the Morgul-Bismark Road Race on Saturday, not far outside of town and on Sunday, the North Boulder Park Criterium right in the heart of the city. And this was not just any Coors, but a mountainous California/Nevada/Colorado edition that featured the La Vie Claire team, rebadged as Celestial Seasonings Red Zinger for the event, of Lemond and Tour winner Bernard Hinault. Both were notably now using the new "Look" ski binding style pedals.

Greg had been disappointed to finish second that July to his team leader Hinault in a race many, including Greg, thought he could have won. Doug Shapiro beat his more celebrated teammates Phinney and Kiefel to the Tour de France start line as well, becoming only the third American to ride the event. The final winning margin after over 2500 miles and over 100 hours of racing was just over a minute after Greg waited for an injured Hinault on the mountain stage to Luz Ardiden. In a breakaway with third-placed Stephen Roche, Greg's French team staff misinformed him of the gap to Hinault behind. Rather than aid Roche in moving past the Frenchman, the American was ordered to wait. He later realized that the gap to Hinault was much larger than he was told, and he had thrown away a winning opportunity. He did, however, win the final time trial, another historic American first. Hinault, meanwhile, won his record-tying fifth Tour to join all-time greats Eddy Merckx of Belgium and Frenchman Jacques Anquetil but promised next year he would work for his American teammate.

After crashing on the floor of an older swimming friend who was attending Colorado University, we rode our bikes out to the racecourse. I had never seen so many people gathered on the roadside for a cycling event! The American cycling cult, stronger in Boulder than perhaps anywhere else in America, was out in force! We didn't catch Greg, the race leader, prior to the start but we strategically waited by the doping control trailer after the race. No one else was there. Within five minutes, the door opened and out popped my main man, Greg! "Hi, guys" he boisterously exclaimed! "Are you bike racers?" "We are!" we proudly responded. He signed our hats and our race programs, smiling and taking time to talk with us and more importantly listen to us. I told him I knew he would win the Tour next year and he said he appreciated that. What an ambassador of the sport and just a nice guy. That day he made it clear...he was one of us!

Because of the low key and tightly knit nature of the US cycling scene, we met some of our other heroes at the 1985 Coors. The first was Andy Hampsten, the only rider who had been able to challenge Lemond in the mountains at the Coors. Lying second overall, he was wearing the purple King of the Mountains jersey. Fittingly, he was sitting on the asphalt and signing a friend's cowboy hat when we met him. I was star-struck as he had won a mountain stage at the Giro d'Italia (as a guest rider with 7-Eleven but now back with Levi's/Raleigh) that spring against the very best in the world. I asked him about that and the progress of the "US Amateurs" in Europe. "Oh, no he responded...we're all professionals now!" I was so embarrassed...I mean, duh! But the truth was that the words US and Professionals were only connected to a few guys until now! And in the previous years leading up to the Olympics the media's focus, and mine, had been on "our" progress on the international amateur scene. So, while I felt like a knucklehead for misspeaking, in hindsight I understood why I had. The US pro scene had developed fast!

After our chat with Andy, we made our way over to the 7-Eleven van. Ron Kiefel had made history in May by winning a stage of the Giro, the first American to do so, beating even Greg to the punch. It was the first time an American had won a stage of a Grand Tour. He was easy-going and friendly and hopeful of racing the Tour next year but noted how incredibly difficult racing in Europe was. Our real 7-Eleven experience happened after the stage as we were riding back into town. Topher and I were rolling along, recounting the day's events, when the whole 7-Eleven team (Kiefel, Phinney, Bob Roll, and even director Jim Ochowicz!) came riding by! So, we tagged along with our heroes, all easy-going and accommodating, unable to believe our luck. Friendly, accessible, all while taking on the world and winning…it was truly a magical time in American cycling history!

Meeting my hero at the 1985 Coors Classic-Greg Lemond.
Photo credit Dave Campbell

CHAPTER FIFTEEN:

THIS IS A PERFECT WORLD,

I'M RIDING ON AN INCLINE

Topher's parents allowed him to choose where he wanted to live for the final two years of High School, and I was thrilled to have my number one music and cycling buddy back with me in Cowboy Country. He brought more home-made note pads, but they said "C & D Racing" now. I was sure he would help make "being stuck in this place" so much more bearable. The "big city kid with spikey hair" (he had lived in St. Paul, MN) was a huge hit at Lander Valley High School. His locker was next to Wade, a buddy since kindergarten and we all took the same advanced Math and Science classes. His appearance, and reception, were not unlike Kevin Bacons in "Footloose", albeit without the fist fights, truck races, and dance contests!

We split a subscription to *Rolling Stone* magazine and really focused on the album reviews and especially the "College Radio Charts". Each issue had a Top 50 albums chart based on sales, but the real gem for us were the Top 10 albums being played on COLLEGE RADIO. There we could find the quirky post-punk sort of music we were interested in. We learned from *Rolling Stone* that much like bike racing, the bands we loved were becoming more accepted by the mainstream. The first were the Replacements, who signed with a major label on the back of significant critical acclaim and released "Tim" that autumn, and even appeared, infamously, on "Saturday Night Live".

Of course, getting our hands on those albums in Lander, Wyoming was no small feat. We established a network of other students who were into less mainstream music and more interesting bands like Echo & The Bunnymen, Hüsker Dü, The Cure, REM, U2, The Alarm, New Order, and the like. In our Wyoming high school of about 650 students, that meant approximately eight other kids, and we connected with every one of them and actively recruited others. We all deeply felt the dreamy soundscapes of the Cure, the swirling psychedelia of Echo, and U2 and The Alarm's calls to arms urgency for social justice. It seemed to raise us above the mundane musical and cultural world we felt we were trapped in. Additionally, "our music" seemed to speak deeply to our teenage frustrations and our quest to make some sense of the world instead of just offering trite celebrations of partying and romance. In hindsight, I suppose it uplifted our humanity.

When ANYONE got ahold of a cutting-edge album, usually by travelling to a bigger town, they shared it with the rest of us. The quest for new music in Cowboy Country paralleled the pursuit of cycling information, events, and training partners....there weren't very many of us, so we had to really work at it. But like cycling, it gave us pride and ownership. We couldn't hear our music on the radio, so we had to seek it out and create our own community. Most mornings before class over the next two years would involve Topher, our musical co-conspirators, and I meeting and trading cassette tapes. Most of our classmates didn't understand our fascination with this "new music". I remember one of my old soccer teammates mocking us in Chemistry class with comments like "Topher is like wow, here's another band no one has ever heard of-let's buy it, Dave!" Milleson chimed in with "Echo and the Bunnymen? What kind of name is that, are they gay or something?" We were undaunted, offering up our own jabs at their pop and heavy metal tastes while continuing on our quest.

The de facto English College Prep course for Juniors was Intermediate Composition, taught by Mr. Roger Mork. Initially, Mr. Mork came across as a little bit intimidating and very academic, having been educated at Middlebury College in Vermont and then Oxford. But in reality, he was a well-read old hippy who loved rock and roll, especially Bruce Springsteen, Neil Young, and Bob Dylan. We saw and felt the significance of this music that he readily shared and we saw him as one of the few "cool" teachers. It was in his class that I fell in love with writing, especially since he gave us free reign on topics. He allowed us to write about the things we were actually interested in. One of the first assignments was "No Books Research" and I joyfully penned my own album reviews on a trio of works I had found especially interesting that fall: REM "Fables of the Reconstruction", Talking Heads "Little Creatures", and The Hooters "Nervous Night". Mr. Mork became integrated into our underground tape exchange network and later turned me on to Paul Simon's incredible "Graceland", which I ordinarily would have avoided in my quest for more "underground" music.

In addition to the Student Council and some demanding college prep coursework, the fall of 1985 was focused on getting into December camp at the Olympic Training Center. I took Typing class and stayed late for extra help preparing my race resume and application. I asked Bob from the bike shop and Bruce, my swimming coach, to write letters of recommendation. Autumn was usually a time off for me with some independent work in the weight room to prepare for swimming, but this year I continued riding as well as lifting and kept a close eye on the mailbox, hoping for an acceptance letter from Colorado Springs. I spent a lot of time on my "Racer Mate" in my bedroom when snow, cold, early darkness (or all three) kept me off the road.

The letter from the US Olympic Committee arrived in mid-November and I was thrilled to be one of 120 riders accepted. It read "Room and Board is provided by the US Olympic Committee.* Your only expense is travel to and from Colorado Springs". There were release forms and parental permissions to sign and return. We had to "confirm our intention to participate by this date or lose our spot to the next person on the list" ...no chance of that! 1985 would also be the first year Junior women were included: 20 of the 120 riders would be girls! Bikes were expected to arrive "clean and in perfect working order but tools, glue (we all rode tubulars back then even for training), grease

*Of note: after disappearing in the mid 90's, the camps returned a few years ago... at a cost to participants of $10,000!!! But it did include special commemorative clothing with the USA Cycling logo. Huh

and work stands will be provided by National Team Mechanics! Help and advice is only a THANK YOU away!" I was overwhelmed with pride, excitement, and expectation...this was going to be incredible! The camp would be held December 13-30 and so I would miss a week of school, with the bulk of the camp happening over Christmas break. Academics were very important to me and my parents, so I would need to do some schoolwork in advance, take some with me, as well as make up some tests on my return. Pre-Calculus and Honors Chemistry were just a couple of the classes keeping me very busy. Dad assured me he would be glad to drive me down there and then stay with "his folks" in Denver for a visit before driving back. The drive would take about eight-hours...if the winter roads were good.

The letter explained in detail what the camp would entail and what we should bring. A training program for the weeks leading up to camp was also provided as was an address to give friends and family for mail. I had never trained intently for cycling through the winter, deferring instead to swimming during Wyoming's cold, dark, and snowy winter months. In addition to winter riding clothes, we also needed clothes for gymnasium work. The camp would include road riding, cyclocross (?), running, weight training, and basketball. My mom, as always was super supportive and generously purchased some more winter clothing for me: actual wool tights (I only had leg warmers previously), some serious "wind tights" (wool with nylon panels on the front), and a nylon fronted heavy wool winter cycling jacket. She had told her friends, Rick and Ann Allen, both of whom were former NOLS instructors, about the camp and they contributed a Patagonia (!) fleece jacket and pants. She was worried about me missing Christmas with my family and so she arranged for me to ride the bus on Christmas Eve to Denver, a little over an hour away, and enjoy the holiday with her younger sister Mary and her family.

I was asked to bring a cyclocross bike as well as my road bike. I knew vaguely of cyclocross from my *Winning* magazines where I had seen muddy riders running uphill with their bikes slung over their shoulders. 'Cross is a winter combination of running and riding practiced on a variety of surfaces, but not only did I not have a bike, I had never done it! I bought the only bike frame available at Freewheel Sports, even though it was a little too big, and set about building one up with whatever old leftover parts I had in the garage. Any components I needed to buy were "bottom of the line" as money was tight. I was paying for my cycling habit from my new job at the pool, where like many of my swimming teammates I worked as a life-guard. Cyclocross bikes had cantilever brakes for better tire clearance, but my orange Miyata 912 didn't have boss-es for them, so I made do with old steel Mafac center pulls that I got on the cheap. Drew teased me that I would have "the heaviest 'cross bike at the camp"! Having two bikes though, regardless of weight or equipment, made me feel like a real big shot!

A few weeks prior to the camp, I was in Casper for the Wyoming State Student Council Convention and so I called up Mike Stieb. What a nut! He pulled into the park-ing lot of the Hilton where all the students were staying with his stereo blaring and chanting "Nah, Nah, Nah, Nah-Nuh!" along with Talking Heads ("Television Man") on their "Little Creatures" album. His hair was long and stringy, he had multiple piercings in his ear, his clothes were a bar-rage of neon, and his glasses were like Geddy Lee's from the band Rush. I was happy to see him, but he only rein-forced the stereotype to my conservative classmates that we bike racers were a bunch of weirdos! Which, of course, was part of why I loved the whole thing...we were!

Since he had been to Colorado Springs the previous year, he had loads of great advice. The culture of cycling at that time, particularly in Wyoming, was one of active-ly sharing information and helping each other. Everyone in our little cycling world was trying to elevate not only their personal performances, but the sport in general. It was a wonderful time and since cycling information was scarce, it was shared readily. I told him about my gear, and he noted I would need warmer gloves. He assured me that special winter cycling gloves were unnecessary, and to just get some ski gloves with a leather palm. He advised me on tires for the cyclocross bike and what the daily training sessions and weather were like. Road rides peaked at around two and a half hours, and they made you stay in the small chainring and spin. The hardest workouts were circuit weight training and cyclocross and he recommended I practice "cross" a bit beforehand as riding around in the snow and mud with a hundred other kids was tricky!

As the departure date approached, I started receiving the kind of attention you can only get in a small town. A popular girl from the Newspaper class pulled me out of Social Studies class one day to interview me for the "*The Tiger Connection*" school paper and took a quick black and white photo of me in the hallway. The "*Wyoming State Journal*" called as well, determined to make the camp into something it wasn't despite my protestations. Using a photo from a local race in 1984, the headline read "Campbell to train for the Olympics", an embarrassment to me only slightly below the whole "State Champion by just showing up" thing from a couple years prior. The article itself, however, was accurate about what the camp was...a development camp for promising young riders from around the country. Physiological testing would be done to choose forty to fifty riders to return for a more intensive April camp. At the monthly Letterman's Club meeting, Mr. Johnstone, the club advisor and our biology teacher, presented me with a check for $100 to help with my expenses at the camp.

At this point, I still was a very part-time cyclist. This was due to my commitments to school and college prep coursework as well as the swimming team. Swim season began with Water Polo over Christmas break and then went full bore with two a day practices and twice weekly meets from January through mid-March. I was still unclear about how to integrate the two sports. Most of that time, the roads around Lander were unrideable anyway due to snow and extreme cold. Since temperatures well below zero were common, I had never trained as a year-round cyclist. Although I had participated in a few high-level races, I was realistically limited to mainly Wyoming's minimal but growing summer calendar due to my finances and job, excepting the occasional forays to Utah, Montana, and Colorado. Although my parents were supportive, taking me to races all over the country was simply not in their playbook. My father especially did not want to overindulge his kids. Not only did getting invited back for April seem like a stretch, but I didn't even know if I could pull it off if I did. Missing school was stressful for me and a very tough sell to my parents.

Nonetheless, I wanted to learn as much as I possibly could and use the camp to jump-start the year's training. I was determined to make the most of the opportunity. I hacked around in the snow and sagebrush on my new 'cross bike in the vacant lot across the street, learning not to bruise my shoulder when I ran with it up the hills. I sweated like a pig in my bedroom on my indoor trainer and lifted weights at the pool in preparation. The idea of living in dorms with a bunch of bike racers from all over the country and being a full-time athlete, if only for a few weeks, was thrilling. I had seen how strong and savvy John and Mike had become in the seasons after their winter camps and I wanted the same for myself. I wanted my final year as a Junior to be a dominant one, especially in Wyoming. As I pondered all this on my last day at Lander Valley High School prior to departure, Gene Patch, our short and fiery little principal stopped me in the hall. "Campbell, you goin' down to Colorado tomorrow for that Olympic Camp?" "Yes, sir" I replied. "Well, son you give 'em hell down there!" He instructed me with great enthusiasm as he patted me on the back. It was probably the most quintessentially "Cowboy Country" moment in my entire cycling career!

As I packed that night, I had one final well-wisher...my high school writing teacher! Mr. Mork came by with a small leatherbound journal. It was inscribed with a message I will never forget: "The Olympic spirit is difficult to grasp, to catch. Here then is a net for the attempt!" I would use that journal to take notes daily on what we were learning, and I still have both the journal and Roger Mork's friendship, to this day.

The drive down was cold and windy with blowing

snow. The weather made me a little anxious about bundling up and getting out on the road every day. I didn't have much time to focus on that, though, as I had an American History book report to finish up, so most of the drive was spent reading and writing. Less than a year ago, the US cycling program had received some unwanted national attention for a "blood boosting" scandal. It turns out that several of the 1984 Olympic medalists had "reinfused" red blood cells prior to competition in a move, that while not technically against the rules was clearly immoral and a form of cheating. A lot like doping really. In a very prescient comment, my dad told me to "watch out for drugs down there, you don't want to be involved in any of that".

Upon arrival, I checked in and was issued a meal pass/ID card and given a room assignment. The upcoming 1986 World Championships, to be held in Colorado Springs in September, seemed to be a major theme in the US cycling offices with posters and information everywhere. I ran into Darin Dewsnup from Utah; a friend I had made the year before at a race outside Salt Lake City. My roommates were two guys from San Antonio, Texas. Bryce, a bit of an introvert, was mainly a track racer and had brought a fixed gear bike. Andy was tall and skinny and friendly. He was sitting on his bed- "unpacking". He had the closet open and was taking all his clothes, which primarily seemed to be white cotton "Thermal" long underwear, from his duffle bag, wadding them up, and throwing them across the room and into the closet. It was hilarious, and Dad just looked at him and said "Huh. I've never seen anyone unpack like that." Strange unpacking aside, Andy was friendly and easy-going, and it was immediately clear we'd be friends.

The wind and snow we drove through moved into Colorado Springs making road riding impossible on the first day and so instead we went to the gym. We were broken into twenty man groups each with older, permanent resident (PR) riders assigned to lead us. In the gym, Darroll Batke and Kit Kyle led us through tumbling drills on mats so we "knew how to crash" and would hopefully reduce the chance of injury when we did. We did some circuit weight training following some five-on-five basketball where the only rules seemed to be "run, run, jump, jump!" The idea was to keep it aerobic and the fact that I could actually dribble, and shoot (two years of Junior High basketball-B team) made me a veritable star!

We weighed ourselves each morning and took our pulse for 15 seconds upon awaking and then for another 15 seconds after standing. These were recorded daily and posted outside our dorm rooms on a chart for the coaching staff. A gap between the two pulse rates exceeding 5 was seen as a sign of fatigue and cause for a rest day. We jogged down to breakfast, stopping enroute to stretch and do "deep breathing exercises" where we got all the "stale air" out of our lungs from sleeping, actually pushing and squeezing on our bellies! The weather in Colorado Springs, despite its 6000-foot elevation, was much milder than Lander as it was over four hundred miles south, but all those wool clothes I had brought were still essential!

After our day in the gym, the sun came back out and the snow melted, and we rode for an hour and a half on day two. Helmets were optional and most of us wore wool ski hats. We would ride in twenty-man groups, bigger than the race fields in Wyoming! My training rides in contrast were either alone, with Topher, or with a few of the older guys in the club, but never more than five riders. Riding consistently in a big group was key to developing the skills needed to be a good bike racer. The tough riders I faced at RZMC and Nationals, especially those from California and Colorado really had a leg up on me due to the number of riders they had to train and race with. My group was assigned Mike McCarthy, a permanent resident from New York, as our ride leader. He was only a year or two older than us but friendly, outgoing, and encouraging...and very savvy on the nuances of cycling. Despite being such an accomplished cyclist, he spoke to all of us with respect and treated us like we belonged there. Mike would go on to represent the US in the 1988 and 1996 Olympics. In 1992, he became the first ever American to win a World Championship in the Professional Pursuit on the track.

Our rides were always done after lunch, in the warmest part of the day. Gathering daily with over a hundred other cyclists was something I had never experienced, and I absolutely loved it. We were all just goofy teenagers but when we suited up to ride together behind US cycling vehicles emblazoned with large signs that read "Olympic Cyclists in Training" we felt like something more. This setting alone made us feel serious and important. Nobody joked or fooled around, and we all wanted to ride like pros in tight formation, bundled up and working on turning our pedals over with buttery suppleness as we racked up the winter miles of truly serious racing cyclists.

We spun easily on a flat out and back course, required by the coaches to always stay in our small chainring. Riding formation was always a double paceline and we were encouraged to ride close, keep our elbows bent, and always have our fingers hooked around the bars or levers. Lazily resting hands atop the bars could make for a nasty fall if you hit a bump. As a rider who trained and raced in very small groups, such group riding was invaluable. The melting snow on that first day made for a muddy splatter fest, and I could barely keep my heavy, wet, saggy wool tights from dropping down around my ankles when climbing the stairs back up to the dorms. The coaching staff advised me to get some suspenders, a staple for winter training they said, and I promptly did. It was one of the few legitimate camp-related purchases I made with my Letterman's club money.

Most of the evenings after dinner had lectures or presentations ("Chalk-Talks") and I dutifully took notes on all of them in my little leatherbound journal from Mr. Mork. The first was just a video…of Greg Lemond winning the 1983 Worlds!!! We were instructed to not focus on "Look at the wankers, they're off the back" but rather how Greg was racing, his riding style, and his tactics. I had only seen pictures in the magazines and was absolutely thrilled to see all the key moments of the race, it was incredible. The next evening one of Eddie's Polish coaching recruits, a coach named Walter Golebiewski, talked to us about bike position. I was riveted as I had seen in *Winning* magazine how the pros looked on their bikes and I knew I wasn't there. My positioning was so random that my reason for the stem I had on my bike was that it was the only stem in my local shop when I built the bike up! That it was the right length for my body had never been a consideration. The lecture revealed my many shortcomings, and a little time spent with the mechanics the next day helped me rectify some of the issues and I made a note to purchase a longer stem once I got back home.

One of the best things about being at the Olympic Training Center was having a Record Store very close by. I would regularly ride there during our break after the morning's training. And that $100 from the Lettermen's Club for "expenses"? Well, I had planned to use a portion to purchase some cool cycling clothes from the permanent residents on John's advice. At some point, during all the camps the PR's had a garage sale since all those impressionable juniors were in town. But most of it? I spent it on cassette tapes! A classic everyone I knew said was a "must have" was Pink Floyd's "Dark Side of the Moon". This became a regular on my headphones at swim meets to relax during diving and mentally prepare for the 500-yard freestyle. I bought Hüsker Dü's new album "Flip Your Wig". I knew about them from Topher since they were from Minnesota and many of the cool Colorado riders knew them. I loved their raw, angry yet melodic intensity that was perfect for getting fired up for hard training. They were alternative rock before the genre even existed!

I also knew from *Rolling Stone* magazine that The Clash had recently split up, so I grabbed their classic that was sadly missing from my collection "London Calling" as well as something brand new. "This is Big Audio Dynamite" was former Clash member Mick Jones' new band and I also recognized film-maker Don Letts with his dread locks on the album cover. The music of B.A.D. tackled many social and cultural issues and used little excerpts from film, "samples", which was new to most rural white kids at the time. The cassette made its way around the dorms as everyone loved it. Back in Lander, Topher and I occasionally butted heads with classmates who liked more traditional music like Heavy Metal, which we saw as unsophisticated. To my sheer and utter joy, B.A.D. took on these guys in their song "Sudden Impact":

SUDDEN IMPACT!-Big Audio Dynamite from "This is Big Audio Dynamite", (1985)

"Listening to a metal music prank
that leads straight to the bank.
Each grunt and groan took literally,
some tired old rock star's fantasy!"
"Satanic rights to a tune they knew well
to make the party rock like hell.
Hold tight, the ride begins,
macho men with pimply skin!"

The "rec room" at the OTC had pool tables, foosball, and perhaps most importantly a cassette deck. Much like I had found in Wyoming, most of my cycling peers were very interested in the latest music. College radio staples including Echo and the Bunnymen's "Ocean Rain", X "Ain't Love Grand", The Jesus and Mary Chain's "Psychocandy", The Alarm "Strength", U2 "The Unforgettable Fire", and The Cure's "The Head on the Door" were in heavy rotation there all month. Sadly, so was Billy Ocean and Wham! but unlike back in Cowboy Country, Heavy Metal was conspicuously absent. The Country Western that tortured me on Wyoming airwaves, thankfully, was nowhere to be found.

When the PR's had their "garage sale" I snagged a thin but cool looking red and yellow long sleeve wool jersey from a Czechoslovakian team that Tim Hinz, a PR traded for on a national team trip to Eastern Europe. Whether all those stitched on foreign words were sponsors or a club name or both, it was sure to make me look like a serious and worldly cyclist back in Cowboy Country! But the piece de la resistance? Diadora Italian sandals for before and after the races, just like I had seen riders wearing in *Winning* magazine! Blue vinyl but with flashy logos and cork lining. I was so thrilled with them that I wore them to a swim practice when I got home (with wool socks since it was snowy and below zero) and was accused by one of the very cool older girls of "going down to those bike races in Boulder and now you're turning into a granola!" Since I was into punk rock and the punk's hated hippies, I wasn't quite sure how to feel about THAT observation. So, I skipped the wool socks and saved my new sandals for summer wear especially before and after races.

By the end of the first week, Dale Stetina, that savvy rider who made the big break to win the 1983 Coors on the last day, spoke on tactics and training and once again, I was riveted. So much great information was given, and it was information that I was starved for. I stayed after to thank him...and get extra tips. I used his "bluff to win primes" technique quite often in the coming years. The concept was to go early and hard for a prime and then back off approaching the line to conserve energy, a great tactic.

As the camp went on, Ed Burke would speak to us on Nutrition and Physiological testing. Steve Bishop, a national team mechanic explained bicycle maintenance and equipment, National Cyclocross team member Casey Kunselman educated us about the nuances and equipment requirements of cyclocross, and Junior National Coach Craig Campbell taught us to keep a training diary and explained positioning in the peloton. He made the point that only the riders in the first twenty positions of the peloton were racers and the rest were tourists! I really took that one to heart, but everything taught was informative and helpful and I knew it would all help me get better. In fact, these camps had been making American riders better since 1978 when Greg Lemond was a junior! We were just the latest beneficiaries.

Occasionally, Andy and I rode downtown on our 'cross bikes to see a movie. We would leave the OTC after dinner as the sun was setting and lock our bikes out front. The dark ride home on slippery and frozen streets was pure teenage hilarity as we tried not to crash. The first movie we saw together was "American Flyers" starring Kevin Costner as a bike racer who came out to Colorado to compete in "The Hell of the West", clearly modelled after the Coors Classic and another example that cycling was seeping more into the American mainstream. We were super excited to see our sport on the big screen but to real bike racers this movie was ridiculous. Pretty damn ridiculous in fact. The burly Russian with the full beard? Huh. The other movie was "Rocky 4", which put an end to my love affair with the Rocky movies. While the training scenes were okay, Andy and I agreed the whole East vs West thing was just too much. The ending was super cheesy with Rocky giving a speech to the Russians about how "we can all change" and how "two guys killing each other is better than twenty million". In 1985 America, the cold war was very real, but this sappy shit was not.

We did cyclocross training two or three times a week with the goal of building power and bike handling skills. The coaches laid out a course that took around ten minutes per lap in a park about a twenty-minute ride from the dorms. The conditions varied constantly, and we slipped and slopped through mud, sand, grass, and even snow on our knobby tires. 'Cross was extremely hard but also quite fun and a short run up and several barriers forced us to dismount and then remount the bike several times each lap. This was in the days before clipless pedals and getting in and out of our toe clips required patience and practice and I suffered more than a few smacks in the shin by my errant pedal as I learned the technique.

After several cyclocross sessions so rookie 'cross guys like me could (kind of) figure it out, we had a training race down in the park. We were informed that a "special guest" might be there watching. As we rode to the park, the riders all guessed that Eddie B., the Olympic Coach, must be the special guest and this had everyone fired up to perform. Steve Larsen, a California rider and one of the camp's best, broke out his long-sleeved National Champion skinsuit for the occasion while the rest of toiled in our regular wool. Daryl Price, also from California, was the fastest on the day, and years later would become one of the very few Americans to win a World Cup Mountain bike race. I was left in the dust immediately and as I neared the end of the first lap, someone along the course was shouting at me and directing me on where to ride. I didn't know the guy and since we had pre-ridden the course before our "race" started, I ignored him. It turned out he was trying to warn me of a once snow-covered curb which was now revealed as a drop off, due to the hundreds of wheels that had blown through before me. I promptly crashed, basically right at his feet, understanding once I had hit the deck that he was trying to prevent this. I looked up and staring down at me was Eddie B. The US Olympic Coach of the nine medals in LA fame. Scolding me with his thick polish accent, he said fittingly "Silly Junior, you will learn!"

That evening Eddie himself gave our lecture, and I was all ears. The architect of those nine Olympic Medals! The first point he made spoke right to me: "To be successful, you must be crazy for cycling!" Done. He told us in his thick Polish accent we had to "eat like a pig, work like a bull, and sleep like a baby." That was mostly what we were doing at the OTC! I diligently took my notes. He detailed Speed, Power, and Endurance as the key components of cycling and how to train all three. One of his key points was understanding the difference between speedwork (short sprints always at 100% with full recovery) and intervals (longer efforts to build power and without recovering fully) and how to incorporate them into your training. His funny bits and detailed training information were balanced by simple and logical tips like "learn something from every race" and "analyze why you win and why you lose races". We received it like gospel coming down from on high.

The definitive moment of December Junior Camp at the OTC was the progressive ergometer test. Each rider was assigned a time and date and allowed an easy day (we were excused from regular training to spin easily on our own) prior to their appointment in the Physiology Lab. I visited the coach assigned to me, Canadian Neil Stewart, the day before to find out how to handle my test. He advised me to warm up really well before getting there and be "ready to ride damn hard!".

I didn't shave my legs in the wintertime and my roommates thought this would be a big mistake for my erg test. With hairy legs, the coaches wouldn't take me seriously (they'd think I was a wanker!) and so I better shave down. Of course, this conversation didn't happen until late evening. Thus, I had another little chat with Coach Neil when he came in wondering why I was still up after the 9 pm "Lights Out" which a very serious deal in the dorms. "I've got to shave my legs before my erg test, Coach!" I explained and he rolled his eyes, but let me finish up. The following morning, I had a big breakfast in the cafeteria and talked with Tim Daggett, who I had seen on TV in the 1984 Olympics, winning gold with the US Olympic Gymnastics team. The other guys went to the gym to lift but I went back to my room to prepare for my big test, inspired by the words of an Olympic gold medalist. With my headphones blasting my most inspirational music, I bundled up and did a big warm up on my road bike, building up the psyche to really throw down. As my time approached, I put my game face on and rolled up to the intimidating lab building.

The "Erg" was a stationary bike of sorts that could be easily adjusted to your riding position. There were several technicians present who pricked your finger at set intervals to take blood and measure lactate. The other riders explained that this was to "see how much pain you could take" but we would all later understand it was more sophisticated than that. After as much warm up as needed, the test began with a "load" of 3 "kiloponds", whatever that was, for five minutes. Cadence was to be maintained at 90 rpm. Stripped down to just cycling shorts, shoes, and a headband, I was sweating and breathing hard, but it was not super hard. I could ride at this level for a long time. The load was then increased to 4 for the next five minutes and shit started to get real. I was working hard. Very hard. The next phase of the test was a load of 5 until failure. As soon as they turned it up, it was like stomping on a big gear into a headwind…on a climb. Oh boy. It was eyeballs out! I gave everything I had as all the techs screamed and cheered "Go, Go, Go!" and I pounded that monster gear for as long as I could. I only lasted a bit over a minute and a half as my final time was 11:40, which was decidedly middle of the pack when results came out. I believe it was the 50th or 60th best time and as a few of the best juniors weren't even here for December Camp, I wouldn't be coming back in April. To me it was irrelevant, I came to do my best and learn, so my mission was accomplished.

Saddling up to ride Cowboy Country

The dorm legend had it that Derin Stockton, a rider from Santa Barbara rooming next door to me, was so strong they just turned the machine off after 17 minutes. Whether this was true or not is unclear, but by the next year Derin was right up at the front in Pro criteriums with the 7-Eleven team and went on to a long and successful domestic (with a few brief European forays) professional career. Coach Neil met with all of us one on one after the test to discuss the 1986 race calendar as well as our results. My test wasn't very impressive, and neither was my race resume. He was a little stern with me about getting out of Wyoming and doing more of the big races around the country. My parents and particularly my father didn't want "my world to revolve around bike racing" but I kept that to myself. One race, though, that I was pretty sure I could do on the suggested schedule was The Iron Horse Classic in Durango, Colorado at the end of May. A tough road race that paralleled the train tracks running between Durango and Silverton and tackled two difficult climbs that both peaked at nearly 11,000 feet. It also served as the Junior Worlds Trials Qualifier for the western region of the country.

As camp was winding down one of the big topics of discussion was "the new helmet rule". Prior to the 1986 season, cyclists were required to "wear a helmet of padded leather strips or a rigid molded material" and that was it. Many of my peers wore the traditional leather "hairnets" like the Europeans. My mother mandated a "hard-shell", the first of which was that Brancale from the shop in Golden near my grandparents. It was just a plastic shell with minimal padding and with no impact-absorbing polystyrene, so it was only a little better than a hair net. I shortly graduated to a Skid Lid, marginally better than the Brancale and it was what Bob and Drew wore. We thought they were cool, and they were protective enough. Topher got one too and after we raced the RZMC, we wrote the company and asked for sponsorship...and they obliged, sending us each a new Black Skid Lid in the mail! The new helmets would have to meet ANSI Z90.4 standards of approval. Hairnets, Brancales, and even Skid Lids were now out...they were well below the standard.

Apparently, the issue was insurance for bicycle races as insurance companies wouldn't provide it unless competitors were wearing "real" helmets. There were currently only a few helmets on the market that met the standard, and they were big and heavy. We saw them as "touring helmets" and worn by dorks not racers! The Bell "Biker", a veritable salad bowl of a brain bucket with only a few ventilation ports and weighing a ton, was one of the options. The new rule would go into effect the following season, still a few months away. Our coaches assured us more helmets would be on the market soon, so there would soon be better options. Many of my fellow campers at the OTC were quite fired up about it. A petition went around the cafeteria asking for the helmet rule to be rescinded. I remember a rider from back east, Massachusetts perhaps saying "cycling is a sleek sport. These helmets are NOT sleek. I'm not wearing one, and I will go race in Europe instead!" Whoa, this guy lived in a different world than me! My parents had talked about how "Lawsuit happy" so many people were, and this just seemed like an extension of that issue and something we would all have to live with. I remained hopeful, however, that some new helmets would soon arrive in shops, so I didn't have to wear a Bell Biker…they were awful!

My parents picked me up on December 31st and I was happy to be back in Cowboy Country in time to go out drinking beer on New Year's Eve with my friends. And, of course, to share my tales of life at the USOTC in Colorado Springs. The experience of living like a full-time athlete with no responsibilities other than training and resting was unforgettable. I absolutely loved it. I would also recount my adventures with the Lettermen's Club. At my mother's suggestion, I took photos during my time at the camp and shared a slide show at the next meeting as a thank you for the financial help. I was never sure what the traditional "jocks" thought of cycling, so I was thrilled when Chris Vinich, one of the stars of the basketball team said "Wow, they were really checking you out!" when I told the club about the Erg test. Topher was training more too and was fired up about the upcoming season and our friendly competitiveness helped us both. We rode together as often as possible and when we couldn't, the conversation was always..." How many miles do you have in?" He seemed determined to put in extra training, perhaps in response to my time in Colorado Springs. Arriving at the first race with at least 1500 miles of training was seen as somehow significant at this time and we were both keeping track. With our challenging Wyoming winter weather that was no small feat...

December 1985, living the dream at the OTC in my dorm room.
Photo credit Andy Adams

A DAY AT THE OLYMPIC TRAINING CENTER
by Thomas Prehn

A door opened slowly and light spilled out into the darkened hallway. A shadowy figure, only half awake, walked across the hall and knocked three times on the door. Without waiting for a response, the person dressed in a rumpled sweatsuit and slippers turned down the hall and proceeded to knock quietly three times on each door before walking to the next one. By the time he was all the way down the hall, some of the first doors were opening, and the silence of the early morning was abating. It was exactly 7:30 a.m. and the beginning of another regimented day at the Olympic Training Center.

On more than 10 city blocks surrounded by barbed wire fencing and residential neighborhoods of Colorado Springs, Colorado, some of America's top athletes spend their winter months focused on cycling. With marshalled guidance from the coaching staff and support from Olympic Training Center personnel, few decisions are left to the athlete.

Liz Larsen, a member of the national team, laughed as she summed up the life there. "A rabbit wouldn't even have to think to live here."

The environment was designed for optimum training. Little more than a bike, warm clothes and perseverance are needed to live there through the winter months.

On the ground floor of the dorms, the athletes huddled at one end of the hallway. At 7:45 a coach opened the door leading everyone with sub-zero air. The five-minute march to the dining hall halted for periodic stretching exercises. That morning a dusting of snow pulled away underfoot as a group of 15 stopped on the athletic field to go through a routine of stretches in unison. The mountains, covered in a fresh coat of white, rose from the far side of the city. Pikes Peak, its ragged definition stark against the brilliant blue sky, dominated the horizon. Clouds of frozen breath lingered in the crisp, clean air. It would be a great day for training.

Breakfast was a buffet-style feast of eggs, pancakes, French toast, fruit juice, cereal, yogurt and just about anything else a bike would want. At 8:27 a.m. several coaches hurried out of the hall and headed to their office, where national coach Walter Golebiewski conducted a meeting.

"Okay everyone, how are you...

Winning magazine OTC article.
Courtesy Thomas Prehn

Chapter Sixteen:

COME ON DOWN AND MAKE THE STAND

Seeing myself as a serious athlete now, I began eating better and trying to always stay hydrated. In the particularly conservative and self-conscious teenage environment of Cowboy Country, carrying a water bottle around during the school day just wasn't happening. Hell, Topher and I were already drawing a few sneers from the jock crowd for breaking out of the Lander de facto male dress code of Levi's 501s, white leather Nike or Tiger sneakers, and t-shirts! We did radical things like wearing polos, nicer long sleeve shirts, and colored jeans... so rebellious! Thus, my strategy was to get a drink every time I passed a water fountain in the halls of Lander Valley High School. At my high school, however, this often meant taking in a nice big minty whiff from the mound of chewing tobacco invariably left on the fountain drain. Ah, Cowboy Country!

As my local notoriety as a bike racer grew, I gained a modicum of respect from many of my fellow athletes. I also got a bit of resentment and even animosity from some of my more sheltered classmates. One guy in particular, David Blair, took to flipping me off and yelling insults (particularly about my spandex shorts) from his Chevy Luv pickup truck when I was rolling home from training ride down Main Street, the nine block long drag through the center of our little town. As was often the case in my teenage years, a song captured the frustration, building tension, and ultimate absurdity of the moment more accurately than any of my words could.

TURQOISE DAYS-Echo & The Bunnymen from "Heaven Up Here", 1981
"We've got a problem,
Come on over
We've got a problem,
Come on over"

Saddling up to ride Cowboy Country

Full of adolescent male bravado, I confronted him about his finger gestures at a home football game beneath the bleachers and next to the concession stand. It was classic teenage "You got a problem with me?" bullshit. Emboldened by the presence of my friends right behind me, I wasn't subtle. His response was something along the lines of "you think you're so cool out there on your little bicycle, doing your little ten k, in your tight shiny shorts, why don't you get the hell off the road!" "Ten K?" I retorted. "More like 100 k, asshole!" Now, his guys gathered behind him, and they were much older than us and rough looking. I don't know if they worked on area ranches or out in the oil fields, but they didn't wear polo shirts and colored jeans like my crew. They were dirty, tattooed, scarred, scary, and ready to fight! My guys however, were not backing down as insults were exchanged and taunts were made. Fortunately, cooler heads somehow prevailed, and we all went our separate ways. When my machismo calmed down, I realized how ridiculous our conflict was.

"It's not for glory
It's not for honor
Just something
someone said"

I soon made peace with David, we shook hands and laughed the whole thing off. Very shortly thereafter, however, he was tragically killed, driving away from a party my friends and I had been at, where we had all been drinking. He was not the only victim, however, as he hit a carload of other kids, one of whom was my partner in auto shop class. All survived but sustained a variety of injuries, some quite serious. The whole thing really shook me up and made me re-evaluate some of the foolish things my peers and I did. In our rural state that is still home to "drive through liquor" stores, I had classmates who joked "my truck is like my horse, it just knows the way home"! David's best friend Robert Steers later organized a "Students against Drunk Driving" chapter at our school and for a while, these dangerous Cowboy Country traditions of driving drunk or even drinking while driving on rural roads seemed to abate. I will never forget my shock and dismay when my mother sent me a local news clipping in my freshman year of college… Robert had died in a single car crash while driving home from a bar in Wyoming. A sad, tragic, and all too common side of life in rural Wyoming.

Later that year, on a late winter/early spring training ride, suddenly and right out of the blue, Topher asks "You know what we need to do?" As a teenager still finding my way in the world, I was always curious about what I needed to do…perhaps he had the answer! "What"? I responded, all ears for his ideas. "We need to GET LAID!" This hit me like a bolt of lightning…Yeah! He was so right. That is exactly what we needed to do! Why didn't I think of that? He spontaneously burst into song…

DAY AFTER DAY-Violent Femmes from "Violent Femmes", (1983)
"Why can't I get just one kiss?
Why can't I get just one kiss?
There may be some things that I wouldn't miss
But I look at your pants and I need a kiss
Why can't I get just one screw?
Why can't I get just one screw?
Believe me, I know what to do
But something won't let me make love to you…"

Now, of course, I DID think of that…constantly. And, of course, I did have periodic (and brief) romantic encounters and even more periodic and brief bouts of "fooling around". But the ULTIMATE fooling around that our beloved "Femmes" sang about…that was TERRIFYING! Mainly for fear of the ultimate shame of getting a girl pregnant, which could trap a guy in Cowboy Country forever. I would be an embarrassment to my family AND be trapped in Wyoming…terrifying!

Topher had a plan…we needed prophylactics. What? "Condoms, contraception…rubbers, man!" he explained. As a guy who would go on to teach High School Health Education as a career, it's ironic how woefully lacking our knowledge of any such matters was in 1986, despite a TERRIBLE Health class taught by the Neanderthal LVHS Football Coach. A guy who actually taught us a good rule was "Six pack, don't drive back". Topher said "We will just go to the Public Health Office; it's not far from my house." Good to know as according to the guys on the swim team, the only place I knew to find rubbers was from the vending machine at the bowling alley. I still remember a swimming teammate telling me about condoms. He was dating one of the cutest lifeguards, and they were "doing it" but he was afraid of a rubber breaking…so he wore three. You know, in case one broke! This seemed smart to me, so I made a mental note of it…ha!

"Why can't I get just one f#ʿ@k?
Why can't I get just one f#ʿ@k?
I guess it's got something to do with luck
But I waited my whole life for just one…"

Tuesday's during the school year meant Tony's Pizza for lunch. My swim coach Bruce owned the place. A large cheese pizza was the weekly special and only cost $3.99 and fed three of us. The problem was nearly half the student body of LVHS went there for lunch! But we had an angle…the old man in the counseling office (thanks, dad!) could call in our order half an hour before lunch, so every week we had our pizza ready and waiting while those other poor saps had to stand in line.

Shortly after Topher's revelation about sexual conquests, we had enjoyed our Tuesday Pizza and realized that the Public Health office was just around the corner. We might as well stock up on condoms while we could so we would be ready! What we didn't realize is that several freshman girls had climbed into my unlocked truck canopy to sneak a ride back to school.

The ever-confident Topher strode right up to the counter and stated in his most mature voice, "We would like to purchase some prophylactics". Between his newfound vocabulary and his grown up posturing I let out a snicker or two, but we got them, priced reasonably at a quarter apiece. As we headed back to my dad's truck, we saw Kim Reemt's head poke up from the back and we heard quite a few more giggles. I was worried that these young girls, many of whom were very cute, would get the wrong idea about us, but Topher assured me they would understand that, not only were we serious but we were responsible. Mostly they just thought we were hilarious!

My exploration into the world of rock music continued, especially the burgeoning genre of post-punk, pre-alternative offerings from college radio that were continuing to get more mainstream attention. We even had a college radio station from the community college in nearby Riverton, and it played many of the albums we saw in *Rolling Stone*, but the signal was weak, and we couldn't always get it in the car. There were so many great bands, each one unique and all seemingly had something of substance to say. At the forefront of all this, along with my now treasured R.E.M., was the Irish band U2. Topher brought over a video one night of the band playing live at Red Rocks, just outside of Denver, Colorado. It was raining and cold, but the energy in the audience and from the band was irrepressible. I saw more than just a few cycling caps in the crowd, reaffirming the connection between the new music and my new sport. I was almost certain a couple of those guys I saw on screen were at the OTC with me that past December!

Topher and I had a new accomplice in our quest for new, interesting, and meaningful music and he was there with us that night watching the video. Clay Appleby came from "the other side of the tracks" from Topher and I both literally and figuratively. We had some art classes together and the dude, a year older than us, was seriously cool and totally on board with all our music swapping. In fact, he even DJ'd some of the school dances.

I had a great swim season, continuing to squeeze in cycling training whenever possible, but the Wyoming roads were not consistently clear until March or even April. I was still determined to get to Durango at the end of May for the Junior Worlds Trials Qualifier. John had done the race before and encouraged me. I found myself studying the roads outside of town when we drove home from Swim Meets on Saturday nights, seeing if I could pull off a training ride on Sunday morning before my lifeguard shift at the pool. During spring break, I regularly did "daily doubles" of both swim practice and cycling. I raced the 500 again at the state swim meet and this time made the finals. The highlight, though, was our relay team earning All-State honors by placing third. This put a statuette of Wes Williams, Kevin, Jeff Shope, and I into the trophy case at the pool, now known as the Bruce Gresly Aquatic Center, after we lost Bruce in 2015, which was a real badge of honor. Only the very best Lander swimmers were showcased there, and we joined them with great pride.

My junior year of High School was winding down and I wasn't just focused on bike racing and girls. I was starting to wrap my mind around going to college. I knew I didn't want to stay in Wyoming but where would I go? Somewhere cool with lots more going on than anywhere in Cowboy Country-of that, I was sure! Next fall, I had to start applying.

In mid-April I stumbled onto a concert on MTV broadcast live from UCLA. Having never been to a live rock concert, it really helped me understand how much more there was out there and exactly how great my post Wyoming experience could be. VJ Martha Quinn introduced one of my favorite bands, The Alarm, and the atmosphere was incredible. It was an outside show, and the youthful crowd was packed in, climbing light poles, waving flags and holding up signs as they sang along...the energy was palpable. The music was meaningful and heartfelt, and the crowd was electric and engaged. This was part of what could be out there for me after high school. It had already become clear that cycling was an escape from Wyoming, but now I was beginning to understand that college could be too. Perhaps I could be lucky enough to tie them both together! I knew this change was what I believed in...

I BELIEVE-R.E.M. from "Life's Rich Pageant" (1986)
"I believe in coyotes and time as an abstract
Explain the change, the difference between
What you want and what you need, there's the key
Your adventure for today, what do you do
Between the horns of the day

CHAPTER SEVENTEEN:

WHAT YOU NEED

There was only one early season Wyoming road race in 1986, an unsanctioned club road race in April. We could still wear our old Skid Lids and delay breaking out the horrible new huge and heavy brain buckets licensed racing now required. We contested two laps of the Lyon's Valley Loop, 34 miles, and my friend Charles Pelkey, now acting as our USCF district rep, came up with some of the University of Wyoming guys. Topher and I were the only junior riders in the Senior field. Charles told me he was going to attack the big climb on the first lap and if I could stick with him, he would get me tickets to the 1986 World Championships to be held in Colorado Springs in August. Stick with him I did, digging super deep, and we relayed each other to the finish, crossing the line victorious together and I really felt like a big man. In the comradery of Cowboy Country, most of the riders from the senior race huddled in front of my family's TV set after the race to watch CBS Sports annual coverage of "Paris-Roubaix", the only other race besides the Tour with national television coverage at that time. We cheered as 7-Eleven's Bob Roll became only the third American, following Boyer and Lemond, to finish the brutal cobbled classic and marveled at the difficulty and spectacle of this storied European event.

Our local bike shop had new owners that knew almost nothing about racing, so Topher and I worried about our ability to get the best Italian cycling equipment, and we certainly didn't want to pay retail prices. So, we created our own "shop" …C & D Cycle Sport. It was our third and biggest venture yet. Topher again made stationery, on a computer this time, and we sent out letters to distributors. We needed to have a tax ID number, so we filed paperwork with the State of Wyoming, claiming zero sales every year.

Saddling up to ride Cowboy Country

We could only do things COD and we tried to include other cyclists in the community, so our small orders didn't look too suspicious, and we pulled it off! Our distributors often sent promo posters and decals that we not only put up in our bedrooms but displayed proudly in our lockers at school. I thought the poorly translated Italian on one decal struck the perfect chord between humorous and cool..." Be Care! Rust Never Sleeps! Use Alpina Stainless Steel spokes!" No one else at LVHS had THAT in their school locker! Topher wanted Ray-Ban Wayfarers and so we became a Ray-Ban dealer as well. They retailed for $50 but wholesale was half that, so we sold them to our friends at school for $40 and everyone was happy. The things you could get away with in pre-internet Wyoming!

My mom was supportive of me racing in Durango while my dad was resistant but as was often the case in our house, mom won out. The Ford Mustang with the Thule rack would roll down to Colorado once more. My father spent his first two years of college in Durango at Fort Lewis Community College, playing football there in his first year. It would be fun to see his old stomping grounds. The mother of a good friend of mom's lived in Durango, and we could stay with her. Mom always liked to pack in as much as possible, so we would stop and visit old friends The Krieger's on the long drive down.

Fortunately, the weekend before the Iron Horse I was able to do some long, hard miles with the strongest riders in my area. The Wind River Wheelers Spring trip had evolved from the Yellowstone camping of years before into a ride to Thermopolis. We rode from Riverton, about twenty miles from Lander to Thermopolis up Wind River Canyon. It was a bit over fifty miles and we stayed in a campground with pools heated by natural hot springs. We floated on inner tubes while soaking in the hot, steamy, and smelly mineral-rich water. The older riders let me have a beer, my dad once more "drove sag", and a great time was had by all. We rode back the following day and according to many I "wiped out" the older riders in the club hammering a paceline down the same route on which I had infuriated church lady four years earlier. The feeling I got from my local scene was that I was ready.

The Iron Horse had a large and strong Junior field including the 7-Eleven junior team. Coached by Mike Neel (the American pioneer who famously placed tenth in the 1976 Professional World Championship, just behind Eddy Merckx) these guys were the best in the country and looked totally professional. I knew many of them from the OTC and they had both California and Colorado squads. Their kit differed from the Pros only in the substitution of orange for red in the design, while their bikes were the same as Phinney and Kiefel's! Drawing on the teachings from the Training Center, I warmed up well and lined up in the front right behind the "Slurpees", determined to do my best possible race.

We took off fast and I tried to stay near the front. At one point, Steve Larsen, one of the stars at the OTC, attacked and I went with him. This was short-lived, however, and when we hit the big climb, I was in over my head and started going backwards. The rest of my race became a slog to the finish line either alone or in small groups. Starting in Durango at 6400 feet, Highway 550 "The Million Dollar Highway" first climbs Coal Bank Pass (10,600 feet) before descending to about 8000 feet. We then climbed Molas Pass at 10,800 feet before a spectacular descent into Silverton at 9000 feet. All that elevation was packed into less than fifty miles, making for a brutal race. I finished 28th, mid-pack and ahead of many, but never really in the race. Yes, I had trained hard, but my little local scene was not nearly at this level. Many of my competitors had a dozen or more races under their belts and this only my second of the year. At best, I would have had three but the Mother's Day race in Jackson was cancelled due to snow. I still had a long way to go before I was competitive on a national scale...but I remained determined to get there.

On the way home, we stopped for gas in Baggs, Wyoming. My bike was atop our 1968 Mustang and this old cowboy approached me. He was straight out of a movie: well-worn leather boots, Wrangler jeans and a dusty western shirt, big cowboy hat, and chewing on a weed. Now Baggs is truly a "one-horse town": cafe, general store, post office, and gas station all grouped together and a few houses and... that's it. "You a bike racer?" he asked, and I responded "Yep. Just heading back to Lander after a race in Colorado." He continued "Guy from 'round here is a bike racer". Now I'm thinking...ok, surely after racing all over Wyoming the last few years I know the guy. "He done raced the Tour de France! I am thinking, OK cowboy, you are full of it. In the spring of 1986, the US had Boyer, Lemond, and Shapiro who had ridden Le Tour. That was it. "His name is Jonathan Boyer". Whoa!!! So, the guy knows what he is talking about. I learned that, although he grew up in California, Boyer's family had a cattle ranch in Baggs, and he spent summers there as a kid. I scoured my *Winning* magazines back at home and sure enough when Boyer won "The Race Across America" ultra marathon event there was his dad following behind in a big Ford pickup truck with Wyoming bucking horse plates!

After Lemond rallied to win the final time trial in the 1985 tour, Hinault made a public pledge to support the American in the 1986 edition, stating to the press "next year I will suffer for him as he has sacrificed for me". With a strong likelihood of the American 7-Eleven team taking part as well, 1986 could be another banner year for American cycling. Back in Cowboy Country and inspired by both "the Slurpee's" and Greg Lemond, I was determined to make it a big year for me.

The State Championship Road Race was always the focus of the first part of my season. In 1986 it was to be held in Lander on a course I knew well-Lyon's Valley, the site of my first race back in 1981. Shortly after Durango, I rode it with Brian, and we talked about how the race might play out. It was our last training ride together before he moved back to Cheyenne. It was eventful too, as our ride started out sunny, then storm clouds blew in and the sky opened up! It was springtime in the mountains of Wyoming, and we got absolutely pummeled with large hail. Golf ball sized! In one of those amazing "survival" kind of moments, no words were spoken as we both simultaneously rode our bikes into the ditch and ran across a field to crowd out some rancher's cattle for coverage in the barn.

Only then, covered with welts, did we acknowledge what a crazy thing had just happened. Another totally "Cowboy Country" moment!

The Nationals were not being held on the East Coast this year either, but were scheduled for Boise, Idaho which was within driving distance. Although our scene had grown, the small number of racers in Wyoming meant you had to win States to race in the Nationals. This was my prime focus after my winter at the OTC. I wanted to be in the top 15 at Nationals this time, right up there amongst all those guys I was with in Colorado Springs. I rode that circuit a lot that spring and did many sprints up the final climb envisioning winning the state title.

The week before States, a relative newcomer from Sheridan beat me by twenty seconds in the State Time Trial at Farson. I was a little overconfident and he kind of shocked me. I was vaguely aware of him from other races, but he had gotten A LOT better. His name was Chip Whiton, and he told me he was at the OTC in December as well. What? I never saw him! It turns out his parents split up and he spent Christmas break with his dad in Colorado Springs, latching onto some of our rides when we went by his house. What a wanker! Nonetheless, the guy was fast, and I would have to keep an eye on him.

The race was scheduled to be four laps of Lyon's Valley for a total of 68 miles, near the upper limit for junior race distances. I knew this going in and had trained well and was ready. My mom, dad, and sister all had volunteer jobs out on the racecourse. Eight riders were present, a solid field for cowboy country. Our Wyoming District Rep surprised us by saying we didn't have to race that far, and we could go a lap less if we wished. Inside I thought this was bullshit but, on the outside, I succumbed to that weird teenage peer pressure thing of going along with everyone else and not rocking the boat. Of course, I should have manned up and said "let's do the full distance" but I caved. Mistake number one of many on that day.

Race commentators use the phrase "race like juniors" and in my experience up to this point there were two ways teenagers did this. The most common form was a relentless, uncontrolled and irrational style of racing that was just attack after attack like Topher and I experienced in Steamboat. The other form was to just ride around slowly looking at each other, afraid to make a move, and wait around for the sprint. Our race on that day fell into the latter format. Mistake number two.

We rode so slowly and so passively and so completely devoid of aggression that no one was dropped. At the final turn, where my sister was the corner marshal, with only a few miles remaining, Topher finally attacked. I sat in while the others chased. It was a good move, and my rivals worked hard to close it, which played into my hands. There was a short but tough little climb up to the 200-meter mark before a flat final sprint. I attacked at the bottom of the climb and only Chip could come with me. He actually pulled through and I would only have to come around in the sprint, and I would win. I was still a little cross-eyed from my late attack when I jumped on the inside of him at 200 meters, thinking this was clever. Overthinking things, I then decided I should go wide, so I moved over. Unfortunately, I wasn't yet clear of him, so I clipped his front wheel and knocked him down. Mistake number three and with three strikes, I was OUT!

I crossed the finish line alone, but I gave no victory salute. The other riders were far adrift, but Chip was in a heap on the pavement. I had fucked it up, plain and simple and I knew it. One of the most basic rules in bike racing is that you must hold your line in the final 200 meters, and I had not. I continued on long past the finish line, alone with my thoughts and cursing myself. I knew I would be relegated. I was the better rider, but I had handed this wanker MY state title and in MY hometown. I had no one to blame but myself. Sulking back home in my bedroom, headphones on, I found the words for my disappointment in the music...

PILGRIMAGE-REM from "Murmur", (1983)
"Rest assured, this will not last
Take a turn for the worst
Your hate, clipped and distant

Your luck, a two-headed cow"

Outside of cycling, I was working as a lifeguard again that summer, along with many of my swimming teammates. Topher was building houses with his dad, Wade worked with the youth Soccer programs for Parks and Rec, while Dave was washing dishes at the Commons restaurant. I was under specific instructions by "my guys" to keep an eye out for any good-looking girls visiting our town during the summertime. Anyone from out of town was cause for excitement in Cowboy country, especially young women! They had the right man for the job, as I was up to that task and always kept my eyes peeled!

In addition to young people taking NOLS courses, there were University of Missouri Geology camps, gatherings in the city park, and other summer events that brought new and interesting people to our little Wyoming town. On one busy day at the pool that summer, a large group of high school kids from the Midwest came in. The group contained several attractive young ladies, one of whom, Angela, I engaged in conversation on a break from my perch in the lifeguard chair.

She told me they were camping in the City Park and having a picnic that night. My friends and I should come down! We were welcome and she and her friends would love to hang out. Now not only was I psyched personally, but I was helping my boys! They were thrilled at the romantic opportunities. After work, we all showered and changed and hustled down to the City Park, eager to socialize with our (hopefully) new friends.

There were big tents, loads of great food, and Angela greeted us as we arrived. She had a girl for each of my friends, we ate and talked, and everyone was having a great time. Then she said it's time for "the sermon" ...wait, what? A minister took center stage, the girls escorted us each to some seats and we realized we were victims of a "bait and switch". This was a church group! Worse yet, the sermon focused on young men trying to "put the moves" on young women! It was almost speaking specifically to us in that exact moment! The preacher said "Ladies, when you are out on a date, you put a bible on the seat between the two of you, so that when he reaches across for your thigh, he will find the word of God instead!" Angela smiled at me (duped!) while Topher and Dave glared. Wade wisely said, "I'm out of here" and he bolted. This was NOT what we were after!

Before we could extract ourselves from this mess, the girls ditched us, and a guy came over to each of us and introduced themselves. We HAD eaten their food, so we (or three of us, at least) didn't feel right just running away but these guys wouldn't let us anyway! Before any of us knew what had hit us, we each had a guy our age leading us away from the picnic area and out into the playground extolling the virtues of taking Jesus Christ into our hearts as lord and savior. This was NOT what we showed up for! Ultimately, instead of snuggling up to a honey and watching the sunset after a picnic, I found myself sitting on a swing-set with some dude who was holding my hand and encouraging me to take Jesus into my heart! I looked up to find Topher, staring at me in glassy-eyed disbelief in the same predicament as me on the nearby merry-go-round. Both of us holding hands with some guy, intent on bringing us to Jesus. How could a night that began with so much promise come to this? The next day, Topher found a song that perfectly captured our disappointing evening...

ANGELS AND DEVILS-Echo & the The Bunnymen, from "Ocean Rain", 1984
"So, so happy
When happiness spells misery
And mister me hoping to be
Where ugliness meets beauty
Hope if you'll see
The demon in you
The angel in me
The Jesus in you
The devil in me"

Not long after the State Road Race debacle came our annual local event: The Red Dog! Utah rider Darin Dewsnup who had become a good friend at the OTC the previous winter came up to stay with us. Unlike me, he was up near the front at the Iron Horse and had been contesting many of the biggest west coast Junior events throughout the spring. He was intimidating and brought along a buddy, Chris Poole, who was also damn fast. Fort Collins rider Dirk Friel (who would go on to a professional cycling and then coaching career) who had lived next door to me at the training center raced as well, with several other strong Colorado riders. Combined with the usual Wyoming guys, we had the biggest and strongest Junior field the Red Dog had ever seen. A big part of this growth in our race was that only a few days after the Red Dog was the Casper Classic, two hours away and now a stage race featuring a huge cash purse and all the best riders in the country!

The first stage of the Red Dog was now a mass-start hill climb leaving from the southern edge of town, going along Red Canyon, and finishing atop Limestone Mountain. A barren, windy, tough haul that gained over 2000 vertical feet in just twenty-six miles. After six rolling climbs in the first ten miles, Darin hit the front on the first long steep grade up to Johnny Lee's corner. It took everything I had to hang on but by the time the dust settled it was just Darin, Chris, and myself left to make the climb up to Red Canyon. I was under pressure several times more but "hung tough", as Brian had taught me. My tactics were not very sophisticated at this point and so I charged hard in a big gear at 200 meters like I did in every sprint, while the more patient, savvy, and appropriately geared Darin came around me right before the line. Many strong riders were left behind and I had stuck with the strongest to contend for the win in my home race but I would have to learn more nuance in my sprinting tactics.

My Laramie friends Charles and Danny, both ace time trialists, were fired up about my chances and so they loaned me fast wheels and an aero helmet for the afternoon time trial. The French Roval wheels were rare, exotic, and way ahead of their time. They featured deep section rims, a low spoke count, radial lacing on both the front and rear non-drive side, and hidden nipples. I gave everything, but the concentration and smooth effort required for a fast TT was still a bit beyond me. I was beaten soundly by both Darin and his buddy Chris, who now overtook me for second on GC. Not good. The final road stage was on my beloved Squaw/Baldwin Creek route that I had ridden countless times with my Rocky theme song finale, presenting me with a perfect opportunity if there ever was one!

Again, Darin made the big move on the longest climb and the breakaway was once again the three of us. I needed to win the stage and earn the time bonus to move past Chris into second overall. Darin was too far ahead for me to chase overall victory. Chris had told me how "hard core" Darin was…he would do seventy-mile solo training rides, every week! While this impressed me, it also INFORMED me on what I needed to do to step up to that level. I wasn't doing that…yet. The following year Darin would race both domestically and in Europe with Plymouth/Reebok, the best junior team in the country. But here in Cowboy country in my home race, I needed to redeem myself. I wanted to win. And I did, coming around Darin right at the line, just like I had done in my imagination so many times throughout the previous years. My own underdog victory came on the roads where I had imagined those "Rocky moments" so many times while out training. It was very close, but my dad noticed that I punched the air after the line because in those sorts of finishes, the riders nearly always know who got the win. Inspiration and focus were keys to my success but could I find them on a bigger stage?

My swimming buddy Wes, also a lifeguard at the pool, joined me the next week for the Casper Classic. He did the Citizen's race and to save money we stayed in the dorms at Casper College. The total purse for the event was $50,000! The junior field was huge and full of talent, and I got it handed to me stage after stage, intimidated by "the big guns". While Darin was in the top ten daily and overall, I was often dropped and placed in the middle of the field. Wes was great company and loved much of the same music and while we enjoyed the weekend, I vowed the rest of the summer's racing would be different.

From that point on, I had a great season of regional racing, winning two of three stages and the overall at both the Sweet Pea in Bozeman, Montana (earning my first ever leader's jersey) and at the Snake River Stage race in Jackson. I was trying to emulate the Wyoming juniors that came before me like John and Mike, who had dominated the regional scene in their last year as juniors. Chip was not at any of these races. It turns out there was a criterium in his hometown of Sheridan at the end of August, right before school started. This would be my perfect opportunity to make sure everyone knew who the best Junior rider in the state really was! I would whip his ass in front of his friends and family in possibly my last race as a Junior.

All through my July of cycling, of course, I was also following and being inspired by an historic Tour de France. The presence of the first ever American TEAM-7-Eleven as well as Lemond, a favorite to win, meant the race was now getting much more coverage on CBS Sports and in the newspapers. The 7-Eleven team included Americans Phinney, Kiefel, Grewal, Shapiro, Heiden, Roll, Jeff Pierce, and Chris Carmichael as well as Raul Alcala from Mexico and Alex Stieda of Canada. Lemond was joined by Andy Hampsten and Canadian Steve Bauer on La Vie Claire. From just one rider five years ago, we now had TEN Americans in the race!

The biggest Wyoming newspaper, *The Casper Star Tribune*, had daily results and often a story, while the Saturday and Sunday television broadcasts were now much longer and more in depth. The commentators gave a lot of explanations about the sport and its nuances, which was certainly helpful to the general public but became a bit tiresome for those of us established cyclists. Greg was coming off a consistent spring but had only scored one win-a stage of the Giro. His third in Paris-Nice, second in Milan-San Remo, and fourth in the Giro were unfortunately giving him a reputation in Europe of a team leader who didn't know how to win. Meanwhile, his teammate Hinault had changed his tune and seemingly forgetton his promise, by stating that "the opening time trial will show who the leader is in our team." Both riders were using new "step-in" pedals that were similar to a ski binding. They seemed easier to get in and out of than toe clips and straps, which also made your feet sore on long rides. Not something

Saddling up to ride Cowboy Country

I could afford nor readily available but they seemed to be a great advance!

Canadian Stieda, a criterium and track specialist for the Slurpees, shocked everyone by attacking in the first road stage and staying clear long enough to mop up all the bonus sprints. He came 19th in the prologue and was not far behind in overall time. With a team time trial in the afternoon and his unknown status, the peloton let him go. Even though he was caught before the line by a small group, ultimately finishing sixth, he took the yellow jersey of race leader. Since he was first over the climbs and all the intermediate sprints, he took ALL the leader's jerseys in fact! It was an incredible moment for North American cycling as not even Lemond had worn yellow in the Tour.

The 7-Eleven team's performance in the afternoon Team TT, however, was in the words of commentator Phil Liggett "a different kettle of fish". Years later, a cycling teammate would describe the footage as best watched with the comedy soundtrack from Benny Hill! There was a dizzying array of crashes, flat tires, and general chaos, and the team dropped an exhausted Stieda. Several teammates helped him to the finish, but he came within just a few seconds of being eliminated from the Tour! Things went so poorly that Phinney, an Olympic medalist in the team time trial along with Kiefel, had to endure the humiliation of being asked by a European journalist if they had ever ridden a team trial before! What a day for the American team…from hero to zero in just a few hours!

American cyclists competing in Europe at that time were nothing if not fearless and none more so that Phinney, who got into the break the very next day and lifted the team's spirits by winning the stage into Lievin! After Lemond had become the first American to win a stage in 1985 (the final time trial), this was the first American road stage victory. Sadly, little more would be heard from our Colorado heroes as they slogged their way through probably the most difficult Tour of the past twenty years. An interview with Phinney on CBS Sports really summed up what riding the Tour was like "Ah, it's about 50% faster, 200% longer, and ha, ha…100 % harder! There's nothing like it, it's unbelievable. It's really unbelievable!" He sounded just like Topher and I describing the racing in Colorado! The rugged Roll would be their best finisher in 63rd overall, over an hour and forty-three minutes behind, with only five of ten riders making it to Paris.

Greg, meanwhile, found himself playing second fiddle yet again to Frenchman Hinault, who could make history in his final Tour, if he became the first rider to win it six times. Greg lost a little time in the first time trial due to a puncture while Hinault won. Hinault then blind-sided his American teammate by attacking early on the first big mountain stage and moving into the yellow jersey with over five minutes advantage. Greg shocked us all, when he told CBS Sports that "If I want to be frank, I probably should have never come on La Vie Claire. Because I feel too close to Bernard Hinault, too close to his strength and I always end up having to take the second position and uh, it's my fault!" He also insinuated that the Tour was effectively over with the lead his teammate now held.

Seemingly drunk with his own power and ego, Hinault attacked early and alone on the descent of the Col du Tourmalet in the following day's stage thirteen. It was the first of four massive climbs enroute to a summit finish at Superbagneres. The La Vie Claire team was shocked as his tactics went explicitly against their team's plans. Fortunately for Lemond, other teams chased and the mighty Hinault ran out of steam. A select group of favorites caught him on the descent before the final climb. In the definitive book on the race "Slaying the Badger", Richard Moore writes that when Lemond asked him how he was feeling, "he just grunted. I didn't care. I was just seething".

On the tough ten-kilometer climb to the finish, Lemond's American teammate Hampsten attacked. Andy was my mother's favorite since he was from North Dakota, where she was born. Because of the lag in print coverage, we only learned during the TV coverage of the Tour that Hampsten had made history a couple of weeks before the Tour by winning the Tour of Switzerland. The Swiss race was basically the fourth most difficult (and prestigious) stage race in the world! It was the first victory by an American rider in a major international professional stage race. Lemond had supported him there and now Hampsten was returning the favor.

Saddling up to ride Cowboy Country

On our couch in Lander, we were going CRAZY! Greg bridged up and two Americans were at the front of the Tour on a key mountain stage. By the finish, Greg had won solo and had taken back all but 40 seconds of Hinault's seemingly insurmountable advantage. Moore reported another uniquely American moment from Grewal (now up to 24th place before having to drop out with bronchitis), "who stood out as a maverick even on a maverick team like 7-Eleven". As he rode past the struggling Hinault, he reportedly said "You blew it, Bernie. You fucked up!"

The infighting in La Vie Claire continued as Lemond and his wife Kathy complained to the press. On stage seventeen of twenty-three, finishing atop the mighty Alpine pass of the Col du Granon, third placed Urs Zimmerman of Switzerland attacked. Greg went with him, Hinault was dropped, and by the summit my main man Greg was in the yellow jersey of race leader of the Tour de France. His lead was nearly three minutes, but his French teammate kept insisting the race wasn't over. Greg was beginning to look like a nervous wreck. Hinault broke away again on Stage eighteen on the road to Alpe d'Huez but Greg's teammate and friend Bauer helped him bridge up. Ultimately, they laid waste to the rest of the field over the final two climbs and finished arm and arm atop the famous L'Alpe d'Huez. Now securely in first and second, we all anticipated the word from Hinault-the race was over.

Instead, on CBS Sports, we heard this feisty little man say "The Tour is not finished. There could be a crash, many things could happen. We will let the time trial decide." Greg's discomfort was palpable. The Campbell family, deeply drawn to this soap opera, all hoped Greg would win the final time trial the day before the race ended in Paris. He didn't. Hinault did, but only by 25 seconds after Greg crashed in a corner and had to change bikes. He was clearly a worthy winner and Hinault shepherded him on the final day down the Champs-Elysees. Hampsten meanwhile, finished fourth overall, and earned the white jersey as best young rider. Could we potentially see two Americans duking it out for future Tours? They were joined by Inga Thompson of Reno, Nevada, the latest in a long line of world beating American women. She had won two stages, placed third, and won the Queen of the Mountains jersey in a now very competitive Women's Tour de France. We were all ecstatic at the historic moment…an American atop the final podium in Paris and only five years after our first rider even got into the race, a staggering progression!

Meanwhile, news had filtered back from the National Championships in Idaho. Doug Smith, a permanent resident at the Olympic Training Center who had been very friendly and helpful to riders like me, had won the senior men's road race in a bold solo move. Riding for the Wheaties/Schwinn team, he would become the first ever cyclist to appear on a Wheaties cereal box. Awesome! And Chip? He rode a few laps and then quit! Fellow riders reported him changing into street clothes and then watching from the sidelines. That was BULLSHIT! Wyoming only got one rider in the race and so you had to REPRESENT! It was your responsibility, your veritable duty to give it everything and show them Cowboy Country had some real racers. What a tosser! Now I really had to go up to the Sheridan Crit and kick this guy's ass!

My big plans changed when I broke the frame of my beloved Atala Italian racing bike a few days before the big race. The crash was a slow speed case of teenage male bumbling, only a block from home. That same pretty girl down the street who shook me out of my Tarzan phase all those years ago, Debbie Skorz, was back from college and sunbathing in her backyard. I was rolling slowly down the street, listening to the bike, as I had been doing some derailleur adjusting back in the yard, when I spotted her bikini-clad body glistening with suntan oil. It grabbed my attention so intensely that I smashed into the back of her dad's pickup truck parked in front of their house!

Embarrassment quickly swept over me, as did fleeing the scene of the crime. I picked myself up, realized Debbie hadn't seen my endo, but her dad came out the front door wondering what had happened and if I had hit his truck. I assured him it was just a little tumble because I was looking down at my derailleur and I had not hit his truck. Actually, my front wheel had wedged under the rear bumper, and my carcass had slammed into his tail gate! No damage had been done to the old and well-weathered vehicle, but the big issue was my bike! The top and down tubes were cracked at the lugs, and the fork was bent back…it was ruined!

I called Lennard Zinn, a frame builder in Boulder I had met at a past Red Dog race, about repairs. Replacing tubes and lugs was not an inexpensive endeavor but it could be done. It would require a repaint as well, which was intriguing as, even though it was "pro team issue", I never loved the drab grey with blue paneled scheme of the bike. A new frame and fork were at least $350, assuming I could get it wholesale again, which was doubtful even through "C & D". The prices of Italian frames had risen a lot recently. The repaired frame but in a new color scheme would be $275. I didn't have that kind of money, and it would also take a couple months. And what about the rest of the season and kicking that wanker's ass in Sheridan?

Enter Drew Leemon, my long-time local cycling buddy, who would step up to help not for the first nor the last time. He had that Team Miyata, which was full Dura Ace, that he was happy to loan it to me. It was a little small, but I could make it work. On went my race wheels and my junior gears. A close inspection of the Sheridan race flyer showed a significant prize list, with gift certificates to the local shop for the top three finishers and loads of cash primes. Given my dilemma with my broken frame, the race now took on a new dimension…I had to win as much money as possible!

I got a ride to the race in Sheridan with a local cycling friend, Darin Tams, and his folks. I offered to chip in for gas, but they insisted I didn't need to. Financially, I was off to a great start. The mission was two-fold and a bit tricky: kick Chip's ass and win the race but also win as much prime money as possible. In consideration of the second goal, I brought along a freewheel with SENIOR gears (12 tooth cog) so I could put on bigger gears after the junior race and, like Topher had shown me the year before, race against the Senior men and try to win some more cash primes…I needed the money!

The criterium course was a one-mile circuit at a VA hospital. There was a short but tough little climb just after the start/finish, followed by a slight downhill section and the rest was flat. The turns were all nice, wide 90-degree corners. There was a decent sized Junior field including a real threat to my plan, Joe Strandell from South Dakota. He was strong and savvy and a fast finisher, having beaten me for the win in a road race in Sheridan the previous summer. There were five primes on offer, three in cash, and the winner of the 20-mile race got a $50 gift certificate at the local bike shop.

Pretty early on the bell rang for a $20 prime and I came around Joe to take it. Looking around I found Joe, Chip, and I had gotten a gap on the others, so I drove it up the hill, with Joe coming through strongly to cement our three-rider break. The next prime was merchandise, so I let Joe have it. Chip was pulling through, but he didn't seem particularly strong. Our gap was growing each lap, and the break seemed certain to stay away. The next cash prime was only $10, and I just pipped Joe to take it, while Chip was barely hanging on. One more merchandise prime, which I didn't contest easily went to Joe, and I decisively grabbed the final prime for $20 cash. I expected some kind of attack from Chip, but it never came, and I once more beat Joe in the final sprint, more convincingly this time with Chip a complete non-factor. Feeling redeemed, I thrust my arms skyward with great joy. It is worth noting that I never saw Chip Whiton again.

I had $50 in cash and a $50 gift certificate for the local shop. I hoped they would still be open, and I could swing in to grab some cool swag on the way out of town. For now, I went to work on my bike while the women raced. The August midday sun was blazing hot and there was no shade to be found as I worked on the grass near the start/finish area, conscious to drink lots of water. Freehubs, which allowed cogs to be easily changed, were not yet ubiquitous and all my wheels had the less expensive freewheel system. As such, I had brought a big crescent wrench and a freewheel tool (as well as my little workstand and a screwdriver to readjust my rear derailleur) to pop off my junior 15-22 six speed cluster and replace it with a 12-21 seven speed, so I could take on the big boys...I needed the money!

The 30-mile Senior men's race (an OPEN event-so all categories were present, although in fairness I think only one rider was a Cat 2) had SEVEN primes, all of which were cash. I still felt strong and was hopeful of taking at least a couple. When I won the first cash prime, sprinting from second position out of the final corner, the older riders were supportive of "the young kid". After I took my second in the same way, they started to grumble a bit and to make my life more difficult. Since I was the fastest in the sprint, riders would jump early or attack on the little climb right after the finish line. It was down to me to cover all of these efforts since well…I needed the money!

It got harder, but I kept winning the primes. Every single one in fact! They were worth $10 and occasionally $20 and with about ten laps remaining; I was running out of steam. The little climb after the finish was getting more difficult each lap. At this point, the race announcer (Dale Jacobsen, one of those cool veteran racers who had traveled to the Park City race in the "Wade-a-bago" back in 1983 with me) had received some visitors. Angry wives and girlfriends of the older riders came up to protest that this young kid was taking all "their" prize money! So, now hanging on for dear life, after over forty miles of racing and nearly a dozen all out sprints under the hot sun, the prime bell rang again! I came back to life, happy to know I could perhaps win one last cash prize. It was to be the eighth and final prime lap of the race. But there was a special caveat. Dale's voice boomed out over the PA "Attention riders: this cash prime is for SENIOR RIDERS ONLY. SENIOR RIDERS ONLY. This means NOT you Dave!". The older guys snickered, and the Category 2 from South Dakota threw down a fierce attack on the little climb. My day was over but what a day it had been, a special effort, a day to set apart…

SET THIS DAY APART-Hipsway, from "Hipsway" (1986)
"I set this day apart
To take the burden, take the pain
I set this day apart
I take the burden, I take the pain!"

My legs were gone, and my tank was empty. I went out the back as soon as the climb began. Winning the Senior Men's race had never been in my plan as I knew they had gift certificate prizes, and I needed cash. It certainly would have been cool, but in hindsight I had literally gone a perfect eleven out of eleven on sprints contested, a frankly remarkable achievement and one to be proud of. I made as much money in that race as was possible. I was toasted, but my mission had been accomplished. I had noticed a pretty girl my age sitting out in her yard at the top of the hill watching the race. She had been cheering "the young guy" she kept hearing about over the PA.

So, I spun around, quit the race, and chatted her up! Like many, this bike-racing thing was new to her, and she offered me a cold soda from her cooler, which I gladly accepted while I explained some of the nuances of the sport to her…my sport! My prime haul from the Senior race was $100 bringing my day's total to $150, over half of what was needed to repair the frame. All achieved in less than two hours "work". This was another one of those "delusional days" that many bike racers experience, forgetting the cost of our exotic machines and the travel expenses. Not to mention all the time spent training. The cash earned, the great swag I scored with my gift certificate on the way out of town (A nice "Local Motion" shirt I could wear on the first day of school and some bike parts), and the phone number from that pretty girl all stoked these fires of delusion nicely…swelling my head to suitably ridiculous proportions!

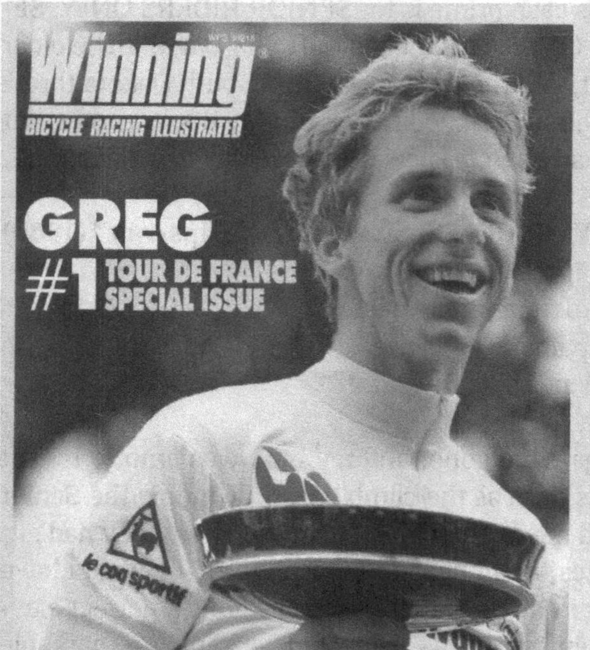

The Winning magazine celebrating Lemond's 1986 Tour win.
Courtersy Winning Magazine

CHAPTER EIGHTEEN:

THE WORLD CRASHES INTO MY LIVING ROOM!

As my Senior year began, my bike was shipped off for repair and I was immersed in college applications and college-prep classes. Calculus class was especially intense. It was an AP class before LVHS had AP classes and only twelve of us stepped up to take it. I was blessed with great classmates. Thank heavens for Wade's help with homework over the phone on most weeknights. Whenever the challenging math stumped him, I would call future doctor Kirk Bollinger, as the class came easy for him. I also had the assistance of Frosty Sprout, a brilliant eccentric and real cowboy who went to school at MIT, eventually writing a math textbook. The fall of my Senior year was mostly memorable for America hosting its first ever Elite Men's and Women's World Cycling Championships! Charles had been calling and giving me reports on the track events since I was in school. As soon as that morning's Calculus class was completed on Friday, September 5, though, I jumped into Drew's car, and we headed for Colorado Springs to watch my heroes race for the rainbow!

Drew had friends in the area we stayed with (we cyclists in Cowboy Country ALWAYS did things on the cheap) and the Pro Road Race was held Saturday while the Women and Amateur Men competed Sunday. Both races were on a circuit at the US Air Force Academy on the outskirts of town. When we arrived Saturday morning, the first thing that was clear was that Colorado Springs was NOT Boulder. Unlike the huge crowds that turned out for the Coors Classic, attendance at Worlds was pretty sparse. The weather didn't help either as the air was cold, and damp and the skies were grey. The course was a rolling 9.5 miles on perfect, glass smooth pavement through the Academy grounds. The pros would do an astounding 17 laps for a total race distance of just under 163 miles. Damn!

As we walked up to the start line from the massive grass parking area, I finally saw those big yellow Campagnolo signs from my poster up close. Present in every finish line shot I had ever seen from a World Championship, I now realized the side facing the riders counted down the final distance remaining, starting at 300 meters and posted every 25 meters all the way to the line…cool! The short laps and high speeds meant we saw the riders almost every half an hour. Little pockets of fans from each country were situated all around the course, complete with patriotic clothing and flags. It was so awesome!

We made our plan to view the start from the hill above and then walk the entire course to see the riders at many different points but arriving back to the finish line for the final laps, since I had grandstand tickets from Charles. As we walked around the course, we happened to run into a young entrepreneur named Jim Gentes who had a unique new helmet he was showing to all gathered. We all had just endured a year of riding in bulky, heavy helmets (Mine was a Vetta Pro and it was terrible) under the new rule, but this was easily half the weight and very comfortable. It was just polystyrene foam lacking a shell and instead had a Lycra cover. It was called a "Giro". Jim asked, "Would you wear it?" and "how much would you pay for it?" Turns out this clever guy was really onto something, and those helmets would be ubiquitous the following year, nearly a peloton standard, as he almost singlehandedly rid the sport of bulky, heavy brain buckets.

The American team, especially Roy Knickman, were consistently on the front, despite Lemond playing down his chances in the press. With a "home" course, and medals in three of the previous four Worlds, the newly crowned Tour Champion should have been primed for victory, but he was tired after a long season. The bitterness with Hinault still lingered from the Tour, and things hadn't gotten any better at the Coors Classic, which preceded the Worlds. Hinault won and Lemond, the 1985 winner, was second but they bickered the entire time. We watched the definitive breakaway go on the short climb on the backside of the course, driven clear by Frenchmen Charly Mottet and Fignon. It was thrilling to see Kiefel make the split, but he was dropped before the final lap. Italian Moreno Argentin, an ace in hilly road races (winner of the 1985/86 Liege-Bastogne-Liege Classics) left the break in the company of German Rolf Golz and Mottet. In the finale only Mottet remained but Argentin was clearly the strongest. He embodied all my imagery of a classy Italian cyclist from the tricolor trimmed azure jersey to the deeply bronzed legs seemingly sculpted by Michelangelo himself. Onboard a beautiful celeste Bianchi, he easily disposed of the Frenchman in the sprint. Lemond finished seventh after a half-hearted sprint for the bronze, which was won by Saronni.

Another enticing aspect of visiting Colorado Springs was that in Colorado you could drink beer (3.2% alcohol content) at the age of eighteen. I had just turned eighteen a couple of weeks earlier. After the race, I walked to a "3.2 bar" near Drew's friend's house, listened to some music and felt like a big man! I decided that the Worlds, held on a circuit, was the best way to watch bike racing and I would have to one day make it to another one, preferably in a cycling hotbed overseas.

The women's and amateur races the following day were even colder and rainy and not much fun to watch. A frozen Rebecca Twigg launched an attack on the last lap but crashed out leaving Frenchwoman Jeannie Longo to solo in for her second (of ultimately five) World Road title. We were thrilled when Janelle Parks-Graham ecstatically won the sprint behind to claim a silver medal for the home nation. As the fog descended over the amateur men, we headed for the car and the long drive home, listening to most of that race (dominated by the East Germans) on the radio. Although hosting the World Championships showed that cycling in the US had come a long way, it was only massively popular in a few isolated pockets and was still very much a cult sport.

The repaired Atala, now painted yellow (Wade said I should name it "Koladi-Ola" like the song by the synth pop band Yello) with blue decals was back in Cowboy Country a few weeks later and needed to be rebuilt. I would be contesting the 1987 season against the Senior Men. My strong results as a junior meant I could skip the crash-prone Cat 4's and race as a Category 3. Most of the strong Wyoming riders were in this field as Danny was still our only Cat 2. That winter would be my last as a swimmer and even though I had little passion left for the sport, it was my Senior Year, and I was the team captain. I lifted weights all fall in preparation and planned to give it everything for my last hurrah.

Another quintessential Cowboy Country moment came later that fall when a few classmates and I were painting the window of the local Dairy Queen for the upcoming Homecoming week. The parade went down Main Street, so students decorated the windows of businesses with some sort of giant Tiger conquering its rival for a class competition and to get everyone fired up for the big game. I think I had come up with a "Raiders of the Lost Ark" Theme for the Seniors. I had a deer tag, but the hunting season was nearly over, and I still hadn't found a nice buck in my area. Granted my interest in hunting was minimal and I hadn't worked very hard at it. However, someone spotted a nice buck near the rifle range and Dad pulled up in the truck with my rifle on the gun rack and said we should go try and find it. So, I set down my paint brush, leaped into Dad's pick up and we charged the barely five-minute drive out to the range. The buck was still there, and I shot it. Dad stayed to gut the deer, and I drove back in town to finish my art project while mom retrieved Dad and my deer. Only in Wyoming!

Meanwhile, Topher and I were both on the Student Council and determined to have decent music at the spring formal dance. We wanted a live band and not a DJ. To this end, we reached out to booking agencies for lists of their acts and what kind of music they played. When we found interesting candidates, we would go listen when they performed nearby. This was a bit tricky, as we were underage, and the bands mostly played at bars. Somehow, we could always talk our way around it. We would order cokes and sit in the back as we worked hard to find some cool music in Cowboy Country. It was not an easy task. Nearby Riv-

Saddling up to ride Cowboy Country

erton was a bit bigger and had more nightlife, so we often went there on our quest. We frequently ran into Clay Hendrix, that quirky old bike racer, who now owned a bike shop in Riverton. Later, over Christmas break, when Wes was home from college, I borrowed a friend's ID to go out to a bar with him. Wyoming had a drinking age of 19 then and we were the last holdout in the country to adopt the nationwide age 21 standard. We saw Clay again and he took great pride in asking if I was "looking for bands tonight". Touche!

The Cycling World comes to America. September 1986 Colorado Springs
Photo credit Dave Campbell

1986 Worlds Colorado Springs, caught spectating as Janelle Parks-Graham (center) races to silver.
Courtesy Winning Magazine

CHAPTER NINETEEN:

FATHER TO SON

By the spring of my Senior year, I was dead set on leaving Cowboy Country to attend college out of state. My mother had given me several books detailing the top colleges and universities around the country and I had studied them intently throughout the fall and winter. My grades were good, my test scores solid, and I had loads of extracurriculars, so I was excited to attend a "really good" university. Far from the safety of home. I was particularly interested in one where I could ride my bike year-round on the west coast. One where things were HAPPENING... live music, especially new cutting-edge music, cool people I could really relate to, more cyclists, record stores, etc. The important stuff! My top choices were the University of California-Santa Cruz and UC San Diego. My mother, who grew up in North Dakota and left to go to college in Colorado, understood where I was coming from and was supportive. My father? Not so much! A song from the Alarm nailed this conflict perfectly and was regularly on my headphones as I logged the miles in Cowboy Country...

FATHER TO SON-The Alarm from "Strength" 1985
"Today I can't find nothing nowhere
Tomorrow I might find something somewhere!
Give me a future now,
I need it so badly now,
Oh...for tomorrow!"

My Dad could not understand why any Wyoming kid would not want to attend the University of Wyoming in Laramie. I fancied myself to be a good student and UW had no pedigree at all in mind; one only had to graduate from a Wyoming High School and TAKE the ACT test. The score was irrelevant. Additionally, it was in Laramie, dubbed "Laradise" by many with more than a hint of sarcasm. Only about 25,000 people lived there, and its 7200-foot elevation made for some tough weather. The wind blew constantly and winter temperatures with wind chill were borderline frightening...and not at all conducive to year-round cycling. The mascot was a damn Cowboy! I was not at all interested; I was determined to leave Cowboy Country far behind.

My father countered that it was a veritable bargain, I could almost certainly land a significant scholarship, and it had one of the best student-to-teacher ratios in the country. These ranking systems for Universities (UCSC and UCSD were near the top) he assured me, meant little and "were based on silly things like how many books there are in the school's library!" UW was a great school, and it made sense to go to your local University. His arguments fell on deaf ears, as there had never really been a time when I had truly considered going to college in my home state. The friction that had already existed between the two of us only intensified as I continued to insist on attending college out of state.

"I see these signs of black times everywhere I run
I can't stand it another day
I gotta move away!
I gotta move away!"

He was so desperate to convince me to stay in Wyoming that the guy who always asked "Where is all this going, this bike racing thing? Where is it taking you?" appealed to my cycling passion. "You know you could operate pretty good with your bike racing out of Laramie. Colorado and all those races are close by; it's not far at all down to Boulder." He wasn't wrong...but I saw the University of Wyoming as "safe". They had a cycling club, but I knew most of those guys and I could beat most if not all of them...when I was sixteen! UW was an easy, predictable, and non-challenging choice. Limiting and lacking any sort of prestige in my eyes. Most of the people I grew up with would go there and I was ready to spread my wings and take on new challenges.

I wanted to meet new people and hell, "find my tribe". There were 160 people in my graduating class, and I knew every one of them. Most very well and many since kindergarten! Many of these people I grew up with said "You spent a thousand bucks on a bike? That's crazy… you could buy a truck!" or "You go out and ride fifty miles? That's crazy!" Let alone Wyoming's musical environment! "Who the hell are Echo & The Bunnymen? Why don't you listen to Bon Jovi"? many would say. I wanted to leave that crowd behind. I imagined that on a more liberal and enlightened campus I could find more people like me. Where things were really happening. I saw college as the ultimate opportunity to make something for myself, to go where no one knew me and had any preconceived notions of "the son of Bruce and Carol Campbell" …and that meant going far from home.

Tensions between my father and I were high as we visited the California schools over spring break. My mother, as was her way, arranged things, including a meet up with a college friend of Dads to appease the old man's frustrations. I was certain, based on all the things I had read in those books about choosing a college, that one of these schools was going to be perfect for me. It started promisingly enough, in the car on the drive south from the airport, a local radio station (91X) had played the incredible new U2 album "The Joshua Tree" …in its entirety. U2 never even made the radio in Cowboy Country, so I loved this! While I intently studied the UC-Santa Cruz student newspaper the first night at the hotel, I was encouraged-Big Audio Dynamite was playing on campus the next month. Now this was what I was looking for-surely California was the place for me.

The tour of the campus the next day, however, revealed the truth. Despite my desire to spread my wings, school in California was a bridge too far for this small-town boy. Santa Cruz was like a summer camp for hippie kids… no grades, a beautiful lush green campus, and very, very alternative. As it turns out...too alternative for me. When we stopped for lunch, I couldn't even order a Ham and Swiss sandwich. All the offerings were vegetarian and all the pretty girls I saw on campus had hairy legs and armpits or dressed like Janis Joplin. I was far, far from Cowboy country. It would appear too far. Here was a guy who shaved his legs on a campus where the girls didn't shave theirs! San Diego was even farther away from what I wanted with its suburban campus and California car culture, even though my old swimming teammate Jeff Shope, now a student there, gave us a personalized grand tour and he loved it there. My Dad wasn't even sure if "the truck would be a legal vehicle out here, what with all the emissions laws they have in California". Both UCSC and UCSD were out.

I received scholarship offers from the University of Oregon and Oregon State University, both of which we had visited back in the summer of my sophomore year, and each seemed like they would fit the bill quite nicely. Things were happening there, they were big but not too big, and I would be far from home...this could work for me. They were also places I could ride year-round. Meanwhile, though my father, in his role as LVHS Guidance Counselor, had one final play. He had convinced me to apply for the "Wyoming Alumni Scholarship", which no one from our school had ever gotten and he was convinced I could land. The Alumni scholarship would pay for four years at the University of Wyoming and was awarded to a "well-rounded student, who while strong academically, was also deeply involved in school and community activities". "That's you, David. This scholarship is perfect for you!" Well...I got it, and my dad was thrilled but I already knew UW was not for me.

"Stop fighting the system,
Cause the system won't break!
Get your hair cut boy and learn from my mistakes!"

Senior Awards night is a big deal in a small town and all the top graduates would put on their Sunday best and be there. Graduation was just a few short weeks away. The host? Bruce Campbell, LVHS Guidance counselor of course! Springtime meant cycling for me, and Awards Night just meant I had to really hustle back from training in time to pack in some dinner and get cleaned up for the big show. On the way back into town, in my beloved Red Cinelli "winged C" t-shirt, while passing the Rifle Range, I was crowded by a pick-up truck. Fittingly for Cowboy Country, he had a gun rack, acted as if he owned the road and treated me as if I was some kind of menace with no right to be out there. These sorts of drivers never seemed to take the time to see how fast a racer such as myself was riding. As a result, he not only crowded me but ultimately turned right in front of me. Frustrated, I yelled at him and of course, he yelled back. As I rode off, I gave him the finger and the whole ordeal reinforced just how ready I was to put this place behind me! I couldn't wait to move on to "someplace so much better" in college.

While I "shoveled in" (Dad's words-didn't he know what Eddie B. taught us at the training center about training like a bull and eating like a pig?) my dinner, with my mom reminding me what time we needed to leave for the Awards night, the phone rang. Dad answered. "Red T-shirt, huh? Out by the Rifle Range, you say? And he gave you the finger? Well, I'm sorry about that, Tom and you can bet I'll be having a talk with him!" GULP. When saddling up to ride in Cowboy Country, particularly in a town I had lived in my entire life, I was out on the road with my mom and dad's friends and neighbors. Everyone knew me. Few people rode bikes on the roads outside of town and only VERY few rode them as far out and frequently as I did. Despite the way I was sometimes treated out there, such responses from an angry young man were "pretty damn ill-advised". And "pretty damn counterproductive" if I wanted to be treated with respect! "I was going to lose any kind of car/bike confrontation". Such was the content of the lecture, and thankfully it was brief, if due only to the timeline for getting to Awards Night.

"Now I said to my father,
Father give me a break!
There's a million more chances

Saddling up to ride Cowboy Country

That I'm born to take!"

My father presented the Scholarship to me with great pride, and my mother-the world's greatest scrap-booker, documented the moment with numerous photos. I promptly declined the offer from the University of Wyoming and began to seriously consider the University of Oregon. Our neighbor Carolyn Gilbertson had gone to school out there and loved it. The town of Eugene was featured in my *"Sport Style"* magazine where it was hailed as a veritable hotbed for outdoor and endurance athletic enthusiasts. My parents noted that Eugene was "very liberal." The deal was sealed when a pamphlet arrived in the mail that detailed the school's club sports program which included cycling. The pamphlet included photos of the annual Campus Criterium that looped around the Student Union. A race I would go on to win during my sophomore year. I was going to flee Cowboy Country to be a Duck! Danny advised me to get an aluminum bike (all that rain) while Mr. Petersen, my Calculus teacher, told me I was going to "grow mold in my arm pits". Could it really be THAT wet out there?

I saw High School graduation as a beginning and not an end. I enjoyed High School and had many great friends, but I now had the opportunity to move on to something bigger and better. I was even brave enough now to get a "new wave haircut" since I was on my way out of this cowboy town! I knew I would always stay in touch with Dave, who was headed to Casper College. Wade and Topher would be at the University of Wyoming and Wade got a nice scholarship. But I was getting out of Cowboy Country! This was my attitude throughout the final days of my High School experience and all the hoopla that went along with it. And as people spoke of the actual graduation ceremony and how emotional it would be, I just laughed at these cliches...I knew I would NOT be crying!

When we all gathered for the big night, I was alongside Topher of course. He was antsy, fired up, and of course, our conversation turned to music. We had both been listening to the new Replacements album "Pleased to

Meet Me" extensively. Topher needed reminding of lyrics for the "Alex Chilton" song because he wanted it "in his head "as we marched in. "I'm in love-what's that song? I'm in love with that song!" The one I had in my mind, the mind of an angry young man, was the album's opener "IOU" ..." I want it in writing-I owe you nothing!" Get me out of here-I'm done. On to bigger and better things! Right before we marched in, I saw Owen and Shirley Jones, my cycling buddy John Griber's parents who had driven all the way from Jackson over Togwotee pass to be there for me. Smiling and excited, they rushed over to wish me well, a touching sentiment from our tight-knit Wyoming cycling community. Touching yes, but I still wanted to just get this over with!

Well, I cried. Eventually. We marched in, we sat, and the speakers spoke. We filed up and received our diplomas. We had been told in rehearsal, NOT to throw our hats (someone could lose an eye!) and I really tried to remember that. But when the big moment came, "it just happened", perhaps all those movies where kids throw their hats was just engrained, but I remember seeing it mid-air and thinking "Oh yeah, we weren't supposed to do that!" Then, as we milled around and embraced each other I saw our Valedictorian Kirk Bollinger. And he was tearing up. This was a guy I had called on the phone many times for help with AP Calculus. He had been so patient with me and so helpful. One of the many incredible and generous people I grew up with here in Cowboy Country...and I lost it! I cried the tears I swore I wouldn't...and it felt great! The truth was, this was a great town filled with kind and generous people where I had made so many wonderful memories, I was just ready for the next phase. Again, I found the expression for both conflicting emotions in a song...

THESE IMPORTANT YEARS-Husker Du from "Warehouse: Songs, and Stories" (1987)
"We're all exchanging pleasantries
No matter how we feel
And no one knows the difference 'cause it all seems so unreal

Saddling up to ride Cowboy Country

You'd better grab a hold of something
Simple, but it's true
If you don't stop to smell the roses now
They might end up on you"

Expectations only mean you really think you know
What's coming next, and you don't!
Yearbooks with their autographs
From friends you might have had
These are your important years,
you'd better make them last!"

Alternative hairstyle, alternative senior photo, surely alternative music was playing. Summer 1987. The photo shoot was a prize for a race win.
Photo credit Dave Campbel

CHAPTER TWENTY:

CELEBRATED SUMMER

My swimming career may have been over, but I still worked at the pool. Upon graduation, I took the Water Safety Instructor course so I could teach swimming lessons as well as lifeguard. My pool connections would soon prove to be of additional usefulness. I had always suspected some of the older lifeguards snuck in after hours and one Saturday after a home sweet meet, I found a bottle cap on the bottom of the hot pool. How cool would it be to soak in the hot tub with my buddies (or a girlfriend!) and drink beer? Well, one summer afternoon at work my magic moment arrived when I oversaw the keys and was charged with locking up. So, what did I do? I assigned a schedule for the guards, gave myself the first break during which I raced down to the hardware store on my bike and made a copy of that pool key!

In addition to the focus of graduation, I was still training intently for the State Cycling Championships in June. I was on my own now, though, as Topher took a summer job at his uncle's horse racing track in Minnesota and wasn't around. I missed his energy and companionship and found the barren and windswept spring roads less inviting on my own. I had to work harder to stay motivated. I was focused on the road race, and it was a big step up: the Senior Men raced 100 miles instead of the 50-60 we raced as juniors. The Cheyenne course would feature a long climb, not my forte, so I trained regularly by riding up Red Canyon to the top of Limestone Mountain and back. With a summit of over 8000 feet and over 3000 feet of climbing, I hoped suffering alone on the rugged and wind exposed sixty-mile round trip route would prepare me for my latest challenge. I was stopped one late spring day at the top to refuel and pull on a jacket before the descent when Carrie Boedecker, one of the prettiest girls in our class, who I had basically crushed on since kindergarten pulled up with her boyfriend in his truck. "David, are you okay? Are you lost or stranded? Do you need water? What are you doing all the way out here on this mountain?" Such an incredulous reaction to my rides was quite typical in Cowboy Country. "I'm fine, I'm just out training" I responded with a grin.

People in Lander talked about how much they loved the mountains, but most of that came from what I saw as relatively passive activities. I came to understand that from your car or campsite, you saw the mountains but from the saddle, you experienced them. You feel the steepness of the climb, smell the trees and the sage, and feel your body responding to the lack of oxygen when riding hard at altitude. The wind doesn't just blow through the window, it batters you in the face, blocks your progress like a wall, and then refreshes you on the descent. To me, pushing myself deep on the bike in "my mountains" brought a certain authenticity to my life. I was living, breathing, and truly experiencing the beauty of my rugged and challenging homeland.

The first state championship event was the time trial, in its now traditional location in the barren, windswept and sparsely populated cycling mecca of Farson, famous for a general store that sold giant ice cream cones. There was almost nothing else there. My goal was to go under an hour and the only piece of aero gear I had in 1987, other than my brake levers, was a spandex swim cap to stretch over top of my helmet. I knew this was cool because I'd seen Alexi Grewal do it in the pages of *Winning* magazine. Going under an hour for the 40 km test was my goal and I strapped my Casio wristwatch to my handlebars to keep me focused. Thrashing in and out of the saddle and unable to stay on top of a gear, I watched the hour tick by with the finish line still a couple hundred yards away. I placed ninth and was none too pleased with myself.

Feeling defeated, I drove home to work my evening lifeguard shift at the pool. My mother phoned me during my break and told me I needed to call Charles. He was in Farson, and he needed me for the TEAM time trial, which was 62 miles long and scheduled for the following morning. One of his teammates was sick. Jeff Handwerk, a cool guy from Casper and an ace time trialist was on the team along with a UW guy I didn't know named Mike Shappell. I couldn't really wrap my head around this. My legs were sore; I had to work until 9:30 pm and the race was early the following morning...and a two-hour drive away! Besides, based on the day's performance I was no time trialist. But Charles was a good friend and he really needed me, a point re-iterated by my mom. I argued that he had won the individual title and would surely rip my legs off...I would only slow them down. I called Charles. He kept convincing me I could do it and he finally got me on board when he told me what great training it would be for next week's road race.

My sweet and supportive sister Amy drove so I could catch a few more z's on the drive over South Pass to Farson. She would follow the team with our spare wheels during the event, acting as our support vehicle. I prepared like it was a road race and wore a jersey with pockets to carry food since 62 miles at full blast was no small undertaking. This being Wyoming, there was only one other team to contend with, Brian's crew from Cheyenne, and Charles was certain we could beat them...so I could win a Senior State title!

The first hour of the race was the worst. I suffered immensely on the wheel of my older and stronger teammates. I never missed a turn, although I kept my pulls short and hung tough, hoping to survive the distance. I was suffering so profoundly and was so oblivious to everything except the wheel in front of me that I hit a big rock that my teammates had all avoided and I flatted. The team rolled slowly on. My sister, who had watched more than a few races with me, leapt out of the truck with the wheels and we did a quick change. The guys later told me they picked a highway marker and decided if I hadn't come back by that point, they were going to carry on without me and apparently, I barely made it. I was the only one who brought food, and the second hour was totally different. I felt better and took longer pulls. In the final miles, I was our strongest rider and ultimately brought us across the line in around two hours and twenty minutes, a speed of well over 26 miles an hour, quite respectable. We smoked Brian's squad, and I felt like a big man…I could ride with the best seniors!

Or maybe not. In the next weekend's road race in Cheyenne, climbing out past Curt Gowdy State Park I got dropped like a rock and limped home in fifteenth place. Nonetheless, I was pleased with finishing my first ever 100-mile race. It was my first time feeding by musette (cloth bags), where my sister was once again an ace helper, standing out on the roadside to feed me. I bought THE ONLY musette bag at Freewheel Sports, white and emblazoned with the Campagnolo logo. When we practiced handing up the bag in front of the house, loaded with two water bottles and a sandwich inside, we broke the strap, so in our Wyoming cycling spirit of "do it yourself" mom reinforced it on her sewing machine. My dad, who had a rifle match in the area, was there for the finish and had a bucket of ice and water ready to pour over my head after a particularly hot and windy day.

Or maybe I could ride with the big guys, if the race was a criterium! The next weekend Dad drove Darin (whose folks had driven the previous year) and I to Sheridan for the State Criterium Championship and I dominated. Granted, the strongest riders hailed from Laramie and Jackson and none of them made the trip North to this new title event, but there were some strong riders there and I smoked 'em! I attacked early on the little climb, three of us went clear and I convincingly won the final sprint. Dad was quite proud and took some photos. I had claimed two state titles in my first year as a Senior. Not the most prestigious ones granted, but hey, not bad!

Greg Lemond had been shot in a bizarre hunting accident that spring and as a bike racer myself I was frequently asked about this around town and at the pool. He had reportedly lost 65% of his blood volume and nearly died. No one, including me, knew if he could come back but we certainly hoped he could. Meanwhile, Andy Hampsten carried the torch for the American presence in Europe. He was now the leader of the 7-Eleven team and narrowly won the Tour de Suisse for the second year in a row. Key to his victory had been the help of his teammate Ron Kiefel, who snatched a bonus sprint away from a rival at the last possible moment. In the world's biggest races now, our guys were up there! Despite Greg's absence, and largely due to the 7-Eleven team, interest in cycling continued to grow among average Americans and we had even more television coverage of the Tour. Unfortunately, Andy struggled at the Tour, but Phinney won another sprint stage and in an incredible finale, Jeff Pierce broke away alone to win the prestigious final stage on the Champs Elysees. My swim coach Bruce even had it on the TV at Tony's Pizza! This was real progress!

The next major event for me was my hometown Red Dog race. Bob had moved away, and the shop had new owners, Terry and Kris Hayes. They were helpful but inexperienced, so I became the main promoter. Bob had shown me how the Highway Department would loan you cones, flags, and vests for the marshals and the local beer distributor was always happy to give us race numbers. We kept the time trial out on North Second Street as an opener as well as the closing road race around the Squaw/Baldwin Creek loop, but we wanted to bring back a criterium. Topher's parents had built a home in a new housing development not far from my house and I always thought it seemed like a cool spot for a crit. I talked to City Hall and the police department, and they said if I obtained permission from every resident on the course, I could do it. My evenings after working at the pool were now spent going door to door to sell my event. All the residents were supportive, so we coned off the street, put marshals (my friends, neighbors, and family) in place, and with no police involvement or even fees in 1987 Wyoming, we had a criterium!

The only problem was we didn't have an announcer. Brian had always done it, and he had moved back to Cheyenne. Enter my buddy Clay, now living on his own in a little apartment and scooping ice cream at "Hooligans" on Main Street. Topher and I had attentively watched "Sid and Nancy" on his VCR over there a few weeks back. He was worried he didn't know enough about bike racing, but he was bursting with personality, he had his own sound system and great taste in music, and I offered him fifty bucks, so he was in. He ended up doing a great job, although I was hoping to impress him by winning. I could only manage third behind a fast new guy from Casper named Dean Golich who surprised me by going long in the final sprint.

There were other races that summer but my expanded duties at the pool meant I only raced a few and all were in Wyoming. For several years, I had competed in the local triathlon but always on teams…and we always won. Triathlons were new and the sport was growing quickly. A couple of fellow lifeguards, Jay and Don were now triathletes. One day at work they were sassing me about being just a cyclist, "you couldn't go so fast on your bike if you had to swim first! Triathlon is hard and you don't even run!" Hmmm. This got my competitive juices flowing. These were nice guys and even though I wasn't a "triathlete" I still thought I had the fitness to beat them. The last Wyoming bike race was the Dead Dog in early August, and the local triathlon was several weeks later, so I had some time to start swimming again and become a runner. I decided to train in secret and then show up unannounced and let them have it!

The Dead Dog in Laramie was significant because, following our team time trial win, Jeff's Casper "Bike Stop" team started recruiting all the best riders in the state. In the Dead Dog I think they had at least nine riders of twenty in the field and they raced like a real team. This was a fairly new dynamic in Wyoming. I followed my now typically lackluster time trial by getting dropped on the big climb in the road race, leaving the crit as my last chance to do something. "Bike Stop" sent rider after rider off the front, until Jeff Spencer, maybe the nicest guy in the Wyoming peloton and a student at the University made a move that stuck. He had loads of friends and family cheering from the sidelines and his team was blocking for him. But as the end of the race approached, his gap was coming down and he was dying…it looked like we might catch him right at the end.

Golich, who whipped me at the Red Dog, was on the

"Bike Stop" squad and had never been known as the best team player. I thought he was cocky, and I didn't particularly like him. Interestingly, he would go on to a very successful coaching career, even advising Armstrong during his heyday. For maybe the first time in my cycling career, my "race radar" came on, time seemed to slow down, and my focus sharpened on the key elements shaping the final moments of the race. I focused in on Dean. I could tell he was just ITCHING to go. Brian was announcing and as he rang the bell for one lap to go, Jeff was dangling just in front of us. As Bob Roll would say, he was "dying but not yet dead", and his teammate Dean shot out of the field like a rocket. Exactly as Eddie B. advised us back at the OTC, I "glued up" …right onto his back wheel. Dean blasted around the course and never once looked back. Everything fell into place, and it felt all too easy. It seemed almost magical as we blew past Jeff on the backstretch, and I launched off Dean's wheel out of the final corner for the win as Brian yelled at the top of his lungs "It's little Davey! It's little Davey!" and I thrust both arms skyward with great pride. Thanks in no small part to improved American race coverage on television and print, and immersing myself headlong into my sport, I had truly learned how to "read a race".

I now had three weeks to become a runner. The local triathlon was a 1500-meter pool swim, 40 km bike (twice around the hilly Squaw/Baldwin loop), and a 10 km run. I swam a few times in preparation and knew I would be fine. The run would take much more work. I started with walking a block, jogging a block, which seemed just ridiculous, but my running friends insisted it was necessary. On my next training session, I ran a full mile and damn near crippled myself with shin splints. My cycling fitness seemed to mean nothing when it came to running. So, I built up slowly. By one week prior to the event, I did a full triathlon training session from the pool parking lot with transitions and a five-mile run, which boosted my confidence. I was "running" only eight-minute miles, so I would need a BIG lead off the bike. Clay had discovered this fabulous new band, Concrete Blonde, on MTV's "120 Minutes" which highlighted alternative music. Their debut album had been on heavy rotation for me all summer. I especially ran this lyric through my head as I trained for the triathlon and visualized Jay and Don not being able to lose me…

OVER YOUR SHOULDER-Concrete Blonde from "Concrete Blonde" (1986)
"Wherever you go
Whatever you do
Whatever you say, I'm watching you.
Oh! no.
There I am.
Over your shoulder
Over your shoulder
Over your shoulder
Oh! no. There I am again."

Specialized triathlon gear of any sort didn't yet exist, so figuring out clothing was another part of the puzzle in this new sport. I would swim in a Speedo and then pull on a one-piece skinsuit for the bike and of course, glasses and a helmet and cycling shoes. For the run, off went the "zoot suit" and on came running shorts and of course a swap of shoes. I wasn't "tri" enough to forego socks. The Speedo would do all three legs with me.

My two lifeguarding buddies were surprised but not shocked to see me on race morning. Drew, a woeful swimmer, but great cyclist and runner threw his hat into the ring as well. I came out of the pool second, just behind Jay, two years older and a former swimming teammate. He transitioned faster but I caught him in the first mile on the bike and in an effort to psyche him out, I blew by him like he was standing still. Fueled by the idea that these guys doubted me, I found the capacity to go deeper than ever before, riding so hard that I could hardly see, and practically blinded by my effort. Clay, now an employee of Bruce's at the pizza parlor, was sleeping in a lawn chair out on the bike course, supposedly marshalling traffic. I startled him when I blew past and ultimately built an eight-minute lead on the bike. Wade rode alongside me during the run and fired up about leading, I managed a seven-minute pace, cruising to the win with a few minutes to spare. The triathlon was fun, and I certainly shut Jay and Don up.

By now Topher was back in town, leaving the next day for Laramie and the University of Wyoming. He and Clay wanted to celebrate my victory with me, and I had the perfect place...the City Pool! Well after closing, of course. It was to be the first of many visits over the years, carrying on all through Christmas and summer visits home from college. The drinking age in Wyoming was nineteen, so Clay could buy the beer. The pool was covered with neoprene mats to hold in the heat, and we came up with the brilliant idea after a few beers, of trying to run all the way across the pool on top of the covers. Hilarity ensued with the chubby Clay not making it far, me doing better and Topher rocking it, using this hysterical high-kneed technique to make it all the way to the other side. The mat was curling under, and he was knee deep in the water, but raucously cheered on by Clay and I, he made it!

The next teenage male idea crossed over from funny to stupid...they would part the covers, and I would dive into the gap off the high board and then swim to the side underneath the covers. What could possibly go wrong? Indestructible young men we were! The impact was disorienting, and the darkness beneath the mats was complete. I tried not to panic but I could see the headlines in the local paper "Intoxicated lifeguard drowns after winning local triathlon". During a few seconds that felt like an eternity, I found an edge to orient myself and then swam to the side as calmly as I could manage. The guys were impressed, and I didn't mention how scary it was. I suggested we go back to the hot tub and chill with another beer.

There was one more cycling event in 1987, just a couple of weeks before I left for college at the University of Oregon. Brian, now a DJ in Cheyenne, had put together a fund-raiser for the "Make-A-Wish" foundation. Burger King gave $500, team jerseys, and placed donation boxes in all of their "restaurants" across the state. Five Wyoming riders would ride 100 miles each in a bit of a circuit around the southern part of Wyoming. It was only a few days after

Saddling up to ride Cowboy Country

my nineteenth birthday, upon which Clay took me out for a free drink at every bar in town. Lander is a small town but there are a lot of bars! We had a blast, but I didn't feel so good until the day before the big event.

Brian promoted it on the air in Cheyenne and even got me a slot on the Lander radio station to pump it up. The local paper, of course, did a story as well. He had a friend drive a Winnebago behind for the riders to sleep in and to pick up collection boxes along the way. We met the group on the Highway outside of Casper in the heat of the day and I rode the wind blasted stretch back to Riverton. The route was fairly flat, and I was thrilled to have a tailwind for the last stretch and I clocked a 4:27 century...I finally rode a decent time trial!

1987 Sheridan, Wyoming State Championship Criterium.
Photo Bruce Campbell

CHAPTER TWENTY-ONE:

This Must be the Place

Prior to starting college at the University of Oregon in Eugene, I took a road trip to Laramie and then on to Boulder. U of O was on the quarter system and didn't start until late September, about a month later than my Wyoming friends. I had tickets for a concert in Denver at the famous Red Rocks Amphitheater and since my job at the pool was over, I devised a week-long trip. I almost couldn't believe it when my parents approved and let me take the truck, but hey, I was nearly a college man now!

I packed a sleeping bag and crashed on the floor in Topher's dorm, and we watched a UW "Cowboys" football game. Wade was pledging a fraternity and not around much. Many of my former classmates were there and although it was college, it really felt way too much like an extension of high school to me, reinforcing my decision to flee Cowboy Country. I did, however, meet a cool girl in Topher's dorm who also rode bikes and remembered me from winning the Dead Dog Crit...sweet! Topher could see the sparks flying and I didn't see him again until the next morning, finding much cozier accommodation for my last night at UW...very sweet!

The next stop after Laramie was Boulder, Colorado where my old swimming teammate Wes was attending CU and had an apartment with a couple of guys. Wes took me to a "New Wave Bar" on campus that played the music I loved. I think it was even called "Pogo's", like the way punk rockers danced. Many of the kids had mohawks and wild hairstyles and we guzzled that 3.2 beer by the pitcher. The next night we were at the Red Rocks venue I had previously only seen in the U2 video for a "New Wave Festival". The lineup was Gene Loves Jezebel, New Order, and then Echo & the Bunnymen. Gene were an energetic opener, New Order was a boring synth band, and Echo were real showmen and rocked it! It was an awesome experience, and the real-life venue proved even more spectacular than in my imagination. I was really living the dream now and I was convinced U of O would be more of the same...parties, cool people, great music, and a bigger cycling scene. The next day I was off to Denver to visit my grandparents, who, as they had generously done for all their grandchildren, were paying for half of my college education. Shortly thereafter, my parents drove me out to Eugene, and I couldn't believe all the trees...we didn't have many of those in Wyoming!

Back in Lander, most of my classmates had seen my cycling as an oddity. The standard comment was, "You spent $1000 on a bike? You could have bought a truck!" It was like a broken record, as was the incredulousness about my training. Even my lifelong friend, Dave said "So let me get this straight...you guys shave your legs, lube your butts, and wrap yourself in Spandex? You're only a few steps away from being drag queens!" Most of them didn't get it, couldn't relate, or thought I was just plain weird. Couldn't they see the grandeur and the epic nature of being out on the open road for hours in the elements battling an entire peloton? The serenity to be found in the suffering? Their sports interests were very traditional and institutional. As such, independent and individual sports like mine seemed of little interest to most of them.

It was the same with the music...if it wasn't in the Top 40 or a Metal party anthem, or God forbid-Country Western, most weren't interested. At the State Swim Meet, my Senior year there was a mall near our hotel, and I was always looking for an opportunity to find and buy new music. I came back with Hoodoo Gurus "Mars Needs Guitars", which had been prominent all winter on the college charts. In a move that typified most of my peers musical attitudes, Paul Susich, our distance coach turned his nose up at it instantly. "Who the fuck are the Hoody Gurus? In twenty years, nobody will remember them, but they'll remember the Eagles!" Eugene was immediately different on both fronts. Once I settled into the Wilcox dorms in Eugene and started meeting people, the response I got to my cycling hobby were things like "cool, I'm a rock climber!" or "That's awesome, I run" or "I'm a mountain biker". Everyone seemed to be able to relate. Within just a few days and right in my dorm complex, I found some other bike racers! Most of them also had great music on their bookshelves they were eager to share and discuss. I had found my tribe!

The country roads around Eugene were seemingly made for cycling and I couldn't get over how many trees there were. There were flat roads, lumpy roads, and roads with long climbs, all easily accessed from the bike paths running throughout town. Not the barren, sage brush covered, windy terrain of Cowboy Country. And there were so many riders! The days of lonely rides fueled solely by my imagination were replaced by strong, competitive groups that really pushed each other. The U of O cycling club regularly had twenty fit and savvy people on our rides (Monday, Wednesday, Friday) and the Eugene Cycling Club (ECC) rides on Tuesdays (Sprints), Thursday (Club Races), and weekends (Long) were even bigger and faster, often with forty riders. Most of the group rides had more people than many of our race fields in Wyoming.

The music scene was just as heavenly as several record stores were within walking distance of campus and there were regular concerts at the student union. My roommate Jeff (assigned by chance but we got along great) brought home a poster one day, "isn't this a band you like?" and it was Concrete Blonde! Continuing in the independent ethos that I loved, the poster featured the artwork of Johnette Napolitano, the lead singer. Seeing such an artist anywhere in Wyoming was impossible and here they played within walking distance at the student union for like five bucks a ticket…I was in heaven!

That first year of college was really marked by two "pilgrimages" to California, both involving U2. Jeff was also a huge fan, and we sat on the two dorm pay phones, one on each floor, for several hours to score tickets for their "Joshua Tree" tour that November in Oakland. They had become the biggest band in the world and Topher and Clay saw them a week later in Denver. Our show was on a Sunday night, so we travelled all day Saturday. It was billed as a Bill Graham "Day on the Green" meaning General Admission and featuring two other bands...The Bo Deans and The Pretenders, both of whom we loved. 58,000 people attended and *Rolling Stone* magazine reported it as one of the biggest concerts of the year. Jeff borrowed his parents' car, and we piled in several other people, including a girl-friend I had at the time who knew people at nearby UC-Davis, giving us a place to crash. The concert was epic, and we drove straight back through the night, rocking out to all U2's albums because somebody (me) had a Chemistry midterm exam at 8:30 am on Monday morning. We made it with just fifteen minutes to spare! The opening track from the album nicely captured the feelings of freedom I experienced in that first year away from home.

Where The Streets Have No Name-from "The Joshua Tree" (1987)
"I want to run, I want to hide
I wanna tear down the walls that hold me inside
I wanna reach out and touch the flame
Where the streets have no name, ha, ha, ha
I wanna feel sunlight on my face
I see that dust cloud disappear without a trace
I wanna take shelter from the poison rain
Where the streets have no name, oh, oh
Where the streets have no name
Where the streets have no name"

The other pilgrimage came in March for spring break when I joined Jeff's family for their annual Palm Springs trip. I brought along my bike as Eugene would host an epic stage race in mid-April...the Tour Willamette. The same hilly five-day event that was contested a few years back by Karl Maxon and his Gianni Motta teammates prior to racing the Giro. I trained every day, but I also partied too much with Jeff. My longest training ride was out to Joshua Tree National Monument where I met Jeff and his cousins. To the music of U2 we climbed rocks all day and explored the incredible area that graced the album cover of "The Joshua Tree". Considering I first heard that album on spring break the year prior, I certainly got a lot of mileage out of it. As the years went on and I came to see my home state of Wyoming differently, I would regularly cue up "In God's Country" from that seminal album, or "A Sort of Home-coming" from "The Unforgettable Fire", on the long drive home to Lander. I would play those fitting tunes right as I crested the last hill after leaving the reservation, and my hometown finally came into view. Because as much as I wanted out, I found that I loved coming back home. I realized Cowboy Country was a very beautiful and special place!

Most of my collegiate teammates were Category 3s and 4s and so I enjoyed my first real experiences racing as a team. Being a cyclist in Eugene meant riding in the rain...a lot. This was a bit of an adjustment, but you could ride year-round here as it didn't freeze, which was a revelation. I had never ridden so much through the winter nor raced as often in the spring. We cleaned up the basketball court after home games to fund gas and entry fees and we used State Motor pool vans to travel.

At the annual campus criterium, the Collegiate race field lulled in anticipation of a field sprint and my race radar came on. As the group bunched up, I attacked on the back stretch and went clear. Still holding a nice gap coming out of the final corner, I was ready to sprint up the final hill and win on campus! Instead, I yanked my foot out of my toe strapped pedal and time stood still while I struggled to get it back in, losing valuable time and momentum. All my dorm buddies were watching, and I suffered a crushing fourth place that should have been a win.

Cycling technology was rapidly changing and I had recently upgraded to the indexed (click) shifting I first tried two years prior in Washington. I decided I should save my pennies for some of those "clipless" pedals like my main man Greg. I did and found them to be a major improvement in comfort and efficiency. You could crank down the spring tension, so you never pulled your foot out! We sent a team down to San Luis Obispo for the first ever Collegiate Nationals and I was named the first alternate, but everyone was healthy, so I stayed back in Eugene and studied. The 1988 team wasn't very competitive at the national level, but we had potential. Collegiate cycling was growing fast all over the country and was even featured in *Winning* magazine. I struggled a bit with learning how to balance studying, life in the dorms, and being a bike racer but had fun and learned quite a bit…on and off the bike. The dorms had an end of year "Air Band" competition, and I got Jeff and a couple other friends to embrace the energy and anger of punk rock. We performed in the cafeteria as the Sex Pistols, going all in of course, and although we scared quite a few people with our intensity, we had a blast!

Shortly before my parents came to pick me up and take me back to Wyoming, I saw Mike Keep at the Student Union. Mike was one of only two Category 2's on our collegiate team and had his ear to the ground for everything cycling. He had been at the OTC the year before me and knew lots of national level riders. He had big news: Andy Hampsten had won the Giro d'Italia! "And I guess it was totally a classic win under epic conditions" he told me as he related stories of a massive snowstorm over the Gavia Pass and how the American team hung tough supporting their leader and triumphed over the Europeans. This was another watershed moment in American cycling history… "our guys" had now won two of cycling's three Grand Tours. 1981 was the first year Americans even rode the Giro and Tour and by 1988 "we" had won both? The progress "we" had made was just incredible to me.

I returned to Wyoming for the summer to work at Freewheel Sports under Terry and Kris. Fired up about cycling, I was excited to beat up on my Wyoming friends with the excellent form I had built in Oregon. Within just a few days of being home, however, and under my parents' roof (and rules) I immediately second-guessed my choice. I was training alone and travelling to races alone. A week after arriving home, I made it into the breakaway at the State Criterium Championship in Cheyenne, elevation 6000 feet. I hoped to defend my title but instead I felt asphyxiated and could barely pull through, let alone sprint. The adjustment back to altitude killed me. There were fewer events now in Wyoming and my forty-hour work week meant travelling out of state was out of the question. It became clear that I had made a mistake in returning to Cowboy Country.

I had grown my hair long and pierced my ear and my father made it clear on a regular basis just how much he hated this. I decided I should have stayed in Eugene. Thankfully, Topher, no longer racing nor enrolled in college, had a cool apartment loft across from the movie theater on Main Street with Clay and I spent a lot of time there with other non-conformists. Topher and Clay had become the "leaders of the counterculture" in Lander and there was always great music, movies, people, and conversation there. The dreaming and scheming that went on there was critical for all of us and helped us collectively escape the perceived repression of Cowboy Country as we vowed to never to be swallowed by its cracks.

SWALLOWED BY THE CRACKS-David & David, from "Boomtown" (1986)
"We were on top of the mountain that summer
Thought we'd never be swallowed by the cracks
Fallen so far down
Like the rest of those clowns begging bus fare back
Swallowed by the cracks
Our pride worn down talking times gone by
Like everybody else
Swallowed by the cracks
We would never be swallowed by the cracks
We would talk through the night
About what we would do
If we just could get started…"

I helped promote the local Red Dog race again, this time with the brilliant help of Drew. We didn't even try to do a criterium this time and revived the hill climb road race up Limestone Mountain. A strong group of Masters racers from Sun Valley, Idaho raced the Cat 3's. These guys were ski racers and were trying out some "new tech" at our little race. In the road races they used a U-shaped extension in the middle of their handlebars and for the time trials they used these crazy "DH" (as in a downhill skier's tuck) handlebars I had previously only seen in triathlon magazines. I didn't get it. At this point, the triathletes were doing all sorts of crazy things from the perspective of road riders, like racing in Speedo's and using these ridiculous handlebars, and we widely dismissed them as geeks, tri-geeks. A few riders' asked Drew if these handlebars were "legal" and he just said "Sure, why not!" We wouldn't see or hear much more about them for about another year...

I took great pride in winning the final road race in a reduced field sprint, again on the Lyon's Valley loop, and throwing up my arms in victory in front of friends and family. I wore my U of O team jersey with pride and was thrilled to find the entire Lang family cheering the field up the climb, so I threw down a big showboat attack just for them! Brian was announcing at the Casper Classic in July, now basically the biggest race in America outside of the Coors Classic, and he had a free hotel room at the Hilton where I could stay. Racing in the Cat 3s, I was thrilled to see several familiar faces from Eugene who had made the long trip out for the big prize money. I nearly won the Road Race to Independence Rock, but my standard sprint tactics of "stomp on your biggest gear from 200 meters out" failed me in the headwind as a couple of riders slipped by right at the line. Still, it was super cool to hear Brian screaming over the PA "It's little Davey, it's little Davey!" once again.

The calendar got pretty thin after Casper and a mid-July stage race in Jackson was the only other Wyoming event I contested that summer. For the first time since its inception, I missed the Dead Dog in Laramie. I struggled to stay motivated on the barren Wyoming roads, out training solo, particularly after wrenching on bikes for eight hours at the shop. I desperately missed the cycling community and organized weekly rides of Eugene. The long road trips all alone on top of a full-time job were tough as well. Crazy to say it, but I seemed to be "burned out on bikes" ...I didn't know that was possible for me!

Still, Topher and I road tripped down to Boulder to see the last two stages of the final edition of the Coors

Classic. Boulder during the Coors was the gathering place for the American cycling faithful. The crowds were enormous, as usual, and we even ran into Andy Adams, my OTC roommate who came up from Texas to watch. Davis Phinney, Boulder's favorite cycling son, and the "King of the Criteriums" won the race overall. He had been inspired to race bikes after watching this very event go by his house when he was a kid. Far from being just a sprinter, he was now an all-around rider who had finished both the Tours of Italy and France that summer. We were blessed to again ride back into town with the gregarious 7-Eleven team after the Morgul-Bismark Road race.

"The Slurpees" were so easy to talk to, fun loving, and simply fabulous ambassadors for the sport of cycling. Bike races in Boulder were the closest thing we Americans had to the fervor of Europe. The crowds were huge and boisterous for the final stage, now held on the CU campus. Phinney's main challenge came from the feisty Alexi Grewal, leader of the small Crest team and he fought hard until the very end. We crowded the podium and cheered the 7-Eleven team, including Women's winner Inga Thompson, who had dominated the race. American cycling at this point, was chock-full of sponsorship dollars, and Phinney joyously gave the keys to his prize: a beautiful red BMW to his sports director Jim Ochowicz. The whole weekend reminded me how much I truly loved cycling and reinvigorated me. I made a promise to myself that I would re-commit myself to cycling the following season.

Andy Hampsten-Giro d'Italia 1988, Gavia Pass.
photo courtesy Steven Hampsten

The glory days of American cycling, 1988 Coors Classic, victorious 7-Eleven team drives away in BMW race prize.
Photo credit Dave Campbell

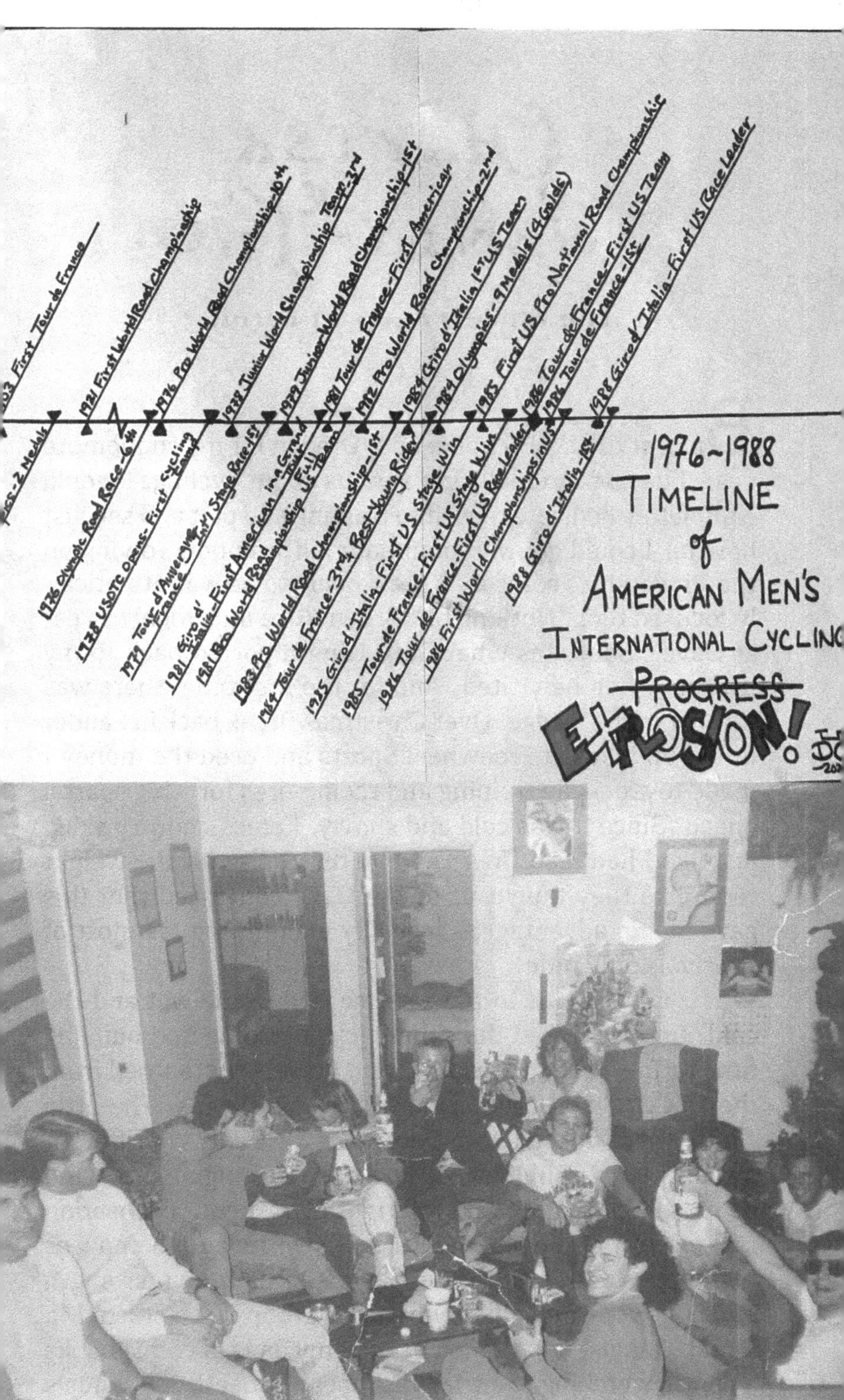

Clay Appleby's loft-The counter culture convening in cowboy country. Christmas break 1988-89.
Photo credit Rhonda Illka

Chapter Twenty-Two:

The Wheels Keep on Turning

Back at the U of O in Eugene, Oregon for my sophomore year, I decided to really get serious about cycling. I would completely dedicate myself to training and diet and see just how far I could go. My roommate Jeff was now rowing on the University's eight-man crew boat, so he was athletically focused too. "Nothing but Brown Rice and Yogurt to eat at Dave's house" is what Gary Lang reported back to my parents when he visited. And for the first time, there was no beer in the 'fridge. Over Christmas Break back in Lander I built up bikes at Freewheel Sports and used the money I made to stockpile training and racing tires for a big season ahead. Since it was cold and snowy, I cross-country skied just like I had read Greg Lemond did. I also hit the weight room like they taught us at the OTC, convinced that this gave me an advantage, especially in sprinting, as most of my rivals only rode.

Often alone in the early season in the wet and the cold, I rediscovered the simple joys of riding and building fitness. Based on my readings and the lessons learned from the OTC, I devised personalized training plans. The little climbs that I slogged up in December were entirely different by February. I could now call down to the engine room and be reassured that I could roll right over them, a sensation and pattern of development I still love today. The speed, the deep power, and the sensations of your own strength building were magnified when the group rides started in March. Maybe it harkened back to my days of comic books but just watching the road disappear beneath my wheels for hours on end while feeling so strong and so smooth, flying along under my own power...well, it felt a bit like being a superhero! And clad in brightly colored spandex to boot!

This all coincided nicely with the arrival of some new, driven, experienced, and talented members onto our collegiate team. Their enthusiasm was infectious and our comradery in training and travelling created the magic of really wanting to do our best for each other. Our team captain, Brad Gebhard was the winningest rider in the Northwest, a past member of the National Team, and had been living at the OTC off and on for the last several years. He was generous with advice and a great leader. The level on our local training rides continued to rise and I found myself regularly hanging tough with the best riders in the state...a much more competitive state than Wyoming! A second year of consistent year-round riding and racing in big groups allowed my pack skills to develop even further and instead of just hanging on or trying to stay up front, I actually started understanding and using the ebbs and flows of the group. I learned to move up efficiently, saving energy by working the little seams and pockets created as a mass of humanity on bicycles rolls down undulating roads. Brad taught me how to control my breathing on climbs so I could be there for the sprint at the end. My unabashed love affair with all things cycling was back...

HEAD ON-The Jesus and Mary Chain, from "Automatic" (1989)
"As soon as I get my head 'round you
I come around catching sparks off you
I get an electric charge from you
That secondhand living, it just won't do
And the way I feel tonight
Oh, I could die and I wouldn't mind
And there's something going on inside
Makes you want to feel, makes you want to try
Makes you want to blow the stars from the sky
I can't stand up, I can't cool down
I can't get my head off the ground"

Our first team success happened in mid-April at the annual campus criterium, the very event I had seen featured in that U of O Club Sports pamphlet back in Wyoming, which helped seal the deal for me attending college in Eugene. With a few laps to go, I got into a strong three rider breakaway and my teammates controlled the chase. In a veritable story book ending, I won the sprint, joyously thrusting my arms skyward in front of my classmates and my new community in Oregon. Set in the center of our campus, people really turned out for this event. Full of confidence, I raced in several weekend events with the Cat 2's, while still a 3, and placed in the first five every time. We won the Northwest Regional Collegiate Team title convincingly to qualify for Nationals in Colorado. The early May Tree Top Classic in Yakima, Washington featured a nice prize list, a large competitive field, and was my last race as a Cat 3. I was second in the Road Race and won the Criterium and came home with $225 in cash, heady stuff in a time when my rent was only $175!

Our five rider men's team were all Cat 2's now and we even had a small Nike sponsorship for clothing and shoes, thanks to none other than Tom Prehn. Oregon's wet but mild weather meant we raced every weekend from early March onward, something I could never do in Cowboy Country. Steve Marcy, one of the new arrivals and a fierce competitor, convinced his athletic wife Katy to race so we could field a three women team as well. Our clean-ups of MacArthur Court gave us just enough money for plane tickets to Colorado Springs...if we each also threw in eighty bucks. The host school Colorado College put us up in the dorms and my folks drove down from Lander to watch. The National Championships featured 175 men and 105 women and was held in Colorado Springs, with Saturday's 78-mile road race held on the 1986 Worlds course at the Air Force Academy. Sunday's Team Time Trial was on State Highway 94 east of town, site of our daily rides back at the OTC. The downtown criterium was the finale and the backstretch passed right in front of the movie theater that Andy and I rode to on those cold winter nights back in December of 1985. The serendipitous completion of the circle of my cycling journey was seemingly everywhere.

The 6000-foot altitude of Colorado Springs meant

we riders from the Willamette Valley in Oregon (elevation 426 feet) would need to stay within ourselves on the hilly road circuit. As such, we didn't go with the early break-away, some of whom survived until the end. Only about forty riders were left in the main field, and I jumped early for the hill-top finish sprint for seventh place. Someone flashed by right before the line and it was Brad. Steve was not far behind in eleventh. We had placed three of our riders into the first eleven in a field of 175! We were sixth in the next day's team time trial and Steve and I each won a points prime in the criterium. Both my aunt and uncle from Denver came out to support me for the evening criterium since my folks had to start the long drive home. The last lap of the crit was a crash-fest that impacted all of us in the finale, with our ace sprinter Keep only managing 17th while Steve was again 11th. Steve ended fourth in the Omnium while Brad and I were in the top twenty. Colorado University won, while our University of Oregon squad ended fifth in team scoring (combined men's and women's), despite our women not scoring a single point. We basically had the best men's team in the country.

Collegiate Cycling in 1989 was as much "do it your-self" as any of my experiences in Wyoming. We made our own money, designed our team jersey, crashed on the floors of host families, and did homework in the van. There was even a national collegiate newsletter, and the task fell to me to pen a piece on our team when we were chosen "Club of the Month" based on our performance at nationals. Riders from all over the country, many of us with several weeks of coursework remaining in the school year, congregated in the halls of the dorm after the race. We drank beer, the first for me in several months, traded jerseys (I brought home a cool red, white, and blue University of Arizona Wild Cats one covered with little cat tracks), and packed our bikes back up in the cardboard boxes we had begged off local bike shops. It was a super cool scene. The soundtrack to our revelry was R.E.M., Cowboy Junk-ies, Concrete Blonde, The Waterboys, The Jesus and Mary Chain, and other bands outside the mainstream just like us! College radio rock was not just my cycling soundtrack but seemed to be enjoyed throughout American cycling culture.

Brad picked up a *USA Today* in the airport and we carefully studied the finale of a brand-new American race on the Eastern seaboard...the Tour de Trump. This cocky real estate tycoon had put up a big prize list, drawing many of the world's top teams including Panasonic, PDM, 7-Eleven, the Russian National Team, and a recovering Greg Lemond and his American Coors Light squad. The Slurpee's Norwegian ace Dag-Otto Lauritzen had clinched the overall after finishing fourth in the final time trial. As Brad pointed out, he used those weird triathlon handlebars, like I had first seen at the Red Dog. His teammates Ron Kiefel and Sean Yates, who placed first and second, also used them. I still didn't get it as aerodynamics at that point mostly meant having a flat back. Brad explained how you used the bull horns for starts and to accelerate out of turns but that having your hands out in front of your face closed off your chest from the parachute effect, putting you into a position like a downhill skier and letting the air flow around you. These were the future for time trialing he assured me.

I made plans to return to Wyoming for the summer, determined to not make the same mistakes as the previous year. I contacted "The Bike Stop", the biggest shop in Wyoming with the best team and they were thrilled to have me for the summer. Terry and Kris gave me some flexibility in my work schedule so I could travel to races further away. There was only one serious rider in the area, Clay Hendrix-that quirky but strong Masters racer, and he lived in Riverton, 25 miles away. I made plans to meet up with him before work, often at 5:30 or 6 am, to train. I was a Cat 2 now and couldn't wait to use the best form of my life to dominate my homeboys. On one of my first training rides back home, out near the Reservation, Mr. Johnstone, the teacher who had been so supportive of my OTC trip in high school, saw me and pulled his truck over to say hello. A former college football player at the University of Wyoming, he had read about my Colorado Springs performance in the local paper. "You were top ten in the College Nationals, David! That's All American!" he beamed. Here was another example of the good people here, folks that really cared about me. I had to admit it felt good to be back in Cowboy Country.

Until the altitude got me. Again! It KILLED me. Within a week of returning, I did the High Uintas Stage Race in Evanston, Wyoming and was certain things would somehow be different this time. The first stage was an 80-mile point-to-point road race from Kamas, Utah into Evanston. Wade was living down there for the summer with his dad (working night shift security at the State Mental Hospital-ha!) and could drive my truck back. Kamas sits at 6000 feet elevation and the route climbed over Bald Mountain Pass at 10,700 feet and then descended into Evanston at 7000 feet. I was dropped like a stone and struggled through rain, then snow as first the Cat 3 field, then the Cat 4 field caught and passed me. Despite my great fitness I lacked red blood cells, so I was just worthless for a couple of weeks. I phoned it in for the time trial, then rallied for third in the criterium. Future USA Cycling President and many times Masters National Champion Steve Johnson attacked out of the field with just a half lap to go to win decisively and my old buddy, John just nipped me in the sprint behind. I hoped to recover and acclimate for the upcoming Casper Classic, which was not only at altitude, but against the very best riders in the country, some even among the best in the world!

With a $50,000 purse and a field that included Olympic gold medalist Steve Hegg as well as Thurlow Rogers and the Coors Light team, Casper was now the second biggest race in the country and the biggest for amateurs. To say lining up against this Pro/Cat 1,2 field only two months after my Cat 2 upgrade was a bridge too far is an understatement. I dropped out after three of the seven stages. I'll never forget the sound of eventual overall winner Rishi Grewal's double disc wheels coming up on me in the time trial, catching me for thirty seconds after less than three minutes out on the course. It was humbling to say the least. Crushing would be more accurate. Fortunately, Kent Olson, the manager of "The Bike Stop", helped ease my pain by paying me to work his little "pro shop" in the

Hilton after each stage. I was also assigned to collect water bottles (in exchange for a bottle with the Classic's logo) from the visiting pro teams to display in the shop. One day, a nice young kid came through with a bottle from the Belgian ADR team to trade. Greg Lemond's European team! I told him thanks, but we only wanted bottles from teams that were here racing. After all, ADR was in France racing the Tour. He looked at me with a puzzled expression and then left. It was rather strange.

He returned shortly with a very fit looking guy with a curly mullet not unlike my own, and little John Lennon glasses-his older brother who was racing. His name was Joe Parkin, future author of one of the finest books ever written on cycling in my opinion, "A Dog in a Hat". Joe was very friendly and an extremely unique cyclist in that era. Like perhaps only Bob Roll before him (and at Bob's suggestion he explained), he had crossed the pond to race in Belgium shortly after discovering the sport. He went alone, without a team and with only a few contacts, to race professionally at the age of 19! Talk about "do it yourself!" He was, in fact, on the Belgian division of the ADR team and he shared stories of riding the Midi Libre stage race in France, Paris-Roubaix, Ghent-Wevelgem, as well as the World Championships the previous year. We had a stack of *Winning* magazine back issues in our "pro-shop" and he showed me his photo at the head of the field during the '88 Pro Worlds. I had wondered who that guy was! American cycling had reached the stage where guys like Joe were inspired to try to make it on their own over in Europe. In just a few short years…incredible!

Back in Lander a couple of weeks later, Terry, Kris, and I promoted what would be the final Lander Stage Race. Given the emergence of the mountain bike and the decline of road cycling, at least locally, we redesigned the event. Thinking that we were ahead of the times and perhaps we were, we called it the "Ride the Winds" weekend. Saturday morning was a new longer Time Trial that was technical, twisty, and rolling in contrast to the traditional flat out and back affairs of the past. Saturday afternoon would be the Lyon's Valley Road Race and then on Sunday we held a mountain bike race high up on the Louis Lake Road. Known locally as "the loop road", this single lane gravel road connects Sinks Canyon with Red Canyon. Starting on this gravel road and then linking into a trail, our course wound through Worthern Meadows (9000 feet elevation) in the Shoshone National Forest. The road races would be scored as a two-stage race with the Mountain bike race prized alone. Sue Lang, who owned Cat's Cradle pottery, generously agreed to make mugs for the top finishers in the Mountain Bike event.

Despite, or perhaps because of, the success and sheer size of the Casper event, many of the small Wyoming races of my youth had disappeared, and field sizes had shrunk. In true Cowboy Country fashion, however, we made the best out of what we had. Charles won the time trial but for the second year running, this time against the Cat 2's, I won the road race, in a sprint of course, where I had finally learned some tactical nuance. Thanks in no small part to the group rides and club races in Eugene, I now tailored my efforts and gear selection to the situations demanded by the wind, the course, and my competition. I borrowed one of the shop's rental bikes for the mountain bike portion, my first ever foray into the off-road world. We had three distances (10, 20, and 30 miles) based on a circuit and I won the twenty-miler from a mainly local field while my out-of-town road rivals, all veterans of other mountain bike races, rode the thirty-mile event, which finished in a cold mountain rain.

All month long, we all had been intently following Lemond's return to the Tour de France after his shooting. US cycling coverage, particularly of the Tour, had finally gotten to the point where commentators stopped explaining the sport to the novices, and just covered the race, something all the racers like my friends and I were grateful for. After some glimmers of form throughout the spring, my main man Greg nearly quit the Giro. Following an iron injection (he had not received such an intervention since the 1987 hunting accident) and despite the lead pellets he still carried in his body, he began racing like himself again, finishing second in the final time trial in Italy. He opened his comeback Tour with fourth in the prologue and was cautiously optimistic but remained uncertain of his climbing ability going forward. He hoped for a top twenty placing overall and a stage win. All of America seemed to cheer when Greg won the 73-kilometer long stage five time-trial into Rennes on July 6th and, for the first time in three years, pulled on the yellow jersey! He was using those "triathlon handlebars" that I first saw in Cowboy Country. The inventor, Boone Lennon, was one of those fast masters, and a ski racer, from Idaho who tried them out at our little race the year before...small world!

Since the TT, Greg had been engaged in an incredible battle with Parisian Laurent Fignon, the 1983/84 champion, with the leader's jersey passing back and forth between them and both winning stages. Lemond would fall behind in the mountains but recover in the time trials. It had been an incredible race and ended Sunday, July 23rd, the day of our local mountain bike race, with a unique 25 km final time trial into Paris. Greg trailed by 50 seconds, a margin most saw as too much to overcome. My mother had been left with strict instructions to videotape the coverage on CBS Sports. This was 1989 after all and we stopped at a payphone at a little store on the highway to verify that she had taped it and to see if my group of wet and cold racing friends could all come over and watch. Even though we told her not to tell us what happened, she hinted that it was good. She was fired up, saying "It was so exciting, I had to stop vacuuming to watch, you are going to love it!"

Several carloads of cyclists booked it back down the mountain and my mother enthusiastically welcomed us all. She'd made popcorn and she wanted to watch it again with us. Interviewed on his massage table the day before, Greg told the cameramen "It is not impossible, but it will be very difficult." That phrase alone would motivate and inspire me for nearly three decades of racing to come. Greg had always been an innovator, and he made great tactical and equipment choices. This day, however, would be his finest hour. He used a rear disc wheel and tri-bars on his low-profile time trial machine and wore a stub tailed Giro aero helmet. He eschewed time splits along the course, knowing his rival's pace was irrelevant, he had to go as hard and fast as possible...and hope it was enough.

Fignon rode double discs and went without a helmet on the hot summer day. He had reportedly been seen testing some crude aero bars on the course in the morning but chose to race without them. Lemond would later reveal another confidence booster he received on the day prior. On the train transport to the stage start in Versailles, Fignon "congratulated him on his second place". Since both had been coached by the same director, Guimard, who advised all his riders that "the race was never over until the final finish line", Greg knew his rival was making the fatal error of overconfidence.

Commentators Phil Liggett and Paul Sherwen, still in the early days of their partnership, seemed just as excited as we were. For perhaps the first time, we got to see nearly the entire race, albeit a 27-minute stage. As they called out the time gaps, it was clear it was going to be close...in the words of Liggett "desperately close". Lemond alternated putting his head down for extended periods and then picking it up to see the course. Charles, our Wyoming time trial guru who would years later write the special *Velo News* magazine supplement detailing Greg's career upon his retirement, was concerned about Lemond "sticking that helmet tail up into the wind". He seemed to be going super-fast. The last announced gap was 48 seconds only a couple of miles before he finished and awaited the arrival of Fignon. His stunning average speed of just below 34 miles per hour meant it was the fastest time trial ever ridden.

Greg, always nervous and antsy, was alternately listening to a headset of the live feed on Radio Tour and pacing anxiously while running his hands through his sweat-drenched hair. Liggett called out the time gap as Fignon approached the finish line, ultimately running out of time less than 100 meters from the end. Lemond punched the air and then ran into the stands to find and embrace his wife, Kathy. Greg, after nearly dying two years before, had beaten his French rival and former teammate by 58 seconds to claim overall victory in the near 3300-kilometer three-week event by just eight seconds, still the closest finish in the men's race history. In another quintessentially Cowboy Country moment, I watched it following a race with my competitors and friends.

Dad and I drove up to Billings, Montana the next weekend for the Hogback Classic Stage Race. I won the road race and finished second on GC behind Tom Noaker, a Master's National Champion from Utah. A young guy named Levi Leipheimer, a ski racer from Butte, smoked the Junior field. He would later become the 29th American to ride the Tour de France, finish on the podium, and win an Olympic bronze medal. I won a coupon for an oil change prime in the opening crit and Dad insisted we use it before the evening's hill climb time trial, classic! Some Colorado hot shots raced the Dead Dog in Laramie in mid-August and just aced me out of victory in the criterium on the UW campus.

I competed in the local triathlon again at summer's end, but this time got chased down by a "real runner" from out of town and had to settle for second place. My father grumbled at me all summer long with gems like "you treat this place like a training camp", "you contribute nothing to the family", "you act like an old gambler, trying to win that big money one day!" and "where is all this bike racing taking you anyway"? To the next race, of course and as to the previous points, that was my whole plan...so what's your problem? Ha!

Over that final summer of living in Cowboy Country, though, I came to realize the rugged beauty that only Wyoming can offer. The same friends and I who had complained throughout High School that there was "nothing to do in this town" and "I can't wait to get out of this place" discovered the simple joys of our little mountain town. We re-found and truly grasped the beauty and wonder of hiking to the Popo Agie Falls and going down the water slide, backpacking above Fiddler's Lake, and spelunking in Sinks Canyon. I even tried rock climbing. Talking with the NOLS students as they stopped in the shop after completing their courses took on a new dimension. Mostly city kids from the East Coast, they couldn't believe the grandeur of the Wind River Mountains and told me how lucky I was to grow up here. Having finally "grown up", I agreed. Lander, Wyoming was in fact a beautiful place and my travels across the west to bike races had shown me that there were very few places like it left in America. It truly was an amazing place to grow up, surrounded by generous and supportive friends and neighbors. My parents, of course, still live there today. Their neighbors and our dear friends, Phil and Carolyn Gilbertson, both avid cyclists, who encouraged me to go to Oregon and have family there, would go to great lengths, for many years, to come cheer me at Oregon races when they were anywhere nearby...incredible!

Due in no small part to Greg Lemond, who also won a thrilling 1989 World Championship, 1990 was a very healthy year for domestic bike racing. Back in Oregon, there were races every weekend from early March through the end of September. Our Eugene weekly club race, the "Thursday Nighter" had seventy riders turning out, necessitating two groups. There were four elite teams getting "the full meal deal" with sponsored bikes, entry fees, and clothing and Washington had even more. No more cleaning up Mac Court at the University for the five of us that rocked it in Colorado Springs! Brad and Steve were on the Specialized/Bike Gallery squad, Mike and I were on Bassett Press/Giant, Peter went to Hutch's/Cannondale, and many of the best Portland guys were on Nike/Raleigh (Team Oregon). My team manager howled with laughter at some of the names of races in Cowboy Country listed on my resume: Red Dog, Dead Dog, and Hogback among them. There was still an element of "do it yourself", as I typed up team resumes, clipped media highlights, and sent out proposal letters and Mike and I courted sponsors over the phone. I even drew up the design for our jersey. Still in college and putting off adulthood and a real job for at least one more year, I raced sixty-five days that year.

I have been blessed by so many incredible experiences within the world of cycling and have been fortunate to have my own cycling circle continue to complete itself throughout my life. In a Portland criterium in 1991, I was in the winning break with none other than Tim Rutledge, who rode the Giro d'Italia with the pioneering Gianni-Motta team back in 1984, showing us all what was possible. By 1993, Davis Phinney, Ron Kiefel, and Roy Knickman were finishing out their careers by racing domestically for the Coors Light team. I was fortunate to get to race against these pioneering Americans who inspired me and so many others of my generation at our local Tour Willamette stage race among other events. I even got to compete against Olympic champion Alexi Grewal, now approachable and friendly.

The Eugene race was used as a prep event by the top American teams for the biggest race in the country, The Tour Dupont (formerly Trump) in May. When mechanical misfortunes caused me to miss the time cut in the last road stage, the promoter offered me the microphone for the final stage. I interviewed both Ron and Davis, true ambassadors for American cycling that fired up my imagination back in the mid-80s when they broke new ground in Europe. Would I have been inspired enough to log all those lonely miles without the determination and accomplishment of riders like that? Their honesty about their struggles at the next level, paralleling my own, gave me not just inspiration but hope. I even interviewed Alex Stieda, who took that historic first North American yellow jersey in the Tour, during my first announcing job at the U of O criterium, now the final stage of the Tour Willamette. I'm still announcing regional events in all cycling disciplines to this day.

I traveled to Milwaukee, Wisconsin later that year to race "Superweek" against a stellar two hundred rider pro field, including many riders from Europe, for a purse of over $100,000. The criteriums were blazing fast and I was getting whipped daily. Luckily, back at my host family's house I stumbled onto "Rocky" on TV. I once again took the lessons to heart and when I lined up for the next day's race "I ain't goin' down no more" was my mantra and I rallied to finish with the field in all the remaining events, even getting into a break, and cracking the first thirty a couple of times. The day before I returned home, I received a call to interview for a teaching job in Newport, Oregon. A real job that I not only ended up getting but working at for the next thirty years. Of course, during my time there, and with the support of some great students, I started a cycling club, and together we founded a mountain bike race, The Coast Hills Classic, that continues to this day. I eventually taught a "History of Rock and Roll" class featuring a special unit on the College Radio Rock of the 1980s, which formed the foundations of the Alternative Rock that dominated popular music in the 1990s. Over a period of at least fifteen years straight, I was able to take at least one student to their very first bike race, much like Drew and Bob did for me.

When I took up triathlon again in 1999, seriously this time, I raced in the first ever Ironman in the continental US...held in Lake Placid, New York. My dad came out to watch the race and the transition zone was in the shadow of the famous Ice rink where we were inspired by that scrappy American hockey team nearly twenty years earlier. Would I even be racing an Ironman without the inspiration of those guys? I have been able to recently mentor my high school math tutor Kirk Bollinger's daughter Kinley in triathlon. She won her age group at Ironman Arizona and qualified for the Hawaii Ironman with a potential that seems unlimited. I was blessed to coach High School Cross Country for twelve years, and in 2006 was fortunate to have an exceptional group of young women who won the district title for the only time in our school's history. To do so, they had to overcome a rival who had won the last twenty-eight years in a row, not unlike the dominance of the Soviet Hockey team. I used bits of Herb Brook's speech to his 1980 Olympic Hockey players to help our runners rise to the challenge and I even showed them the documentary.

I believe passing on what you have learned, and passing on inspiration, to be the most profound lesson from this incredible period of American cycling history. It happened not just on the elite and international levels but right down to the local level, a veritable positive feedback loop. The culture of sharing and working together to make everyone involved better was unprecedented during this era and we need more of it today. Happily, that spirit is alive and well in Bend, where I now make my home. I am a volunteer race announcer and rider coach for the Chris and Megan Horner Cycling Foundation. Chris was the 25th American to ride the Tour de France, ultimately riding seven and became the first American to win the Vuelta Espana in 2013. His wife Megan is a former US Under 23 National Road Champion. It is a grassroots junior development program that provides bikes, clothing, travel expenses, and race entry to all its riders, which currently number over thirty and range in age from seven to thirteen. Additionally, I am currently working with other Oregon cyclists on "M Prove It", a new project to help support and promote Oregon track cyclist McKenna McKee in her quest to make the 2028 Olympic Team.

Incredibly, most of the cycling dreams from my lonely days out on cold and windy Wyoming roads came true. While Wyoming might not have been the best place to develop my racing skills, in the end there probably could not have been a better place for developing a lifelong love of cycling. It took a while, but I finally wore the stars and stripes in international competition. I had the honor of representing my country in the 2004 Long Course (Sweden) and 2008 Short Course (Canada) Triathlon World Championships and I even won a Master's National Championship in 2012, nearly thirty years after my first Nationals. I ultimately competed for thirty-five years and contested about 900 races. Fifty-nine Americans have now ridden the Tour de France and eleven have won stages.

Dave, Wade, Clay, and Topher remain some of my very closest friends and we get together whenever we can. I still stay in touch with my mentors Roger Mork, Drew Leemon, Brian Davis, and Bob Moon. Could that have happened anywhere else but Wyoming? At the high school reunions back in Lander (which I, the guy who had to escape, now organize), it is amazing how many of my classmates, as well as my parent's friends and neighbors are now avid cyclists. Many have even travelled to France to ride the roads and peaks they've seen in the Tour or participate in events like "Ride the Rockies". I love to travel back to visit my friends and family in Lander now, and I tell everyone I meet how great it was to grow up in Wyoming. The small town that I couldn't wait to get out of is now I place I love to return home to. When I ride there now, I can't believe how many cyclists are out on the roads! Saddled up to ride in Cowboy Country!

A SORT OF HOMECOMING-U2 from "The Unforgettable Fire" (1984)
And you know it's time to go
 Through the sleet and driving snow
 Across the fields of mourning to a light that's in the distance.
 And you hunger for the time
 Time to heal, 'desire' time
 And your earth moves beneath your own dream landscape.
On borderland we run.
 I'll be there, I'll be there tonight
 A high-road, a high-road out from here.

1993 Tour Willamette, Eugene Oregon. With Olympic Gold Medalist Alexi Grewal.
Photo credit Michael Adamson

Interviewing Davis Phinney at the Tour Willamette April 1993.
Photo credit Michael Adamsonl

Reuniting in Lander recently, wishing we could still get into the pool. Topher, Wade, Dave, and Dave.
Photo credit Giselle Albertson

BIBLIOGRPHY

Avildsen, J.G. (Director). (1976). Rocky [Film]. United Artists.

Alexander, D. and Ochowiz, J. (1986) Tour de France '86 American Invasion. Alexander & Alexander Publishers.

Badger, Emily, "United States of Innovation: How Colorado Springs Became the Heart of the U.S. Olympic Movement", Fast Company, June, 2012.

Baerwald, D.F. & Ricketts, D. (1986) Swallowed by the Cracks [Recorded by David & David]. On Boomtown. Universal Music Publishing Group.

Bernstein, R. (Director). (1997). Do You Believe in Miracles? The Story of the 1980 U.S. Hockey Team [Film]. Home Box Office.

Berry, B., Buck, P., Mills, M., Stipe, M. (1983) Pilgrimage [Recorded by R.E.M.]. On Murmur. IRS Records.

Blumenthal, Tim. "Giro to Moser" Velo News, June 22, 1984

Borysewicz, Eddie and Riddle, Patty. (2020) Eddie's Side of the Story: The Life and Times of Eddie B. Independently Published.

Buck, P.L, Mills, M.E., Berry, W.T., Stipe, J.M. (1986) I Believe [Recorded by R.E.M.]. On Life's Rich Pageant. Night Garden Music.

Byrne, D., Weymouth, T., Harrison, J., Frantz, C. (1983) This Must be the Place (Naïve Melody) [Recorded by Talking Heads]. On Speaking in Tongues. Wb Music Corp, Index Music, Inc.

Clayton, A., Evans, D., Mullen, L., Hewson, P. (1980) A Day Without Me [Recorded by U2]. On Boy. Island Records, Universal Music Publishing Group.

Clayton, A., Evans, D., Mullen, L., Hewson, P. (1984) A Sort of Homecoming [Recorded by U2]. On The Unforgettable Fire. Island Records, Universal Music Publishing Group International, BV.

Clayton, A., Evans, D., Mullen, L., Hewson, P. (1987) Where the Streets Have No Name [Recorded by U2]. On The Joshua Tree. Island Records, BMG Rights Management, Royalty Network, Songtrust Ave, Universal Music Publishing Group.

Cobb, E. (1981) Tainted Love [Recorded by Soft Cell]. On Non-Stop Erotic Cabinet. Some Bizarre Sire/Warner Bros. Records, Equinox Music.

De Vise, Daniel (2018) The Comeback: Greg Lemond, the True King of American Cycling, and a Legendary Tour de France. Atlantic Monthly Press.

Drake, Geoff with Ochowicz, Jim. (2011) Team 7-Eleven: How an Unsung Band of American cyclists took on the World and Won. Velopress.

The Editors of Velo-News: Blumenthal, T. (Research), and Pavelka, E. (text). (1983) Ten Years of Championship Bicycle Racing. Velo-News-Barbara George.

Farriss, A., Hutchence, M., Farriss, J. (1985) What You Need [Performed by INXS]. On Listen Like Thieves. Songtrust Ave, Sony/ATV Publishing, LLC, Universal Music Publishing Group, Warner Chappell Music, Inc., WEA, Mercury, Atlantic Records.

Frantz, C., Byrne, D., Harrison, J., & Weymouth, T. (1985) Perfect World [Performed by Talking Heads]. On Little Creatures. Downtown Music Publishing, Warner Chappell Music, Inc. Sire Records.

Frantz, C., Byrne, D., Harrison, J., & Weymouth, T. (1985) Television Man [Recorded by Talking Heads]. On Little Creatures. Downtown Music Publishing, Warner Chappell Music, Inc. Sire Records.

Gano, G.J. (1983) Day after Day [Recorded by Violent Femmes]. On Violent Femmes. Slash Records.

Gordis, Kent K. "Straddling Two Generations: An Exclusive Interview with Davis Phinney". Winning Bicycle Racing Illustrated, July 1984.

Hood, Ed. "George Mount-The Original, Colorful 'Salty' American Racer". Velo Veritas, 17 April 2014, https://veloveritas. co.uk/2014/04/17/george-mount-mar14/

Jones, M.G., and Letts, D. (1985) Medicine Show [Recorded by Big Audio Dynamite] On This is Big Audio Dynamite. Columbia Records.

Lehrer, Rich. "Hell Bent on Glory: The US National team Sweeps Through Europe Like a Whirlwind". Winning Bicycle Racing Illustrated, July 1984.

Lennox, A. & Stewart, D.A. (1982). Sweet Dreams (Are Made of This) [Recorded by The Eurythmics]. On Sweet Dreams (Are Made of This). RCA Records, D-n-a Ltd., Neue Welt Musikverlag Gmbh & Co. Kg, Bridgeport Music Publishing, Spirit Music Alpha.

Letts, D., Roberts, G., and Jones, M.G. (1985) Sudden Impact! [Recorded by Big Audio Dynamite]. On This is Big Audio Dynamite. Columbia Records.

Mankey, J.A., and Napolitano, J.L. (1986) Over Your Shoulder [Recorded by Concrete Blonde]. On Concrete Blonde. Concord Music Publishing LLC, Sony/ATV Music Publishing LLC, Warner Chappell Music, Inc.

Martin, Pierre; Penazzo, Sergio; Bratino, Dante; Schamps, Daniel; & Vos, Cor. (1984) Tour 84. Kennedy Brothers Publishing Ltd.

McDermott, Barry. "Goldilocks 1, Bears 0". Sports Illustrated, 13 July 1981, https://vault.si.com/vault/1981/07/13/goldilocks-1-bears-0-actually-the-soviets-did-win-the-team-title-in-the-coors-classic-but-nevadas-greg-lemond-stunningly-took-individual-honors-to-become-the-uss-fair-haired-boy.

McDonald, E. and Peeters, M. (1985). Father to Son [Recorded by The Alarm]. On Strength. IRS Records.

McElhone, J. Skinner, G., Travers, H. (1986). Set This Day Apart [Recorded by Hipsway]. On Hipsway. Virgin-Nymph Music Inc.

Moore, Richard (2011) Slaying the Badger: Lemond, Hinault, and the Greatest Tour de France. Yellow Jersey Press.

Morton, R. (2023, November 27). Personal communication.

Mould, R.A. (1985). Celebrated Summer [Recorded by Husker Du]. On New Day Rising. SST Records, BMG Rights Management.

Mould, B. (1987). These Important Years [Recorded by Husker Du]. On Warehouse: Songs and Stories. Warner Brothers Records, BMG Rights Management US, LLC, Warner/Chappell Music, Inc.

Pattinson, L.T., McCulloch, I.S., Sergeant, W., De Freitas, P. (1984). Angels and Demons [Recorded by Echo & The Bunnymen]. On Ocean Rain. Sire Records, Zoo Music Limited.

Peters, M.L., Kitchingman, D.W., Macdonald, E.J., (1984). The Stand [Recorded by The Alarm]. On Declaration, I.R.S. Records, Arlovol Music.

Ringholz, R.C. (1997). On Belay! The Life of Legendary Mountaineer Paul Petzoldt (C. Newman Bohn, Ed.) First Edition. The Mountaineers.

Reid, W.A. & Reid, J.M. (1989) Head On [Recorded by The Jesus and Mary Chain]. On Automatic. Blanco y Nego Records, Domino Publishing Company Limited.

Sergeant, W., McCulloch, I, Pattinson, L., and de Freitas, P. (1981). Turquoise Days [Recorded by Echo & The Bunnymen]. On Heaven Up Here. Sire Records, Warner Chappell Music Inc.

Taylor, J., LeBon, S., Rhodes, N., Taylor, A., & Taylor, R. (1982) Hungry Like the Wolf [Recorded by Duran Duran]. On Rio. EMI Records, Gloucester Place Music Limited.

Seven Ages of Rock. Program 6: Left of the Dial. Directed by Sebastian Barfield, Andrew Graham-Brown, Anna Gravelle, Alastair Laurence, Robert Murphy, and Francis Whately. Interview with David Fricke. BBC Worldwide, 2007.

Simmons, G. (1974) Nothin' to Lose [Recorded by Kiss]. On Kiss. Casablanca/Warner Brothers Records.

Sullivan, F. & Peterik, J. (1982) Eye of the Tiger [Recorded by Survivor]. On Rocky III Motion Picture Soundtrack. Warner Brothers Music Corporation..

Watt, M. (1984). History Lesson, Part II [Recorded by The Minutemen]. On Double Nickels on the Dime. SST Records.

Westerberg, P. (1984). I Will Dare [Recorded by The Replacements]. On Let It Be. Twin/Tone Records, BMG Rights Management, Warner Chappell Music, Inc.

Westerberg, P. (1984). Seen Your Video [Recorded by The Replacements]. On Let it Be. Twin/Tone Records, BMG Rights Management.

Westerberg, P. (1985). Left of the Dial [Recorded by The Replacements]. On Tim. Sire Records, BMG Rights Management, Warner Chappell Music, Inc.

Westerberg, P., Stinson, T., and Mars, C. (1987). Alex Chilton [Recorded by The Replacements]. On Pleased to Meet Me. Sire Records, Nah Music, Done to Death Music.

Westerberg, P. (1987). I.O.U. [Recorded by The Replacements]. On Pleased to Meet Me. Sire Records BMG Rights Management.

Westerberg, P. (1989). Achin' to Be [Recorded by The Replacements]. On Don't Tell A Soul. Sire Records, Nah Music.

Yates, P. (Director). (1979). Breaking Away [Film]. 20th Century Fox.

About the Author

Dave Campbell was born in the small mountain town of Lander, Wyoming in 1968. His world exploded when he found the sport of bicycle racing in 1981, ultimately winning ten State cycling Championships in Wyoming and Oregon over thirty-five years of racing. He became a 1989 Collegiate All-American while attending the University of Oregon, where he earned a degree in Health Education with a minor in Biology. He earned a master's in science education from Oregon State University in 1998. Dave taught Health and Science and coached Cross-Country at Newport (Oregon) High School from 1993 through 2023. He completed the Ironman Triathlon in 1999 and represented the US at the 2004 Long Course World Triathlon Championship in Sweden and the 2008 Short Course Triathlon World Championship in Canada. He won the US Masters National Tandem Road Championship in 2011 and lives with his wife and dog in Bend, Oregon. Dave is a volunteer coach and announcer for the Horner Cycling Foundation, writes for "Cycling West", and announces cycling events across the state. He writes the "clips and straps" cycling history account on Instagram and has been writing about cycling in state, regional, and national publications since 1992, but this is his first book. He still rides often and visits "home" in Lander, Wyoming every summer.